I Didn't Save the President's Life

(I Only Saved His Pants)

By Raymond L. Wilkes
November 2007

Indigo Publishing Group, LLC

Publisher	Henry S. Beers
Associate Publisher	Rick L. Nolte
Associate Publisher	Richard J. Hutto
Executive VP	Robert G. Aldrich
Editor-in-Chief	Joni Woolf
Designer	Scott Baber
Print Studio Manager	Gary G. Pulliam
Print Studio Assistant	Chris Bryant
Director of Marketing	Tammy U. Martin
Director of Finance	Monica A. Ellis

Library of Congress Control Number: 2008936461

ISBN: (13 digit) 978-1-934144-40-4
      (10 digit) 1-934144-40-1

Indigo Publishing Group books are available at quantity discounts with bulk purchase for educational, business, or sales promotional use. For information, please write to: Indigo Publishing Group, LLC, 435 Second Street, Suite 320, Macon, GA 31201, or call 866-311-9578.

═══ACKNOWLEDGMENTS═══

My family, Cathy Pittman, Ray Jr., and Pearl. Jack Caldwell, Joe Kovac, Debbie Bartow, Joni Woolf, General Robert L. Scott, all my friends, and our Morning Coffee Club.

DEDICATION

This book is dedicated to all law enforcement officers who are now serving or who have served in the past.

To the families who were left behind when their loved one, who in the line of duty paid with their life.

To my wife Pearl, who went to work so we could make ends meet as my salary was so low we couldn't make it on my income alone. She knew how much I loved my work, and stayed at my side, in good times and bad for these last sixty-one years.

General Robert L. Scott was one of my heroes as I followed his life from early boyhood and to his death. He was a motivator of mine to write this book. He never read any copy of it as he died before it was published. The stories I have written had been told to him many times and he insisted that I put them on paper.

FOREWARD

The 1952 write-up in the Macon newspaper was four sentences long.

"Raymond L. Wilkes Selected as Deputy," the tiny headline read.

That was the public introduction of a 25-year-old rookie lawman who up to then, the news item said, had "been working at a Macon store."

The last sentence noted that Wilkes, or as the item put it, "the new deputy," had joined the ranks to replace a deputy named "Uncle Bob" Rodgers, who'd died after "42 years of service with the county."

So it was only fitting that Wilkes would one day become something of an uncle himself, the down-home, down-to-earth fellow who climbed the ranks, became a sheriff and, in the process, sat the good people of Bibb and surrounding counties on his knee when it came time to put his spin on the crimes of the day.

He was the law with a drawl, a true Southern gentleman sheriff. He was politically savvy, a businessman with a badge. He realized fighting crime was like running a public company, one where all the shareholders wanted was to feel safe. He was in office for 16 years, from 1976 to 1992. But it seems longer. The marks Wilkes left on the office, his birthing of the largest jailhouse in the region, his ushering in the era of well-trained, well-equipped officers, have endured.

Now "Uncle Ray" has gone and given the home folks more of himself.

He has tapped into the stories of his life and times, ones only a genuinely interested and perceptive man can recall. In doing so, he hands down a treasure box of Middle Georgia's past -- tales and anecdotes told from a lawman's point of view. If more police officers kept diaries and published them, histories of our country's out-of-the-way places could be written with far more authority.

Wilkes has seen and heard a lot. He has met six presidents and, as the title of this book lets on, even secured a filling-station restroom for one of them.

In the early 1990s, when I was the new crime reporter for The Telegraph, Wilkes would on occasion call me into his office. One time he told stories of a recent trip to Europe, to Switzerland. He knew retirement was looming and he seemed to have embraced it.

Other times he'd talk about growing up in the mill that sat on the very site the sheriff's office was built. Wilkes spoke of his father, William Augustus, a "lint head" who worked for less than $20 a week to provide for his three children. Wilkes understood and appreciated his father's struggles.

"It makes me feel like crying at times, for him to do what he did to give me a chance," Wilkes told me for an article published the week before his 1992 retirement. "If you're gonna have a rough time in your life, it's better to have it in the beginning than at the end."

For that same article, a former investigator who'd been promoted to chief deputy, Harry Harris, offered insight into the man behind Wilkes' public persona.

Of Wilkes, Harris, who died earlier this year, said, "I never thought he was a smooth politician with a slick tongue, but I think he grew into the office. It's real difficult to talk about him because you don't know that much about him. He's a very complex man. His honesty and integrity is not questioned."

A few years back, for an in-their-own-words interview series The Telegraph was launching, I picked Wilkes as the first "interviewee." He didn't disappoint.

For a couple of hours he spoke of his lessons for living, of what he'd learned from seeing the best and worst in people. And of what it is like to have your work, your job and the ways you do it, on display every day for the voters who pay you to critique.

"People in public life can have two answers," Wilkes told me. "One is what is politically good, and one is what's the truth."

As a footnote, you might say people who were in public life can provide even more enlightening answers.

They can write books.

But it isn't too common for hometown sheriffs to write them.

Or, when they do, for the books to be readable.

As he nears 80, what Wilkes has accomplished by chronicling his life and times as a lawman is nothing short of remarkable.

He has painted a picture of not-too-distant times already being forgotten.

— **Joe Kovac Jr.**

INTRODUCTION

I have an excellent memory. I can recall names and events that happened 50 years ago. My children and grandchildren have listened to me recall stories that happened during my early years and then through my years as sheriff. They knew how much I enjoyed telling my stories for others to also enjoy, so they encouraged me to make a permanent record of the stories I had told so often. My children wanted their children and their children's children to know the stories of their grandfather and great-grandfather.

I have worked many jobs and done many things in my life. Trying to compile my stories for others to read has by far been my hardest job to date. To sit in front of a tape recorder in an empty room and tell my stories was impossible for me to do. I tried and failed several times. Because of my dear friend, Jack Caldwell, encouraging me and prodding me over the years, I have finally been able to start. Jack has listened to me and coached me through the story telling so that I now have a written copy. Thank you, Jack, for your faithful support. Your kindness will be forever remembered by the Wilkes family.

So much happens in this world that is bad and ugly and hurtful. I hope to share the lessons I learned through these events. Other things happen that we must try to find the humor in. Humor can lighten our load and help throughout life's journey. Through the pages that follow I hope my children, grandchildren, and great-grandchildren can find humor in events that may have seemed so ordinary. And I hope all those who read see the remarkable in one man's ordinary life.

CHAPTER 1

I was born the son of William A. Wilkes on August 16, 1929, at the Macon Hospital in Macon, Georgia. My mother tells me I was born in the afternoon. I know it had to be a hot day. All afternoons in the month of August are hot and humid in Middle Georgia. My mother chose my first name, Raymond, just because she liked the name. My father highly admired William Lawrence Stripling, a local boy trained by his father in boxing. Thus my father chose Lawrence as my middle name.

My mother and father both worked in the Bibb Cotton Mill Number Two off Oglethorpe Street in Macon. They lived in a house owned by the mill. It was a hard life. My mother started working there when she was only 12 years old and stopped her employment at the mill sometime during World War II. She often told of the times she and her brother were taken to the mill by her mother, my grandmother. They would play in a large box she had turned over to keep them from harm. Dad worked at the mill 43 years before retiring. When he did retire he was not given a gold watch or even a farewell dinner. He was told please vacate the house within a few days. That is the way it was. No frills. No fluff. Just hard work year after year after year. Then you were to leave the house you had known all your life to go wherever you could find a place to live. It was not as though you could have saved money for such an event as moving into a new home. Money was scarce in those days and it took all you made just to survive day to day, month to month. They were hard years but good years. As I look back I can see they were years that molded my life into what it has become, for all people and places influence us even if we do not realize it at the time. I knew my parents loved us even though their way of showing it was not an open display of affection. My father would eventually die from brown lung disease due to the dustiness of his work environment.

Mill village people kept to themselves. They didn't exactly mix in and mingle because of the rejection they suffered by those who lived a life outside of the mill. We didn't reject them. They rejected us because we came from the other side. People from the mill village stuck together through thick and thin. It was really a city within a city with people banding together for the common cause—survival.

I had to work hard and scrounge to get from the place in life where I started to ending my career as the sheriff of Bibb County. It was that hard work from a simple beginning that made me desire more out of my life than my father had. I wanted a better life for myself and the family I would one day have.

═══ CHAPTER 2 ═══

When I was a child about eight, I had an encounter that showed me just what I was capable of when I knew I had to take action. In the summertime of my childhood, lavender flowers would be blooming and bees would fly into the center of those little flowers. Whenever we saw a bee fly in we would close the blossom with the bee trapped inside. We would then pull the bloom off the stalk and put it into a quart mason jar. I had a jar and I was catching bees. I don't remember what I would do with the bees but it was a fun activity.

On this particular occasion a boy in the neighborhood, who was probably 13 or 14 years old, came up to me and said, "Turn the bees loose." I said, "No. I'm not going to turn them loose." He puffed himself up real big and said once again, "Turn them loose." I stood my ground and said, "No. I just caught them." Well, he slapped me and knocked me around, eventually grabbing the jar out of my hand. When he did that my brother jumped in there right quick and took up for me. My brother probably didn't weigh 90 pounds himself. He was tall but he was so thin he didn't really amount to any size. We all had brothers and we fought for each other.

The boy who had hit me was a husky boy. He threw my brother right to the ground, still pounding him. In the mill village they were repairing a lot of the houses; I looked around and I saw a two-by-four lying on the ground so I grabbed it. I went to where he was giving my brother 'what for' and I wore him out. I started to hit him and every time the wood struck him he would grunt. He couldn't even get off my brother, Harold. I tore him up. I hit him all over his shoulders and all over his back. Then when he turned Harold loose I took off. I didn't go around the corner until I looked both ways for him real good.

That summer I had to go to summer school. It was located where the old vocational school was located. I had to walk up New Street and then up Orange Street to get there. One day this bully was waiting for me on Maple Street. He grabbed me and knocked me around a little bit. After that he never bothered me any more. I guess he considered us to be even then.

CHAPTER 3

When I was a little bitty fellow Mr. A.C. Bailey, who later in life killed a fellow in Macon and went to prison, ran a wood yard; this was during the Depression. He owned an old wood truck with solid rubber tires on it. You can figure out how old the truck was by the tires. He was a strong fellow. He would load slabs at the sawmill. He had some people helping him but he would load slabs. The sawmill wanted the wood square so they ran the tree through the big rip saw, cutting the bark and part of the wood off to square it up. Mr. Bailey loaded it and then hauled it back to Macon. They would give that to you if you hauled it off.

Once back in Macon he backed his old truck up. Then he had an old rip saw with a big leather belt going from a pulley on the saw to a tire. He cranked up the old truck and put it in drive. The other tire would be off the ground so the saw would begin to spin. Then he would make a jig so he could lay the slab down and push it to the end. When he cut it off they would always be the same length. He also had a steam operated wood splitter. He threw the wood on the pile and then he would pay the little boys to go over there and bundle wood. He had a lot of wire rings someone had made for him. You would take the ring and put the wood in the ring until you got to the last piece. Then you would put the last piece in the center and drive it down with another piece of wood. That was one bundle. You'd start laying your bundles down. When you made 12 bundles he gave you three cents. Then you'd bundle 12 more. We weren't heavy enough to pick up the ring of wood we had bundled.

Well, we had nine cents apiece. The boy I was with said "Let's go to the store and get us a cigar." Mr. Lewis B. Wilson, who owned the store, later became mayor of Macon and had the airport named after him. I never had smoked in my life. I never will forget what he said next, "Get King Edward. That's the best one." King Edward was probably the cheapest cigar on the market. We got a cigar each and then we sat down on some steps where no one could see us. About the seventh or eighth drag on that cigar I could hardly see the ground. My head was swimming around and around. I gave that cigar away and I went home. I have never had another cigar in my life.

Mr. Wilson was also an amateur magician. He would go to the part of the store where there was a bunch of large cans, like dried beans. He would drive you crazy, throwing his voice and saying, "Open the can. I'm in here. I can't get out."

Mr. Bailey's sawmill was across the street from Wilson's Store where the jail is now. At one time there was a chicken place where Hazel Street and Hawthorne Street split. There was an old building where the old foundry was. E. G. Cargill bought the bricks and made the Starlight Grill on Broadway. It featured music in the trees; they actually had someone playing music in the tree. You could park your car under there and buy food. It wasn't a drive-in theater. It was just a big parking lot with food service in the middle of it. They had a disc jockey sitting above the crowd playing music for your enjoyment.

E.G. Cargill bought the building with the bricks, now the site of Department of Family and Children's Services. The bricks would have been made prior to 1860. On Second Street was the old Confederate arsenal. I think they made cannons there.

CHAPTER 4

I remember that I was in about the fifth grade when all the students were told to go to the auditorium. Tables were set up with about eight sets of earphones on each side. You were to sit down and put the earphones on. A record player was also set up at the end of the table. They would play a record and everyone with earphones could hear the record. Then they gave you a sheet of paper with numbers down one side. The records were classical music. The instructions were to put "S" if what you heard was the same piece played twice and "D" if it was different. Well, I thought classical music was kind of a sissy thing anyway. I was more hillbilly in those days.

My turn came up and the music started playing. I said, "This ain't nothing." I put S, D, D, S, S, D, S, S, D, D, S, S, S, and I filled it out all at the same time. They didn't see me filling out my papers ahead of time. When they took the papers up our names were on them and that was the end of it. I forgot all about it until one day Ms. Mamie Robinson called me to her office. She was an elderly lady who had a big bun on the back of her head. When she called you down to her office you could just about guarantee she would wear your jacket out. I was trying to think what I had done that she could have caught me.

I went down to the office and found two or three other ladies were also there. They sat down to talk to me. They were from Wesleyan Conservatory and I had scored higher than anyone else on the music test. They wanted me to go to Wesleyan Conservatory because I had an ear for music and I could pick up the melody. I couldn't carry a tune in a bucket. They then went to Momma and Daddy and told them what a great opportunity it was. I had a hard time convincing them I had filled it out ahead of time. All I could think about was them making me go up there and practice the violin or take all those music lessons at Wesleyan. I had to go through all that just because I had filled out my paper ahead of time. I learned my lesson.

CHAPTER 5

When I was about ten years old we still lived in a mill village, and the Depression was taking its toll. People couldn't work enough hours in the mill to make the money they needed to live on. A man by the name of Mr. Fair moved in next to Momma and Daddy. Mr. Fair worked in the mill as did his wife, Mrs. Fair. They had moved from a street above us. When they moved all us little boys helped them. We didn't get any money. We just got to ride on the back of the truck. They had a big gate on the back of the truck and we would get to ride down and unload the furniture then ride back up to get more of their belonging and ride back down again. I was little and couldn't do much but I rode up there and started carrying chairs and some other small pieces. We all got on the back of the truck and we started down to Bibb Avenue. That was where my Momma and Daddy lived. We got to Bibb Avenue and got the truck unloaded. Then we climbed back on the truck with our legs hanging off so we could all ride back and get some more. I guess I was probably the youngest one on there.

There was a boy named Ernest Davis with us who was probably about 15 or 16 years old. He was sitting next to me and as the truck pulled off to go get some more furniture he turned to me and said, "You haven't done no work," and he pushed me off the truck. I hit the ground on my hands and knees. I had a big cold cream jar under my right hand. The cold cream jar wasn't broken and it didn't hurt me. In those days there was only a small amount of cold cream in the jars and a lot of glass. When I fell on that thing I made one spin. At that age I could really shoot a sling-shot but I never had been able to throw very well. They were riding away sitting on the tailgate like birds. I turned around and with one spin I threw that cold cream jar as hard as I could. It went straight, hitting Ernest Davis in the head and knocking him off the truck.

When he hit the ground I did too. I was gone. I saw he was bleeding but I took off home. As soon as I got there I went to my daddy to tell him what had happened before someone else did. I didn't get knocked around on that one. That boy didn't mess with me any more. To this day I don't know how I hit him with that jar. If I tried a hundred more times I probably would not be able to make that same throw again. They had to take him to the hospital.

He didn't have anything else to do with me after that day. He went into the Air Force and then later he worked for Putzel Electric. I would go in there sometimes to buy something and I would always look at his head to see if I could see the scar.

CHAPTER 6

When I was growing up in the 1940s Boy Scouts were very popular. With the United States being engaged in World War II the Boy Scout Troops were encouraged to be an active part of community life. Companies had recreational activities for people to participate in because they didn't want to lose any of their employees. During that time there were war contracts and companies wanted to provide for their employees and take care of the people. Boy Scouting was one thing that I liked. I got involved in it at an early age and continued through Scouts. I got within four badges of making Eagle Scout but was not able to complete all the requirements.

One of the badges required bird study and bird study was something I was interested in. There was an old professor at Mercer University who had found 50 kinds of birds. I had a little job at the A&P store that would have required me to quit my job if I were going to be able to do all the projects required for the bird study badge and I couldn't afford to quit. I am proud, though. Both my son and my grandson made Eagle.

During that time the Scouts came out to sell War Bonds. They were not called Savings Bonds. They were War Bonds because they were designated in this country during a time of war. I gathered my little paraphernalia and I went to every house in the mill village to sell my War Bonds. I sold exactly none. No War Bonds. People had all they could do to make ends meet for the family. If you wanted to buy a bond you could have $.50 cents taken out of your check every week at the mill and eventually you would own a $25 bond.

I had a job at that time working at the "Macon Telegraph

and News." A fellow there by the name of Blake Jones was the foreman of the printing room. One afternoon as I stood in line waiting my turn to receive the papers I was to deliver that day I was approached my Mr. Jones. He was hunting an apprentice boy. He came up and pulled me out of the line telling me he wanted me to come work for him in the printing room. So I went in there. It was in the summer time and I went down to the press room to start working, helping print the paper. We went to work every morning about 9:00, got the press ready to go, and then as the plates came in we started printing. The first papers would begin to come out about 1:30 in the afternoon. The papers then went on to the delivery area to be taken to other towns. We would pick up our local papers around 3:30 in the afternoon and go home around 4:30 or 5:00. I told them about my Boy Scouts and about the War Bonds. I hadn't sold any and I was down.

Mr. Jones and a fellow named Red Ward, who was Del Ward's father, took me to one side and they said, "You can't sell bonds to people who don't have any money." I innocently asked, "Who do you sell them to?" They both replied, "Sell them to people who's got money." That was a new concept to me. I didn't know anyone who had money. I only knew the mill village. I asked, "Who's got money?" Mr. Ward said, "P.L. Hay." I said, "Who is P.L. Hay?" I was just about to learn who P.L. Hay was. They explained to me, "He owns half of Macon. He owns the Bankers Building." I still didn't know who he was. I was so far down on the totem pole I had never heard of him. I knew all the mill village people but I didn't know anyone outside of the community where I lived. They told me, "All you've got to do is go see him." That sounded easy enough. I had gone to every house in the mill village. Making one more visit couldn't be all that hard so I inquired as to where he lived. "Well, he lives in the big house up on Georgia Avenue," they replied. I had never been there, but they gave me all the directions I would need to find it.

Now remember, I lived on Bibb Avenue, off Oglethorpe Street in the mill village. Although the Hay House is a prominent landmark in Macon today, when I was a young boy it could have been in China and I would not have known the difference. As far as I was concerned it was just another house.

That day after I got off work and took a bath I put on the Boy Scout uniform and began the walk from my home to the Hay home. It was now in the fall of the year.

When I saw the house I was amazed. I walked up the street and stood at the end of the walk leading to the front door. I looked up and I had never seen such big doors on a house in all of my life. I walked up the street and I walked down the street. I would look at the house and say, "I can't do it. I'm going back." Then I said, "No. I came this far. I've got to do it." Finally I got up enough nerve to walk up the sidewalk to the door and ring the doorbell. Well, the nicest old black fellow you ever saw came to the door and he said in a most eloquent voice, "Good evening, sir." I said, "Good evening." He continued, "May I help you?" I gulped and said, "I'd like to see Mr. Hay." He very properly asked, "Whom shall I say is calling?" I gave him my name and then he said, "Would you wait here, please?" He left me standing at the door but I could see Mr. and Mrs. Hay sitting in the next room with a fireplace on the left. They were sitting on the couch in front of the little fireplace.

I didn't see anyone else in the house but them. Mr. Hay must have told his butler to have me come in because the man came back and said, "Please come here." I walked in and to my amazement Mr. Hay stood up. He extended his hand and said to me, "Please sit down." I sat down on the sofa with Mrs. Hay on one side and Mr. Hay on the other side. They offered me a Coca-Cola. Well, all my life my family said when people eat, don't hang around the table. You don't hang around the table and you don't ask for anything and you don't take anything. I wouldn't take the Coca-Cola.

We kind of got past that and all the other little formalities and Mr. Hay said, "Now tell me what brings you here?" I replied in my best voice, "Mr. Hay, I came here to sell you some War Bonds. I'm a Boy Scout and we're trying to help the war drive by selling bonds to help our troops fighting overseas." He asked, "How do you go about buying these War Bonds?" I told him, "Well, you have to fill out this form here and I turn it in to Scout headquarters. Mr. Sullivan will take it to a bank and the bank will call you and they'll process it and they'll deliver the bonds." Mr. Hay said, "Okay. Is this the form?" When I got over the shock I said, "Yes, sir." He proceeded to pull out a swatchy green two-tone fountain pen with a gold tip encased in a gold holder for your coat pocket. It was bigger than any pen I had ever seen. Nobody in my family had ever had a pen. Anyway, he scratched on the paper with the pen a little bit then he folded the paper and put it back in the envelope. He began talking to me and I knew I had to stay a few minutes to be polite. Finally I said, "Mr. Hay, thank you very much. I'll leave now." Mr. Hay said, "Please don't go. Stay and sit with us." Then Mrs. Hay joined in the conversation and said, "Yes, please stay with us." They wanted me to stay but I had gotten my take.

My feet were itching. I had actually sold a War Bond and I was excited to let everyone know about it. I didn't know what was in the envelope but I thanked him very courteously and I walked to the door. He showed me out and I walked casually down the steps and around the walkway, taking care to not cut across the grass. I started walking up Orange Street. I walked looking out of my peripheral vision until I passed the window where no one could see me from the house. Then I took off running all the way to the Catholic Church. When I got up there I took the envelope out and tore it open. When I looked at the paper Mr. Hay had signed I nearly fainted. Mr. Hay had committed himself to buy $50,000 worth of bonds. I looked at it once then I had to look at it again. There were so many zeros they all ran together.

The next morning I was at Scout headquarters bright and early with a $50,000 certificate. When I went to my job at the "Telegraph" later that day and the press started rolling, my name was in the paper. I was leading Macon in selling U.S. War Bonds. Oh, were they proud of me. After that I didn't waste my time going to any homes. I only went to the different businesses in town to sell my War Bonds. I was still number one.

About this time, General Robert Scott came to Macon's premier of "God is My Co-Pilot," based on his book. I was invited to stand on the stage with him and the other dignitaries. I was proud of my accomplishment. When all was said and done I ranked about third or fourth in selling the bonds because some of the boys' fathers were in the banking business. Those boys had to get in on the act too so they out-sold me but I kept working.

Two of the people that bought a $500 bond every week were George and Harry Andros, owners of the Nu-Way Weiner stand. They paid $375 for each War Bond and they bought one every week. George and Harry were both in the military.

I oftentimes think back to the time when, as a boy, I was invited into what is now officially the Hay House, named for the Hay family who gave it to the Georgia Trust for Historic Preservation. I've been in there as a man and when I look up the doors are still tall and imposing. I cannot look at that house though without remembering the scared, intimidated lad who knocked on those doors to sell a War Bond. In retrospect, after I got older, I felt that Mr. and Mrs. Hay were really two very lonely people. They had no visitors come unannounced. If anyone did visit them it was at the invitation of the Hays for a party or some such other social event they were hosting. Generally, everybody coming to see Mr. Hay wanted him to give money to them. All I was doing was trying to help the war effort and help my troop. I was getting nothing out of it for myself. It was a good experience and I found out in a practical way people who are wealthy are still people and oftentimes they spend much of their time alone.

When the war was over I was 15 years old. I was too young to have gone into World War II and then by the time the Korean War came along I was married and had a child so I didn't have to go.

CHAPTER 7

One night during a hot, steamy summer month I was walking down Oglethorpe Street with a couple of boys. Johnny Carr was living in the area. He was a young boy who was later killed in Korea. Johnny and I were standing on a corner of Oglethorpe Street where three stores were located—a Rogers' store, a Piggy Wiggly store, and an A&P store. Winton Bloodworth's drugstore was across the street. We were standing there talking and shooting the breeze like boys did.

One of the boys, who I didn't know, was well built and husky. He started easing slowly away from the crowd. There were about four of us there and all of a sudden I saw what he had done. There was a dog that looked as if he were about to starve to death digging through an overturned trash can, trying to find food behind the store. Half of the dog's body was in the trash can scratching for food. This bully fellow came up behind the poor dog and kicked him about as hard as a body could kick a dog. Well, the dog hollered and his head hit the back of the can and stuff went all over me. This bully walked back up with a smile on his face and I said, "Why don't you kick somebody that can kick back?"

"You look like you can," he responded.

I didn't let him get the words out of his mouth good before I decked him right in the face. I punched him hard enough to knock him on the ground.

When he rolled over he came up with a knife in his hand. I later learned he had gotten the knife while helping his father lay vinyl flooring. He had slipped the knife in his pocket to keep for a later date. We didn't have carpet in those days but they laid a lot of vinyl. It was the kind you could cut with a knife if it had a hard blade on it.

I didn't see the knife until he made a dash to cut me. The knife came right across my stomach. I have never sucked in as deep in my life, trying to get my belly out of the way.

By this point I was terrified. Until this moment, I had never been in a fight with anybody who possessed a knife. Now I found myself in a fight with a bully who had a knife and he had scared the daylights out of me. I started backing up. He was advancing on me when somebody, I never knew who it was, touched my hand with something. I later saw it was a leg bone from a cow. It appeared to be the piece that went from the knee to the ankle of the animal and the meat had been scraped off. It was a green bone. I had the little end in my hand. The big end looked like alleyoop. As he advanced towards me I drew that bone back and said, "Come on." I must have taken heart from the Old Testament story of Samson who, when confronted with 1,000 Philistine warriors, was, by the grace of God, given all the power he needed. He took the jawbone of an ass and killed them all. And here I stood with the leg bone of a cow, thanks to a miraculous source.

When he saw that green bone I was holding, he ran. I don't know who gave me that bone but I was grateful. Every time I see a trash can behind a grocery store I think of my experience with the bone. As I got older I saw the reality of our life then. We were not raised with a silver spoon. We were raised learning on the streets a whole lot of what we know.

CHAPTER 8

During the late '30s and the early '40s people were still not making much money. The Depression had hit hard and even though it was over, people continued to struggle in making ends meet. Many in the United States thought our economy would bounce back instantly, once the Depression was over. It didn't take long before we knew it would take quite some time for our country to rebound.

The typical pay for a mill worker was $1.02 per, hour totaling $40.00 for one week's pay. If they didn't miss a day of work they were given a $4 bonus. The mill had production contracts to meet the demands of the war. The bonus was an incentive to keep men working all week so the mill would be able to stay on target with the contract.

The baseball park was a place I would go when home games were played. On Sunday afternoons the bleachers would be filled with people. In the late '30s many people did not have an extra forty cents to get into the ball game. They did, however, find other ways to enjoy America's favorite pastime.

The baseball park was located near the railroad tracks. Often when the railroad workers were finished with their day's work, boxcars were left sitting even with the fence. Men would sit on top of the boxcars to watch the ball game. Every time box cars were left near the fence men would sit on them to watch the ball game.

When I was 12 years old I sold drinks at the ball park on Sunday afternoon. I had a bucket containing 15 Coca-Colas and one with beer. We had two different kinds of beer. We sold Pabst Blue Ribbon and Hooderpole. Hooderpole was sort of an outlaw brand—a very cheap beer. The long and short of it, here I was at the age of 12 walking around with a bucket full of beer. When I sold what was in my bucket I went back to the concession stand to get another bucket full. No one said a word about it then. Now in 2008 if a person goes behind a bar to work and they aren't 21 years old they will be put in jail. There I was 12 years old selling beer right and left.

The only thing good about selling the beer was I profited two and a half cents on each bottle sold. I only made a penny from each Coca-Cola. The concessions had a little trick. They took your clothes from you and furnished you with a uniform consisting of a blue shirt, a pair of blue pants, an apron, and a cap. When you arrived to sell your wares they gave you the uniform in exchange for your clothes, which they kept locked away. They wouldn't return your clothes until you had accounted for everything you had sold. We had to go through the whole park to pick up the cushions. They wouldn't pay us or give us our clothes until that was done.

Times have really changed. In most ways those were innocent days. We were children with beer in our possession yet we knew it was not meant for our consumption. Most parents taught their children the value of honesty. Today the problem of drinking and drugs is so prevalent the government has taken measures to protect our children. Those precautions were not needed in our day.

CHAPTER 9

We learned at an early age to work hard. Growing up in the Depression everyone in the family played a vital role in the family's survival; no one was exempt from helping to provide for its needs. Those old enough to work found employment wherever they could. Those too small for gainful employment were expected to do their part around the house, taking up the slack of those gone off to work. Although the Depression was, for the most part, over by the time I was old enough to leave home for work, that way of life had been engrained in the family. Times had been harder than anyone could have imagined. Everyone had been affected, some more deeply than others. No one wanted to be caught off guard should the economy collapse again. Our parents taught us to work hard, even if our work was at home maintaining the whole family structure.

One of the first regular paying jobs I had was delivering newspapers. I was about 13 years old at the time I walked route number eight. During the week it started at Tom Cook's Jewelry. His was the first paper I threw. My route took me up Cherry Street into the Bankers Building. I then continued the route up Cherry Street to include an old rooming house, which is now Coke's Camera Shop. In the winter time I hated to go up there because it would be dark. The street seemed very eerie and imposing before daylight.

I remember one particular morning it was raining. Since it was before daylight no one was on the streets yet. I really disliked going to Hart's. Hart's Mortuary was one of my customers but they weren't satisfied with the paper being thrown onto the front porch. I had to go inside and lay it on their table. Invariably there would be a dead body in each room. From the front hall I could see about four bodies in there at one time. I hated going there.

Many mornings I would sit on a paper bag in the Bankers Building stalling for time until the sun began to make a little appearance. Going into Hart's was not as hard for me when there was a little bit of light. But this morning I had to move. I was hurrying along because I wanted to get the Hart's delivery behind me. It was raining and cold out.

There was a lady who would sit on the front porch of this old rooming house. I didn't know anything about mental illness in those days. The fact that she talked to herself all the time was enough for me to want to steer clear of her. She must have been at least 80 years old. She wore her gray hair in a big bun on the back of her head with a large flower sticking out. I don't know whether she bathed or just added to her makeup day after day but her makeup was so thick you could scrape it with a knife. Great Scott, I hated to go up there.

I had two papers to deliver in the rooming house, one upstairs and one downstairs. This rooming house apparently furnished the electricity because at the bottom of the steps was a light bulb about the size of a golf ball. It only illuminated a portion of one step. I was running down the steps this particular morning and here was this poor old lady with her hair dropped down to her waist. She had no makeup on and was in her nightgown mumbling something about wanting a newspaper. She scared me out of my wits. Newspapers were twenty cents apiece but I just gave her one. I tossed her a paper and kept going.

My next stop was Hart's Mortuary. It was a bad day all the way around. The woman had scared me so badly I trembled all the way up to the door of Hart's. It took all the courage I could muster to run into the Hart's building, throw a paper on the table, and run out.

All total I delivered about 110 papers, all in the downtown area. My route consisted of Cherry Street, Orange Street, some houses on Magnolia Street, cut across on New Street, and then I'd come back down. I made $3 to $4 a week but I had to pay for my papers first.

In those days a paper boy would actually buy his papers from the "Telegraph" and then collect the money. Whatever profit I made was mine to keep. If there was going to be a short end it was going to be me. If someone got their paper but didn't pay me I lost out. The "Telegraph" always got their money.

CHAPTER 10

When I was about 14 years old my next door neighbor was Thomas Summers. He had a job at Postal Telegraph operating a Teletype machine. He was about four years older than I and was waiting to go into the armed service. He told me they were hiring messenger boys at the "Telegraph" so I went down to apply, telling them I was 16. I was hired to deliver postal telegrams.

The Postal Telegraph office was located next door to Western Union. Being next door the government could divide the messengers between Western Union and Postal Telegraph. Postal Telegraph was on its last leg at that time but the war kept it operational because of the messages the War Department sent out. When a Teletype message started coming in, the message came on a tape. The operator held a razor blade-type instrument on the end of his finger to cut the messages apart. After they had received the completed message they wet the back on a sponge to activate the glue and then placed the message on a piece of paper. That's why telegrams were always stuck to the paper. The operator had to cut it off and tape it on as he went. To make sure the operator was staying alert a bell would ring signaling a message was coming in. We delivered many telegrams but there was one in particular we really hated to deliver from the Teletype machine.

When a Teletype machine message was coming through, the bell rang once to alert the operator. When the message was normal, the bell rang twice. When the message was going to be that one of our servicemen had been wounded or was missing, it rang three times. When it rang four times, it was a death message. We hated three rings but no one wanted four. Four rings would be the message that someone had been killed. The message generally started off, "We regret to inform you that your son has been …" and so on. It was no problem finding the house and going to the door. The big problem was making sure the person was not home alone.

A lot of times when delivering death messages or wounded messages you would find a young lady there with a small child holding on to her dress. The lady was usually young, in her 20s or thereabouts. I never liked delivering those messages. Most of the time the lady would live at a rooming house. With the war going on anything you could put a bed in was rentable. People rented out extra rooms in their homes and even converted outbuildings into small apartments for rent. Almost everything was rentable.

If I had a message to be delivered that contained bad news I would start knocking on doors until I could find a lady home who would accompany me to the door where the message was going. Often times even if she didn't know the person she would go with me. There were so many people moving in and out in such a short period of time it was not unusual for people to live close by and not know the person yet. She would go with me as I knocked on the door, telling the lady opening the door I had a message or telegram for her. You could see by the look in her eyes she was very fearful. I would then tell her that this was Ms. So and So and she would be with her. I would continue to explain the message was bad and I'm very sorry. I would then hand her the message.

I always felt very bad when I left because the ladies always took it very hard. As a 14-year-old boy I didn't know how to respond or comfort them. What does a 14-year-old boy say to a woman with a small child who has just heard her husband has been killed in the war? We were told to never leave a person unless they had someone with them but sometimes that was impossible. I always tried to find someone to go with me but occasionally there would be no one and I had to just leave the message. It was an awesome responsibility to put on a young man. Delivering those messages and trying to make sure you had done everything you could to console a heartbroken woman was a great task. It was an experience which made a young man grow up extremely fast.

CHAPTER 11

The change in the times of law enforcement came about probably under the Reco Law. This law stated if you could establish there were three or more people who had conspired together to violate a law under the state or the Federal government you had the Reco Law. Things began to clean up. I was 15 years old when World War II was over but during the war the houses of prostitution were on Oak Street. I think Oak Street now is Hemlock Street.

Brown's Grocery was there at the forks. The houses went down Third Street and down Oak Street to the Coca-Cola Company, where there was a bottling company. There was a bee-line going to the homes out there. The war was on and men went in and out quite regularly. Soldiers were here. We were kids but we would go by the houses. We knew what was going on. The prostitutes would sit on the front porch wearing bright silk robes that I'm sure were rayon. All the nylon those days went into parachutes. If we didn't see anyone on the front porch we went to the alley next to the house of prostitution. They had a bell by the back door. We would ring the bell and if we heard footsteps we would run away. Sometimes they would say, "Busy right now," and we'd take off sure enough. That was going on all around.

Dr. Applewhite was the county health doctor. They had to have an inspection every so often. The theory was then that if you eliminate those houses, the soldiers were going to be in the neighborhoods with your daughters. So they permitted the houses to function but made routine inspections of them. Whether that was good or bad I don't know. It was really a big business. It was like the 'ranch' in Las Vegas, Nevada, except it's legal out there.

CHAPTER 12

When I got a little older I worked after school at the A&P Grocery Store on Montpelier Avenue. I would work part time on Friday, all day on Saturday, and part time on Monday. On Saturday I was the fellow who got there at 6 a.m. to help Roy Moates put out the produce. I cut off the end of the corn cobs with a large knife. Then I would cut a small window through the corn husk so a woman could put her fingernail on a kernel of corn. Every piece had to be done that way.

On Saturday I had to fill the potato bins and tomato baskets. If the old man who operated the store saw you standing around, even though you were caught up with your duties, he'd say, "Here son, get up there and tidy up the produce." He'd want to see you pick up a potato and lay it back down. He wanted to see you doing something. Many times we walked around just picking up produce and laying it back down. Tidy up the produce. The store closed about 8 p.m. so it was a long day if you got in at 6 a.m.

There was a store up the street a little ways which was kind of a mom and pop operation. Chichester's Pharmacy was also nearby. I made fifty-two cents an hour working at the A & P. During the summer I would try to work more hours. One week I worked 50 hours. The man I worked for said, "Son, it might be sort of a short week next week. I'm going to hold ten out for you." In essence he was not paying me any overtime. He would beat me out of a quarter an hour for the ten hours. He would keep the overtime down. There was nothing I could do. That was the way he operated.

CHAPTER 13

When I was 15 years old the National Guard had been mobilized. They had gone to war in World War II. I was too young for World War II. When the war was over I was 15 years old, not even old enough to be considered for the draft. I went over to Mercer and told them I was 17 so they let me join the Georgia State Guard unit. The Georgia State Guard was made up of people who were not in the National Guard but had been. It consisted of all those too old and too young to be enlisted with the National Guard. It was under the Governor of Georgia, who I believe was Ellis Arnall at that time.

All states raised their own militia. In the event of riots, fires, natural disasters, and many other emergencies the state would have a force other than the Georgia State Patrol. There were units all over the state. We trained and the Army equipped us. My unit was a machine gun company. We had the 30 caliber machine guns. They trained us to use those and everybody carried a rifle.

Years later I was watching "Band of Brothers," the story of the 101st Airborne. Those people were trained and went all through Europe. The men who survived were like blood brothers they were so close to each other. Later I saw one of the episodes which showed where they trained. They were training at Toccoa, Georgia, in the north Georgia mountain area. I remembered we had trained there and used those same barracks. I felt honored I had slept in the same barracks as the Band of Brothers had many years before me.

Those men were gone but later we occupied those barracks and had maneuvers there. Later we went to Fort Benning for another summer encampment. Fort Benning was for paratroopers. I was a corporal. My Yankee friends couldn't believe I was a corporal. They didn't know what the State Guard was.

The CCC, which was the Civilian Conservation Corps, was mostly located in areas like Macon. The Indian Mounds were developed by the WPA but CCC planted a lot of trees there. The two agencies worked together.

CCC provided one member of a family, a young man, a job. His family got $20 a month and he got $5. The money was sent to his parents. The WPA—Works Progress Administration—was an unusual organization that Roosevelt started. A key component in any WPA program that was approved was that almost all of the money the company received had to be spent in labor. No typewriters, no secretaries, only labor. One project they did in Macon was removing the bricks, beginning at Oglethorpe Street where the Department of Family and Children's Services is, and going all the way to Ocmulgee Street. They took the bricks up, turned them over, put more mortar between them, and repaved with the same bricks because the streets were so worn. By removing the bricks and turning them, nothing had to be purchased except the mortar. The job consisted of labor so it was approved and paid for by the WPA program.

The militia lasted until World War II was over, then it disbanded. I received a discharge out of it. Agencies were still short because our troops were not returning in the same numbers that had left. So many lives were lost it left a gap to fill.

CHAPTER 14

I will always be indebted to my best friend for any success I may have achieved in my life. Through the valleys and over the mountains she has walked the trails by my side. Our relationship did not begin with us having money in the bank or land beneath our feet. It did begin with a friendship that would not wane over the years. She is my friend, my confidante, my soul mate, my beloved wife, Pearl.

When I was 17 years old I told my father I intended to marry Pearl Crumpton. As we sat there together he looked at me and said, "That's a mighty big step, son." That was the only advice I ever got from him about the matter. He never asked me where I was going to live, how much money I had, or how I was going to get by. He didn't say anything else. I guess he felt if the marriage was going to be a flop he didn't want to be a party to it.

At the age of 17 I was still active in the Boy Scouts. We had a good Scout troop. I never made Eagle Scout, coming within four badges of completing the necessary requirements. The guys in our troop all pulled together at everything we endeavored to undertake. There was a really good camaraderie amongst us.

Someone wanted us to sponsor a magic show at the old Bibb Auditorium. I was appointed the job of handling the money booth the night of the show. I was at the booth when my mother, Ms. Caldwell, and another lady came in. I took their money without giving a passing thought to them. A little later my mother came back and said the girl with Ms. Caldwell wanted to know what my name was. I said, "Really?" but I never thought too much more about it. There were no volts of electricity or real excitement on my part.

Buddy Caldwell later approached me saying he had someone he wanted me to meet. He formally introduced me to Pearl Crumpton. We talked a little bit, then said goodnight. As time went on I would visit her at her aunt and uncle's home where she lived. She kept their child at night then went to the GAB College in the mornings. I had a downtown job at that point in my life. She frequently walked to the Crescent Laundry and I would escort her. This visiting and walking routine continued for a time. She was someone I was comfortable with. I enjoyed being with her but I still didn't see lightning bolts. The more I was with Pearl the more I wanted to be with her. Some time later we realized we loved each other and wanted to be married.

I wanted to give Pearl an engagement ring but money was short. We went to Sterchi's Brothers, of all places, to buy a ring. They had a display counter with jewelry encased in it. The lighting inside the display consisted of three large spotlights with bulbs I'm sure of at least 1000 watts each. You could pick up a Coca-Cola bottle and it would look good under those lights. We found a ring with a chip of a diamond in it weighing about a hundredth of a carat. It was an itty bitty little thing but Pearl had her diamond ring. We still have the ring in a safe deposit box. Since then I have been able to buy her another ring.

We decided we would be married in Dublin. Her father got the marriage license for us. We didn't plan a big wedding because no one could afford it. Her family was no better off than mine financially. Our plan was to be married by the judge of the Ordinary Court, which is Probate now.

Pearl and I were married on August 30, 1947. I had $77 in my pocket the day we married. I was wearing a new suit of clothes with a new shirt and tie. I had shined my shoes the best I could. When we went before the judge he was holding our license ready to perform the ceremony. Neither of our parents attended the ceremony. I guess it was just the way things were in those days. There was no fuss or flutter. We stood in front of him and repeated our vows. When it was over I didn't know what was expected of me next so I pulled out a $5 bill and handed it to the judge. I regretted that action the rest of my life. I thought I must have been some kind of dumb bell. Here he was a judge wearing expensive clothes sitting in a nice big office. It took him two minutes to marry us and I handed him a $5 bill that had taken me five hours to earn. Now I was down to $72 to my name.

I had already made arrangements with the Elder Hotel in Indian Springs for our accommodations that night. It was a lovely hotel with a large wrap-around porch. A friend of mine who owned a car drove us to the hotel. We had to leave there on Sunday night because I would not be able to pay the bill. I was now down to $70 not including the hotel bill. We came back to the Macon Hotel which at that time was a pretty decent hotel. It cost $4 a night and it had to be paid in advance. We spent Sunday night there and the next morning I called my best friend, Charles Morgan, to see if he could help me find an apartment.

Apartments to rent were unheard of then. Soldiers were coming home from World War II and construction had not caught up with the demand for housing. Anything with four walls, a roof, and a floor was considered rentable space. Charles said, "It ain't too hot but it's clean." He took us to the house of an old fireman named Mike Mullen. He and his wife were both elderly. Neither one of them could hear very well. The first night we stayed there I thought they were fighting but they were really just talking. They had to yell at one another to hear. When you wanted a bath you had to first light the hot water heater. Then when you finished your bath you turned the hot water back off. We had one room, no kitchen. Our only means of cooking was with a one-eye gas hot plate. Our room was a den, bedroom, kitchen, and dining room all in one.

We lived there for two or three months. My father had given my mother $10 to purchase a wedding gift for us. She went to Kress's

Ten Cent Store and bought us four plates, four cups, and four saucers. Then she picked out four each of forks, spoons, and knives. After she added a frying pan and a boiler the $10 was spent. There were no frills, just the basic necessities of life.

I was working at a company called Delta Tank. Delta Tank was really tough but I was grateful I had a job there. It was the only job I could get and I wasn't about to give it up. It was the only income we had and jobs were scarce to come by in those days. They paid $1.10 an hour for my position as a second class welder. I worked during the day and went to school at night. I was scared to death I might lose my job.

I guess I thought I could support Pearl on my measly salary. I was working and she wasn't. I was paid $44 every Friday for a week's worth of work. By Wednesday we would be broke. We didn't have anywhere to go if we didn't make it. There were no back-ups. Her family was poor. They were dirt farmers in Rentz, Georgia. My family was poor. Her daddy had a hard time making a living on a small farm because he worked by himself. Her mother helped him as much as she was able.

I realized very quickly we would never survive on my salary alone so Pearl secured a job at Southeastern Optical Company.

I worked at Delta Tank next to fellows whose names were Watson Adkins, Weaver, and Hilburn. The four of us ran the hand rig. The hand rig consisted of putting the ends into large 500 gallon propane gas tanks. My first job there I had to use a crow bar to break the heads loose where they were stacked on the yard. In the summer time it was 100 plus degrees. There were no fans or coolers in that building. We had to roll the 200-pound head into the building. I got them in there. I thought I would be smart and wear gloves but at the time those gloves cost $2 a pair. I bought a pair and they didn't last four hours until the sharp edge of the heads had cut my new gloves and rendered them useless. I ended up wrapping rags around my hand to roll those heads in there.

Eventually they moved me up. They put me on a hand rig and I got off that job. I had been to school at night learning to weld. I had to do some electric welding where I was to put three welds on each one of those tanks. When I was through with my end the other fellows tacked theirs on. It then took all of us to roll the tanks through an automatic roller. It was on an assembly line.

I really admired my co-worker, Watson Adkins, because he had been a paratrooper in World War II. He had jumped in Normandy and in Belgium so I really admired him. Somewhere in Watson's military makeup he couldn't get it out of his head that I had dodged the draft. I was a pretty good size boy for my age and he figured I had dodged the draft and missed out on the war. I was 15 years old when the war ended so I couldn't have gone if I had wanted to. Every time I would be in a crowd with those men he would cut me off. I was the youngest one working there at the time so I tried to avoid any confrontation with him.

One day he left his position on the tank and went down to the end of the line. He was doing something down there and I didn't see him. I thought he had gone to the restroom or off for a break. I controlled the air pressure valves. I let the air pressure off and when I did the big rings fell off. It scared the life out of him. He came back up there and he was raising Cain with me. He was fussing and fuming and I just simply said, "If you were where you should have been you wouldn't have been frightened. You aren't supposed to be down there." Well, that was the first time I had ever stood up to him and even then I had tried to avoid him. He was still mad. I began to roll a shell, which is a tank shell where the ends fit in into our line. As I rolled it in there he hollered.

The noise level was so loud in the building that if OSHA had come in and taken a reading of the decibel level, Delta Tank would have certainly been cited. That was the loudest place anyone could have ever worked. You had to say, "Ooh, ooh," in a loud pitched voice to get someone's attention so they could hear you. When you did get their attention you both had to lean forward so you could yell in their ear. It was the only way to be heard.

When Watson yelled I looked back. When I did, he took his welding arc and dropped his shield and struck an arc. Well, I caught a full flash of the light from the welding ark. Everyone knows the light from a welding rod can ruin your eyes.

When I caught the full flash I said, "I'm going to whip your ass." He said, "You've got that to do. Let's go." So we started out. We just walked off the assembly line. I was farther away than he was. He walked over to the tank next to the building. They had a little dressing room in the back where you could change clothes and wash up.

We walked into that dressing room and nobody was in there. There were lockers all the way around the room. He turned to me and said, "You could have hurt me while ago." I said, "I didn't come out here to talk." When I said that he swung at my Adam's apple. I guess that was some type of paratrooper training. He swung right at my Adam's apple but I was really agile. I got under the blow and it just barely grazed my head. His right arm had wrapped over my shoulder and I caught the front of the pair of coveralls he was wearing, twisted them, and slammed him up against the wall with his right arm extended so he couldn't do anything. With my right hand I beat the h--- out of him. The first or second lick I cut his eye.

I kept beating him until a fellow by the name of Billy Luthile walked in. He saw blood all over the locker but it looked worse than it was. Billy said, "For god's sake, quit." He ran out and got the assistant shop foreman, Bob Utley, who later joined the Macon Police Department. Later I hired Bob. Bob Utley came running in there just as I drew back and popped Watson Adkins again. I had been hitting him repeatedly. His head was going up and down and back and forth. Bob locked my arm under his and said, "If you don't quit I'm going to fire both of you."

Those were magic words to me. He scared the h--- out of me because I didn't have anywhere to go. I knew what job I had to do. I held Watson and looked him in the eye and said, "Did you get enough?" He said, "Yeah." I reached down to the floor, picked up his cap, and handed it to him. We stood side by side in a trough to wash our faces then we put our caps back on and went to first aid.

First aid was Hubert Howell. He was the first aid man and the tool man. If you burned your eyes you went to Hubert and he dilated them. I don't know where they got the medicine he used. He was dilating eyes with a high school education. He gauzed and bandaged our wounds the best he could. Watson Adkins had a pretty ugly bandage. It seemed to cover half his head. I wouldn't say it was a very professional bandage, but he was definitely bandaged.

When we returned to the building where we were supposed to be working, all 60 or 70 employees were looking at us. We returned to our place on the line, going back to work. As soon as we started working Watson made that sound again. I turned around leaning over to hear him as he said, "You know you've got to do this again this afternoon?" I replied, "You tell me when and where and it will be no problem. I'll be there." We worked some more and then he made another sound. I looked around to see him reaching over the tank with his hand extended. He said, "I'd like us to be friends from now on." I said, "That's fine with me." He continued, "I guess you know if we had gotten fired I would have had to come to your house to find something to eat." I told him, "It would have been some poor picking." After that we did become friends.

CHAPTER 15

I left Delta Tank trying to find something better. Pearl still had her job at Southeastern Optical Company which was owned by Bausch and Lomb. They were located on the second floor of the Bankers Building. The other end of the floor was the Bankers Life and Health Insurance Company. I didn't know anyone there but I knew Peyton Jones was affiliated with it. He had been president of the Scout Council when I was a Boy Scout.

My mother was sick a lot when I was growing up so I had learned to wash and press my own clothes. I could press a pair of pants with a paper sack by wetting the sack and putting it over the crease I wanted and then putting the crease back in. I was in the market for a new job so I got as dressed up as I could and then went down to the Bankers Life and Health Insurance Company.

When I got off the elevator I saw just how plush it was. I had never been in such a plush place. Thick royal blue carpet covered the floors. In the central office sat a beautiful mahogany desk. The intercom looked like a radio. It was made of wood and sat on the receptionist's desk.

As I walked through the door the lady sitting at the desk asked, "Can I help you?" I responded, "Yes. I'd like to see Mr. Jones." She said, "Is he expecting you?" I said, "No. But he will see me." She looked at me kind of puzzled and then she picked up the intercom and said, "Mr. Jones, there's a Ray Wilkes here to see you." I went into his office knowing I would do whatever it took to get this job.

I introduced myself to Mr. Jones and he offered me a chair. We talked a few minutes about my background and employment history, then he explained a little about the job. One of the first things he wanted to know was if I knew how to drive and did I have a car. His question took me a little off guard. I needed this job desperately but I didn't have a car and I didn't know how to drive. I don't know what got into me but I lied and told him I had a car and could drive. I had never even had a driver's license up until this point, much less a car. Then one day he called me into his office and asked me if I still had my car. I said, "No, sir. I've gotten rid of it." Mr. Jones said, "You need to get one because you're going to start working on a debit." I borrowed $400 from Paul Hickman at General Loan and Finance Company. Paul let me borrow the money on my furniture. Our whole house of furniture combined wasn't worth $400 but he was a friend. I bought my first car paying $400 for a '38 Plymouth.

I was able to obtain my driver's license but I had no driving experience. I learned how to change the gears and do the necessary maneuvers until I was comfortable driving. I was assigned a debit manager named Smith Lawrence. He had been Dr. Patton's roommate at Mercer University but he was a nervous little fellow. I would make a mistake with my driving or pull out in front of someone and he would just about have a heart attack. He always smoked a little cigar and every time we went up to someone's house on a call he would lay the cigar in the floor of the car until we returned. Then he would pick it up and begin puffing on it once more.

Smith was a little fellow. He wore a suit about two sizes too large for him. He was afraid of dogs. One day we started up the porch of a house with a little dog in the yard. He said, "Go on, boy, go on." He was looking over his shoulder and about that time someone opened the door in front of us. I reached back and grabbed his leg making a growling sound. He about jumped over the roof of the house. He leaned against the door of the house and said, "You're going to cause me to have a heart attack. You didn't know I had a bad heart, did you?" I was young so I was always messing with him and giving him a hard time.

I enjoyed working at Bankers Insurance. I stayed there about three years and was able to buy a house on Branch Street. Later I left Bankers to start working at another company and I was totally unhappy there. The guys there told me there was an open debit and if I asked Mr. Chapman he would give me the position. I said, "He won't give it to me." They said they had already spoken with him about it and he would give it to me. I had a good record so I made an appointment to see Mr. Isaac Newton Chapman, Sr.

Mr. Chapman was a man who thought a lot of himself. He was a short man, about 60 years old. His feet didn't touch the floor when he leaned back in his chair. He always wore a vest. He said, "Well, well, Ray. I thought you were finished with the insurance business." I realized it was the same old Chapman I had left and I would just be starting over again. I said, "You know, Mr. Chapman, I really am. Thank you for your time." And with that I walked out. Shortly after telling him I was done with insurance I began working at the sheriff's office.

On September 23, 1950, Pearl gave birth to our first child, Cathy. We were tickled to death. Pearl had a hard time delivering Cathy but quickly recovered. By this time we had a maid in the house to cook and care for Cathy while Pearl and I both worked. When I was off duty we both took care of her. Every time I had a chance to be off a while I took Cathy with me wherever I went. Some mornings Pearl would call me very early to say Clara wouldn't be coming to the house because she was sick or something. I would call my mother and she would always say to bring Cathy right over. I would drive her over in the patrol car.

On several occasions I would get a call while transporting Cathy. I would say, "Sweetheart, you stay right here." I would go answer a burglary call or whatever it might be. She would stay in the car until I got back then we continued our journey to my mother's house. I worked nights and then came home to sleep during the day.

Ray Jr. was born nine years after Cathy. They looked to each other like mother and son. They were both raised in law enforcement. Cathy always took care of Ray. Even today they stick together.

When Cathy was a little girl of nine or ten years of age Pearl would call from work to tell Cathy to take something out of the refrigerator or put something into the oven. When Pearl returned home dinner would be ready. Pearl and Cathy have always been close.

Many years later while I was working for the Sheriff's office I learned from the boys drinking coffee that Mr. Jones from Bankers Insurance Company was in the hospital with cancer and was not going to recover. I went to his hospital room and knocked very lightly on the door. They had a green sheet of paper for visitors to sign. His wife came to the door and said, "Mr. Jones cannot come to the door. He is very sick and he cannot have any company. Do you know him?" I said, "Yes, ma'am. He gave me a job when I needed one worse than any time I've ever needed one in my life. I didn't know until today he was here and I could not let him be here without coming back to thank him for what he did for me. She looked at me and said, "Come in."

I went in and sat down next to his bed. I took his hand and told him who I was saying, "Mr. Jones, I want you to know I went to your office and you made it possible for me to get a job with the Bankers Insurance Company. I want you to know I really, really, did appreciate it and I never forgot what you did for me." He broke down crying and I did too. We both just sat there crying. I know he appreciated my visit more than a bouquet of flowers or anything else because it came from my heart, thanking the man for what he had done for me.

CHAPTER 16

Back in the days of my insurance career I met a fellow who had come back from the Korean War. He was a black fellow and he was trying to raise two calves in the city. He had a bucket with a big nipple on it. He also had a big bag of powdered milk to mix with water so he could feed the calves on Tattnall Place. I went down there one morning to collect insurance and about the time I drove up the cow kicked the bucket over spilling milk all over the ground. He was thoroughly disgusted as he said, "If I could get rid of them I'd do it right now." He said, "I'll take $15 apiece for them." I said, "Okay. I'll take them."

I didn't know how I was going to do it. I was driving a 1947 Chevrolet Cub Coupe. I didn't have a truck. I went home and took the back seat out of that car and then I drove to the A&P and started taking boxes apart. I lined the back of my car with the paste board boxes putting them all over the seat and floor area. I picked up one of those cows and put him in the back of the car. Then I picked up the other one and put him in the back as well. I had called Pearl's mother and asked her if she could handle them. They had a cow that had just come into milk. She said to bring them on so I drove 70 miles with two calves in the back of my car.

I had a fellow with me who had been in the Marine Corp. He stuck his thumb back there and they sucked on his thumb all the way to Pearl's mother's house. We got down there and took the calves out of the car to join their new momma. The momma cow took these two calves along with the one she had herself. Pearl's mother raised the calves for us, then in the fall of the year we rented a freezer. The calves were slaughtered and put in the freezer so we could have beef the whole year.

CHAPTER 17

I did not know it at the time but one endeavor I began on the side would later return a good dividend for Pearl and me. Several years after we were married I would find myself in the arena of buying and selling real estate. It began on a whim but became an investment which allowed us to begin to save money for Cathy's education. Later I would not only buy and sell but also be in the home rental business.

Jim Woods sold me three houses for $7000. All three of them were on Rock Street and Rose Street—the forerunner of the Peach Orchard in South Macon. The houses were in really bad condition but I paid him $1000 down on them. I was paying the monthly payment on them and renting them out. A garbage collector lived in one of them and a lady on welfare lived in another one. Another lady, who formerly owned them, lived in one, operating a little store in the front with living quarters in the back part of the house. They were paying the rent which was helping me make the monthly bank payment on the houses.

I remember the day I was working on the front porch of one of the houses. The porch was in such disrepair you couldn't walk on it without falling through. I had the flooring torn off and was in the process of building a brick wall around it and filling the area with red clay. I was tamping the clay with the cement block. I'm sure I looked a sight as I had rags wrapped around my hands, bending over tamping the red clay down so I could pour a cement slab, with all the dirt and red clay covering. I looked up and Watson Adkins was standing there. He said, "I want you to come over and look at my house. I want to sell it. I heard you bought these." I chuckled and said, "Watson, I haven't bought them. These houses here I paid down on them and that's all I've done. I'm trying my best to get them in shape." He shrugged and added, "Well, come on anyway and just look at it." I said, "Watson, I don't have two nickels to rub together."

It was the truth. I was dead broke. Pearl was working at this time but we had used all the money we had, which was from a tax return, to pay down on those houses. I thought to myself, I'm tired anyway. I'll take a break and go up there to look at the house. We had become friends now and I didn't want to do anything to damage the friendship. I still had an admiration for him.

We drove over to look at the houses. Watson had bought three officer's huts from Camp Wheeler, put them together, and made a three room house. The house had pretty good size rooms. They were about 10 feet by 20 feet, and combined, all three rooms gave the house about 600 total square feet. I looked all around and they seemed to be in good shape. He had also put some siding on the outside. They were fixed nicely. The houses had a pitched roof Watson had put on and he had even planted flowers in the front yard. I thought, I should buy this house and my momma and daddy could live there. I knew when they retired from the mill village they would have nowhere to go. I asked Watson, "What do you want for it?" He answered, "$1800."

I didn't have the money but I went to Mr. Freeman Hart and I told him what I wanted to do with the house. He took me to the bank and helped me get a loan to purchase the house. I bought the house and began renting it. It wasn't too much longer until Watson's mother-in-law wanted to sell me her house so I bought it for $2200. Then the man across the street wanted to sell me his house.

The houses were located on Verbena Street off Pine in the Eisenhower Parkway area. Before you get to the interchange there were houses where Sullivan's Junkyard backed up to them. H.G. Sullivan owned Dixie Auto Parts, which was located there, and also a truck parts and supply type store on Broadway. I gave the other man $5000 for his, all borrowed with nothing as a down payment.

I bought the first houses in 1959 at the age of 30. Shortly after this time a fellow called me wanting to buy the houses. He offered me $6000 for two houses. I didn't take it so he upped his offer to $8000. That scared me. I couldn't dream anybody would want to give me $8000 for those two houses so I told him no. I knew there must be a reason. He said, "Think about it and I'll get back with you." The next morning I went to the county engineers and talked to a friend of mine named Marshall Sanders. "What's going on there?" I asked. I knew Interstate 75 was still potentially on the drawing board but he said, "It's U.S. 80 that's coming that way. We don't have any drawings on it. They've got them in Thomaston." So I drove to Thomaston and inquired at the Department of Engineers. They laid the blueprints out and showed me the route this U.S. 80 was going to take. I looked at those blueprints and I saw that the people owning the property behind me and the proposed right of way, which was nothing but a proposal, would only have 40 feet on the frontage. All the set back lines were 40 feet from the right of way. They basically would have no property left. They didn't have anything but frontage of right of way. Their frontage went up to the right of way but they only had 40 feet left. You couldn't put up a bill board on 40 feet.

It was then I got into negotiations to sell the houses. Dr. Eberhardt and Neal McKinney were the buyers. This guy had been the front man. They offered me $8,000. I did my homework and was able to sell one for $20,000 and the other for $21,500. They also bought some others I owned for $14,000. I bought those first ragged houses in 1959 and eight years later I was able to build this house we live in today in North Macon. I have been here since 1967 so I feel like I have done something right. After we began building the house I didn't have any money left. If someone tried to sell me a car or something else I just wasn't able to purchase it. That's the way I did. I only bought what I could afford to pay for.

I think the Lord moves in mysterious ways. I had admired Watson Adkins for a long time. I would not know that day behind the building as we fought how our friendship would unfold. I knew I wanted to be friends with him I just didn't know it would take several years and a few old houses to accomplish becoming friends.

Pearl and I have always been in business together. Whatever we did we always did together. Her support allowed me to be in any business endeavor I attempted. When someone moved out of one of our rental properties we would start painting right away. As the tenants were removing their belongings from the apartment we would start painting. When renters left I would ask them to take their furniture out of the back room first. We started painting in the back moving toward the front of the house as each room was cleared of furniture.

We had to get it rented as soon as we could. We didn't have the funds to take money from our pockets to pay for our rental property. We would paint all day Saturday then go to church on Sunday. As soon as the service was over we headed home to change our clothes so we could finish painting that afternoon. Someone would move in on Monday. There were times I would have tried to buy more than I could afford at the time. She would tell me we were going to end up in the poor house if we kept buying. It was a good balance of being together and working together and for that there is no substitute.

══════ CHAPTER 18 ══════

I really never had an inclination to be in law enforcement. If asked I would have said I would be a business man. I wanted to own something, to sell something, to make a profit, to employ someone, but I had no idea how. My father would have helped me but my father worked in the mill. He knew what the man across the street knew and the man across the street knew what my father knew. There wasn't a new idea in the whole mill village because the company raised all its superintendents. They sorted through the men, helping some of them through college. Grady Morgan was one of those men. He worked a job in the mill while he went to college at Mercer University. There weren't any new ideas.

Then one day I met a fellow named David Mincey and we became friends. I didn't know it at the time but that friendship would forge a path into the career I would call my own. David was starving and I was too. He was a lawyer with an office in the Persons Building. At least that's what we called it then. Bill and John Hemingway had a little room they used for an office on the other side of David. Neither the Hemingways nor David had a secretary so they had put into use a very practical way of helping one another. When the phone rang in the Hemingway's office and they were not in David would hurry over and in his best cultured voice would say, "Hemingway and Hemingway, David Mincey speaking. May I help you?" The caller would think they were talking to a very qualified assistant. Then if David was away, Bill or John would go to his office and say, "David L. Mincey, Attorney at Law. May I help you? Mr. Mincey is out. May I take your number and I'll have him call you as soon as he returns? I believe he's in the courthouse." So they had a system whereby both of the offices were covered with an in-house answering machine.

I really don't remember how I first met David, but we became friends. Whenever I had time I would go by his office, stopping in to visit with him for a short while. One day I stopped in and he wanted me to meet Jim Wood. Hemingway, Andrew McKenna, and David were assisting Jim Wood in his run for the legislature. His opponent was a man by the name of Red Burkette. He represented Georgia Highway Express Company. The only vehicle Jim Wood had was a Willys automobile that he pushed more than he ever rode in. He ran a campaign of door-to-door calling, walking around distributing business cards. His whole campaign expenditures were $60. I didn't give him a contribution because I didn't have anything to give him. The long and short of it is he got elected to the legislature where he served a two-year term.

Just as it would happen Old Man Ed Taylor, who was also a lawyer, had a falling out with Julian Peacock, the sheriff. Ed Taylor wanted Andrew McKenna or Jim Wood to run against Peacock. So sitting there in Ed Taylor's office Andrew and Jim flipped a coin with Jim Wood winning the toss. He chose to run for sheriff and Andy would be his chief deputy. They asked me to come down to the office and talk with Jim and help him run for the sheriff position. I helped all I could but the truth of the matter is everyone was rooting for him, even my daddy and my momma.

The Senate Chairman of the Commission came here and held a public hearing with the Senator overseeing organized crime. They called Sheriff Peacock to testify. The transcript of the hearing said there was no organized crime in Bibb County. Jim Wood knew better. He used those words as his campaign platform. He said, "Ask the people in Bellevue if there's any organized crime around the Will Parks Clay house. Ask the people of that area about Will Parks Clay." He ran on a platform of eliminating organized crime and bootlegging and found himself elected sheriff of Bibb County.

At the time Jim was elected Peyton Anderson was operating the newspaper. Peyton agreed to pay Jim Wood $100 a week if he would not practice law during the interim period between his election and the time he officially took office. Jim had a lot of power over the deputies and what they would testify to. Jim was supposed to be thinking and studying how to reorganize the sheriff's office and put it together. I think he did. As Jim was coming into office he persuaded Mr. Peacock to agree if there were ever a vacancy let him submit an applicant and Mr. Peacock would approve it. Mr. Peacock would not solicit anyone. Jim Wood would supply an applicant to be hired by Sheriff Peacock and then the man would not be terminated. In those days there was no Civil Service and all deputies served at the pleasure of the sheriff.

Jim Wood had approached me some time earlier and asked if I would like to be a deputy sheriff. I said, "I haven't ever thought about it and I don't know." Eventually a vacancy did arise in the department so I began to think about his earlier proposal. I went home and told Pearl about the possibility of becoming deputy sheriff. Well, you would have thought it was World War III. Pearl cried, "No, no. You're not going down there. You'll get killed down there." I went back and told Jim, "No. I can't do it. There would be too many problems in my house."

I forgot all about it until one day Andrew McKenna, a local attorney and friend of Jim Wood, called and said, "Ray, come down here. I need to talk to you." Andrew was already appointed to be the chief deputy when Jim took office. I went to his office and Andrew said, "We've got a vacancy in the sheriff's office. Each deputy is paid a different salary according to his duties and years of service. This is the lowest paying job in the office because the old man whom you are replacing really uses it for retirement. It's $200 a month for October, November, and December. Then you'll have a raise."

At the time I was employed by Rhodes Furniture Company. Mr. Potts was the manager of the furniture company and Lamar Caldwell wanted him to go to Dunlap Chevrolet. Mr. Potts had hired me to come in and complete his six months because the company structure was changing at the end of that time. The assistant manager would have to do what I was doing, along with his own duties, thus doing away with one of the positions. I worked the six months and then was given the next few weeks' salary. The employees even had a little coke and ice cream for me when I left.

During the time all this was happening Pearl's mother had become pregnant at the age of 40. Pearl had been an only child all those years growing up. Now we were married and Pearl's mother needed her. Pearl went back to her childhood home on the farm in Rentz, Georgia, to stay with her mother and help with the new baby brother, Sammy Crumpton. It was while she was gone this conversation between Andrew McKenna and me took place. When he offered me the position I thought, well, I do need a job. Maybe I should look into this. I went down to the sheriff's office and accepted the job. I worked in that position three days before Pearl found out where I was. She was extremely upset until she found out we wouldn't be eating unless I worked. Then she didn't buck me any more about the job. That is the story of my humble beginnings in the field of law enforcement.

═══════ CHAPTER 19 ═══════

I began working for the Sheriff's Department with absolutely no training. We were placed with a partner and all your training came from him. On job training, OJT. Uniforms were furnished but we had to buy our own pistols. It took about six months to receive a uniform. They did take care of providing those for you. I thought, great Scott, I'm telling you. If everybody gets this same training there isn't going to be anybody left in the department. We'll kill ourselves off.

In those days when you went to work they put you with somebody so your training consisted of what that person knew or didn't know. If he didn't know anything then you would have to figure it out the best you could. If he was quick and sharp then you picked up the same things pretty fast.

Sheriff Peacock asked me the day I was hired, "Have you got a gun?" Not wanting to be without a gun, I had one. When I worked at the insurance company I took it with me collecting on premiums. I had never fired the gun so I didn't know if it would shoot or not. It was called a Harrison & Richardson. It shot .38 shots which you loaded into the front. Anyway, I was proud to get my gun and my badge and go out on patrol.

I guess one of the first things I was involved in would be segregation and integration. In the year 1952 race relations were at a boiling point and the pot was getting ready to boil over. Mr. Reginald Trice of Sinclair Gas Company was ordered by the company to obtain some minority dealers. He had a business on Pio Nono Avenue at Anthony Road. There was a dealer there from the black neighborhood. The next situation was an empty station leased to a black man at Cross Keys. It went from Millerfield Road to Jeffersonville Road, right at Cross Keys. When it became known a station would be operated in the neighborhood by a black man, someone set off a dynamite blast during the night, blowing out the back of the station. The sheriff's department was working the case because it was in the county.

Bill Adams, a former Marine who had fought through the Pacific War, was my riding partner. I always looked to Bill for directions. He was a sharp officer. Bill wasn't too tall and he wasn't too short. When he put on his uniform it fit so well it made him look like a mannequin. The Marine Corps had sent him to England as an Embassy guard. He stopped General Omar Bradley from going into Eisenhower's headquarters. One day General Bradley approached the gate and said, "This is General Omar Bradley." Bill valiantly asked, "May I see the General's pass, sir?" The General pulled out his pass showing it to Bill. Bill said, "Thank you, sir, General. Please pass." When the general went in he commended Bill for being brave enough to require a general to show a pass.

Anyway, Bill and I were working the case. We picked up a lead on some fellows we were investigating. We were able to pick one or two of them. We spent quite a lot of time searching them, then we took them to the station and got them talking. We learned a construction company located east of Bibb County had leased a part of the old Camp Wheeler with a bunker on it. The bunker was where they stored ammunition during the war. It was a Quonset hut covered over with a thick layer of dirt. They confessed they had broken into the bunker and had stolen the dynamite by the case. They had several cases of dynamite.

Dynamite is not dangerous unless you have a blasting cap. Usually you have a blasting cap constructed in one of two ways. It could either have a fuse cut as long as you wanted or it could be electronic, one cap with two wires sticking out. People I worked with in later years who handled dynamite to demolish stills and so forth used a plastic tool when they handled the blasting cap. You didn't touch the blasting cap wth anything metal.

The night Bill and I arrested those boys it was raining. The boys agreed to tell us where they found the dynamite. Bill and I took them to the location so they could show us where the dynamite and blasting caps were. It was in a plum thicket. Well, of all places, Bill put the dynamite and two cases of blasting caps in the trunk of the car. That in itself would not have been a problem except we had a short wave radio in the trunk. I knew diddly about dynamite. I'm telling you, we drove all the way back to downtown with dynamite in the trunk and then put it in the evidence room at the courthouse. There was enough dynamite to take the clock off the courthouse should it explode and no one was concerned about it. Later they got a demolition crew with dynamite experience to come remove it from the building.

I really did not have any concept of what dynamite or explosives were until I went to the National FBI Academy. At one point we were shown diagrams and they explained to us how the atomic bomb was made. When those two spheres are driven together the great force splitting the nuclei of the atom a232 and a235 causes the plutonium to explode and then there would be a tremendous ball of flames. When we got to the National Academy we also learned about dynamite. One stick of dynamite in a sealed off room 10 feet by 10 feet with an eight foot ceiling and one gallon of gasoline poured out on the floor with an electric detonation somewhere has the same power as ten sticks of dynamite. Great Scott, I got to thinking about all the dynamite we were holding and all those electric blasting caps. A blasting cap will go off with a nine volt battery. If you take a battery from a smoke alarm and hold one wire to the bottom and one wire to the top it has the potential to blow and set off all of it.

I thought about it and I got weak in the knees when I realized all the dynamite we were holding in the back of the patrol car with a short wave radio in there and then putting it in the courthouse. We were highly trained people, I tell you. If we had stayed there long enough with the dynamite we would have blown the whole town to smithereens.

CHAPTER 20

One of the earlier cases I worked happened at a time when I was on patrol. John Gibson was in charge of the investigation. When J.Edgar Hoover started the FBI Academy it had four sessions and John had studied in the fourth class in the United States. John taught me an awful lot, especially in talking with people and being able to pick up a lot of information from people. John was a good investigator but he didn't talk much. He was a hush-hush sort of fellow.

John had a lead on an escaped criminal who was believed to have been from Reidsville State Prison and was serving a life sentence. Well, John got a lead on the case so he picked up another officer, Harry Harris. Harry didn't know anything about the case but went along with John. John was good about not briefing you on anything. He just expected you to go with him. John said, "Come on." When John said, "come on," you just went. Harry got in his own car and followed John to the place where John thought the men were. John and Harry each got out of their car and began talking to the man. John talked to the man in Harry's presence then he said, "You come with me." He put a pair of handcuffs on the man and told the other guy to get in the car with Harry to go to the courthouse. As Harry started driving, the man in his car pulled out a gun and said to Harry, "Don't go to the courthouse. Drive south or I'll shoot you." This guy wasn't even a suspect until this point. When John arrived back at the station he waited for a while but Harry never showed up. No one knew where he was. It became a very serious situation. Gibson got really concerned. They called Harry on the radio but he did not respond or show up at the station.

Gibson and Investigator Leaptrot went to the jail to interrogate

Gibson's suspect. They asked, "Who is he?" The suspect said, "I'm not telling you a d--- thing." I don't know which one did it but either Gibson or Leaptrot bounced the suspect off the wall. He was mouthing off and throwing his hands around. They said, "We're going to ask you one more time, who is he?" Finally the suspect said, "All right. Hold up. His name is Emory Alvin Goodman. He's doing life at Reidsville. He's escaped and he's doing life for murder. You're never going to get that man."

That information really sounded an alarm. Everyone started looking for his car. We searched all through the night. We later learned Harry was taking him to a church yard. When Harry pulled into the parking lot the man was holding Harry with a gun. The church was located in South Bibb County. There was another car in the parking lot with a couple of lovers in it. The suspect tied them up, along with Harry, and fled in their car. The young man from the other car loosened his hands enough to be able to reach the radio. The suspect had snatched the wire, disconnecting the radio. This young boy was able to get the radio working so they could transmit a call. When they put out the call asking for assistance, everybody in the sheriff's department answered it. By this time we knew there were two suspects, the one we had in jail and the one we needed to apprehend who had kidnapped Harry. What we didn't know was this man had escaped for murder. We thought the suspect we had arrested was the bad guy but it was really the man running with him.

After we received the call we obtained his picture and criminal records from Reidsville. Then the search was on. We put those pictures out everywhere we could. I was working the south side of Bibb County. Jackson's Court, where there was a bar and liquor store, was a hot place then. Stancil's Drive-in, also on the south side, was a good place to buy a steak. If you couldn't afford a real steak you could get the hamburger steak.

Carl Barker and I were out in south Bibb County working a

wreck. We were just about finished with the wreck scene when we got a call from Tony Lorenz, the dispatcher. Tony asked, "What is your 10-20?" (That means, what's your location?) We told him we were at Heard School, south Bibb County. He said, "Forget it. You're too far out." That night when I first came on shift I had made all the rounds of putting pictures out. I could tell by Tony's voice something was brewing and I knew this guy was still loose. I said, "What have you got, Tony?" He replied, "I just got a call from Jackson's Court informing us Emory Alvin Goodman just left there and he's in a Plymouth Fury heading toward Macon." He gave me the color of the car and the tag number.

Carl Barker and I started riding. I was driving a '58 Chevrolet wide open. When we got to Highway 247 I made the turn to come under the overpass and I'm almost sure we left the ground. We didn't have big springs on the cars like they have now. As I went around that curve we had sparks shooting from the ground. I must have been going 75 miles an hour. I'm telling you, I hung that curve in there and gave it the gas and pulled it out of the curve. I remember Carl was hanging on. We didn't have seat belts. He was holding onto the seat and saying, "We ain't going to make that!"

The one thing Carl could do better than anyone I ever rode with was *see.* He had good vision. He could see everything. We slowed down when went we got near Stancil's and started in slowly. I was going about 35 miles an hour and all of a sudden Carl said, "There he is there!" I made a hard left turn and gravel went everywhere. I slid in there and locked it down. My front bumper was against his back bumper and his front bumper was against the fence at Stancil's. Everybody came running out. I opened the door and stepped out behind the door of my car with a gun in my hand knowing he was armed.

His Plymouth Fury had a back windshield as big as the front windshield. I could see a girl sitting in the front seat with him. Carl was on the other side of our patrol car. I wanted the suspect to come out so I hollered, "Put your hands out the window!" There was no response from him. I called another time, "I'm going to give you a last chance to put your hands out the window. If you don't I'm going to open fire and you're not going to get another chance." Still no response. Well, I had a line of sight that I could shoot through the back window and the front window to get his attention without killing either one of them.

I was shooting a .38 special with a high velocity and a 150-foot range. I had improved a whole lot on my weaponry since the first gun I had owned in law enforcement. The fugitive stuck his hands out the window and immediately we closed in. I saw the gun in the floor of the car and I said, "Don't get killed over the gun because I'll kill you now." I opened his door and jerked him out of the car. The girl didn't know anything. We got him out of there, put handcuffs on him, and turned him in. Goodman was doing life in Reidsville for murder. In all probability he's dead now.

At the time that all this happened, Harry was recuperating from an operation. Gibson just wanted to have two cars down there so he took Harry along. He really didn't think he needed another person. Goodman was bad news. He probably would have killed Harry had he not been able to steal the car from the boy and girl. The couple in the car probably saved Harry's life. Goodman was not going to take Harry along and he was not going to turn him loose.

The fact that the boy knew how to work with electronics helped them tremendously. Talk about things beginning to fall in line for you. Things really fell in line that night when they put the radio back together and connected the wires. We hated to tell Harry's wife that he had been captured, and we didn't know where he was—but someone had to tell her. We promised her we were doing all we could, and in the end, Harry was safely returned.

CHAPTER 21

I was riding with a big fellow named Julian Bowden. Julian was about six feet four inches tall. He was 64-65 years old so he had already passed the time limit for being out on patrol. Julian had come into law enforcement later in his life and he wasn't experienced in hand-to-hand combat at all. His size pulled him through most things. Most people were intimidated by him and just obeyed him out of sheer fear.

One night while I was still brand new with the Sheriff's Department I was riding with him. We got a call from dispatch telling us there was a drunk fellow raising Cain. We went to the location and Julian said to the man causing all the ruckus, "You're under arrest. I'm going to take you in." He began to run so I took off running after him.

He ran up the steps of the fire escape on a house, stopping on the first landing. It was dark as pitch as we ran, me following close behind him. He held on to both sides of the rail with his hands, lifted his feet, and kicked me like an ox. I turned somersaults coming back down those steps, hitting the ground with a hard thud. I knew that wasn't the way to do what needed to be done so I went up again. He kicked me again. The third time I went up I brought him down.

When we got to the bottom I realized it was Stacy Meeks. I had no idea when the chase began that it was Stacy. Stacy was a piano mover. He could pick up one end of an 800-pound piano. He was built like a refrigerator. Julian and I got him into the car and put him jail. He spent his time in jail and was then released.

After he sobered up I didn't see anything of Stacy until about 2 o'clock one morning. I walked into the old steakhouse located on Emery Highway across from the Rainbow Drive-in. I walked through the restaurant finding a place to sit at the counter and he said, "Ray, I want to tell you how sorry I am about what I did." I replied, "Well, Stacy, I'm not mad with you but I think there ought to be an understanding. Next time I come after you, if there is a next time, I'm going to tell you one time to get in the car, you're under arrest, and submit to the handcuffs. If you don't do it I'm going to break your left leg with this pistol. If you still don't move I'm going to break your right leg with the pistol. I'm going to shoot both of your legs out from under you. I just think you ought to know that." I meant every word of it. He said, "You won't ever have any more trouble with me. I'll give you my word. You won't ever have no more trouble." After that we became friends. When he was sober he was just as nice of a guy as you'd ever want to meet.

CHAPTER 22

Brother E.C. Sheehan, the Pastor of Mikado Baptist Church, had a team in a church league playing baseball. Freddie Dawson played in that league. Brother Sheehan was umpiring when Freddie hit the ball; Brother Sheehan called Freddie out. Freddie hit the ground and they had to restrain him to keep him from fighting the preacher. He was going to whip Sheehan. I talked to Sheehan years later when he was an old man and he said he remembered it well. He said, "Freddie Dawson had all the makings of a big league ball player. He could have made the big leagues." I thought the same thing. He came out of Pendleton Homes and was a good looking guy and very personable. The liquor made him go bad.

At one time Freddie Dawson, his brother Ken, and his father were all in Reidsville at the same time. They kept it in the family.

CHAPTER 23

Once I answered a call on Chestney Road, which was Old Camp Wheeler. I was by myself. When I got there I found two black guys standing about two feet apart from each other, eyeball to eyeball. Both of them had their hands in their pockets. I knew they had either guns or knives. I didn't know which but I knew it was something bad. They were fighting mad but they hadn't passed any punches at that time. I took command and said, "Stop, right now! Stop right where you're at and move back! I'm going to talk to you one at a time. I'm going to give him a chance to talk and then you'll have a chance, whichever."

I looked to the one I wanted to talk to first and continued, "All right, what's your name?" The man on the other side said, "His name's Willie James Smith." Willie James quickly jumped in, "I know what my name is." He almost pulled the weapon from his pocket. I said, "I told you we were going to talk one at a time." They seemed to calm a little before the one said, "All right. I'll tell you what it is. My house burned down. I didn't have anywhere to take my goats. I had seven goats. I had them goats out there and he killed my goats. He killed them." I said, "All right. Hold what you've got. Don't say nothing." Then I turned to the other fellow to let him respond. "What do you say about that?" I asked him. The man said, "Yes, sir. His house burned down three years ago. He left them goats out here. I've been putting up with them goats three years. Every night, knock, knock, knock, knock, knock, knock, knock, knock, knock." I said, "What does that mean, knock, knock, knock?" He said, "Under the house their horns hit the wood. I can't even get any sleep with that knock, knock, knock, knock."

I thought for just a minute trying to pull any wisdom I could from under my hat. Finally I said, "All right. Y'all split up. I want one to go and get out of here. You both have a complaint and it ought to be settled in the Civil Court of Bibb County. Now, if you think he's taken some of your property then you sue him in Small Claims Court. He'll have to justify why he killed your goats and you'll have to justify why you left them there three years." They stared at me, then at one another, then backed off. I solved that one and got back in my car. I was glad to get out of there.

═══════ CHAPTER 24 ═══════

In law enforcement we never knew the circumstances we would find ourselves in. Once when I was chief deputy I had a most unusual case. I heard the call go over the radio concerning a woman being killed crossing Franklinton Road. A little brick store was located on the corner with some small houses behind it where the lady lived. Across the street from the store was a grocery store.

When I got there we blocked off the road where she was lying. It was a tragic death; she was killed instantly. Both of her legs were compounded and I could see the bone sticking out of them. Her dress was up to her knees and I noticed she was wearing the kind of cotton stockings poor ladies had to wear. The ladies only had nylon and cotton hose back then. Since no one could afford nylons most of the ladies wore the cotton stockings. I always felt sorry for the ladies. If they wore cotton stockings the poor women had to pull them up on their leg, twist it in a knot, and then roll the edge over the knot. That maneuver would hold them up. There was no elastic in the top of them. This lady was wearing those cotton stockings.

I looked at her dress and it was obviously made from scraps of cloth. I don't think it was made from feed bags like so many of the ladies used to make dresses. It was, nonetheless, made from scraps of different fabrics, all kind of blended together.

I talked to the officers working the traffic accident and took down all the information they had gathered. Then I looked all around to make an assessment of the situation for myself. Lo and behold, I saw a candle sitting on the road in front of her head. I had never seen anything like that at an accident scene before. She was lying on the ground and the candle was on the concrete several feet from the top of her head. She looked like she may have been around 70 years old.

I stopped one of the men and asked, "Are you related to her?" He answered with an accent, "No." Then I asked, "Why are you lighting the candles? Is that a religious custom?" He said, "She's queen of the gypsies." I said, "Queen?" And he answered, "Yes. Queen of the gypsies." Well, that floored me. She didn't look like a queen and she didn't dress like a queen, but they said she was a queen.

Memorial Chapel Funeral Home came out to the scene and picked up her body because they were on call. They took her body into the funeral home and began preparations for burial. Later that evening calls began to come in from all over the country about this woman. People were inquiring where the body had been taken and what the arrangements were. The network was hot with it. Some men approached Bill Snow, Jr. at Memorial Chapel, wanting to rent the chapel. I believe they offered him something in the neighborhood of $3000 to $5000 to rent the entire chapel for three or four days. Bill agreed to let them rent it.

The woman's body was all prepared for the burial, lying in the casket. Now this wasn't a cheap wooden casket. It was the best. R.A. King was the coroner at that time, but he also represented Wilbur Vault Company. Wilbur Vault Company had a motto saying they had vaults that water could not get into. This was a top-of-the-line casket that was very expensive.

Caravans of people all ages began pouring into Macon. The chapel was filled with chicken bones and RC Cola bottles. Kids were running around everywhere playing inside the funeral home. They had the entire chapel.

When the caravan arrived at Riverside Cemetery it was obvious that whoever had purchased the plot had bought a choice part of the cemetery. This particular plot had high visibility from the highway. Eventually everyone arrived and the service began. At one point in the service it required something to be poured over her casket. I don't know if it was in remembrance or some other type of ritual but these people were pouring all types of substances, including whiskey, over that casket. I've seen in the movies where they drop a little sand but here they were pouring.

Coroner King was there to make sure everything was all right with the vault he had sold to these people. The coroner had a little nasal drip causing him to clear his throat every time he spoke. He saw them pouring all that stuff and it made him nervous. The coroner said, "Uhhh, uhhh, look a-here. I can't guarantee that casket with y'all pouring all that stuff in there. No, I can't guarantee it with that." He was all upset about his vault. No one had ever been a part of this kind of burial before. The men involved with the burying couldn't believe anyone would purchase such an expensive vault and then let other people desecrate it in such a manner as was being done.

They buried the lady with the title "Queen of the Gypsies." I watched later when the monument went up. She was buried first class with a very nice high-pitched marble monument.

I can remember that night so long ago, when I looked down upon the body of an older woman lying in the middle of the street and how sorry I felt for her. I had no idea who she was with her rolled up stockings and her homemade dress. The Queen of the Gypsies was killed on a street in Macon, Georgia.

Each year Macon hosts a tour of the Riverside Cemetery called "The Rose Hill Ramble." Tourists come from all over to walk through the cemetery and learn of famous people buried there. I have often wondered if anyone knows anything about "The Queen of the Gypsies."

CHAPTER 25

There is one story particularly touching to me. I was called to go to the south bound ramp of Interstate 75 at the place it goes under U.S. 80, or Eisenhower Parkway. A young man was hit, we think by a truck that got too close to him and knocked him down as he was thumbing. No one ever stopped or acknowledged anything about the accident.

The boy's body was brought in to the morgue for assessment. They ran the boy's prints and no fingerprints were on file. His height, weight, race, possible age, fingerprint pattern, and all other pertinent information were sent to the NCIC, National Crime Information Center, and nothing happened. The body stayed at the morgue in refrigeration for about three months and finally we gave up ever being able to solve the mystery of who this boy might be. We had his photograph but nothing else.

There was a burial space at Evergreen Cemetery located on Houston Avenue. The coroner, Sheriff Jimmy Bloodworth, two people from the funeral home, and I went to the cemetery to have a little funeral service for him. We asked a minister to join us and say a few words on the boy's behalf. We still didn't know who the boy was. He would be an unknown but we had a funeral service and buried him with a Christian burial. His grave was marked as an unknown. We never knew who he was.

I always thought, there is a mother somewhere trying to find her son. Some father, brother, sister, aunt, uncle, someone out there was missing a family member. It was so tragic to me—this young boy, killed in Macon, Georgia, with no identification at all, nothing in his pockets, and no one miss him. That was a misfortune.

CHAPTER 26

A woman was reported missing. She had been seen at her house earlier in the day but no one had seen her since. This woman had taken in a boy who was mentally retarded and he lived in the house with her. I don't think it was co-habitation, she was just taking in a needy boy and befriending him. We didn't know what had happened to the lady but we began an investigation. The boy was brought in for questioning and the interview with him was done very, very carefully because there was already a problem in deciphering truth from untruth with him. Of course he denied any wrong-doing to start with.

I kept working with him and eventually he agreed to tell me he had killed the woman. I asked him how he killed her. He began by telling me she had fussed at him about something earlier in the day. As she was coming around the corner of the house he picked up a large stone and hit her in the head with it. She had died instantly. Then I began to question the boy about where he had hid the body. He agreed to take me to the place and show me where he had buried her.

Some of the other officers and I drove back to the house where the lady had lived. I instructed the men where to begin digging, guiding them carefully so they would not damage or put any other marks on the body. We knew the wounds already inflicted on the body during the murder from the boy's description. I was trying to make sure we did not put any other marks or nicks on the body. I said, "Stop here." No one had touched the body up until this point. It was in west Bibb County where there was a lot of sandy soil. I got down on the ground and began to gently push and pull the sand away with my hands.

My hands reached the body and I kept digging until I could remove as much soil around the body as possible. I wanted to be able to take photographs and then remove the body from the sand to see what really happened. Never before had I dug someone up who had been murdered and was lying in a grave that had been dug to hide the body. She had her clothes on but a shovel can damage a body in a haphazardly pattern. If you are not careful when digging, you will hit the body thinking you are still only digging into dirt. I used my hands as a digging tool because they would inflict less harm to a body than a shovel and I would be able to feel the body as soon as I came upon it.

CHAPTER 27

When Rock Robertson became sheriff there were only 38 people working in the offices. The sheriff's department was really a one-man show. As a deputy we had to help people in all sorts of situations. We were all things to all people. We operated basically on our own. Those days you were an investigator and a patrolman. You could handle a wreck, you could handle a homicide, and you were half-way welfare. If people were stranded you had to help them. Now there are about 270 officers in the department and there are different divisions to handle the cases.

I was on patrol one night in 1958 and the temperature was rapidly dropping. We put our coats in the car because we knew if we had to get out it was going to be cold. We were in east Bibb County on the highway. We turned to the right and started down 129.

After we passed Lee & Eddie's Barbeque I looked and saw an old man and an old woman with two children walking down the street. None of them had on sufficient clothing for the weather. I stopped the car and got out to talk to them. I learned they were going to Florida. They were dead broke so they were walking. We put them in the car, and took them to a place where we could talk to them and figure our next move. The heater was on and it was warm in the car.

After a little conversation the lady informed me the little girl was epileptic and she did not have any more of her medicine. I thought, well, I'm not a doctor. I drove them to Cherokee Pharmacy at the corner of Montpelier and Pio Nono so I could talk to the old gentleman there that I knew. I told him about the situation and circumstances of this family. He said, "Ray, bring them in here and let me see her." I went back to the car and asked them to come inside with me.

When we got in the pharmacist laid three pills on the counter and asked the lady which one the little girl took. That was in the days before generic drugs. If you took a medication there was only one kind and color of it. She showed him which pill the child took, which was a mid-dose. It was for a child but it was a mid-dose. The pharmacist said, "Ray, there isn't a thing I can do without a doctor's prescription. They would take my license." At the same time he was telling me all the reasons he could not give us any medication he was putting the pills in a bottle. He then said, "Of course, if I made it up and set it on the counter and somebody stole it, there isn't anything in the world I could do about that." About that time he turned his back to the counter where we were standing and began to continue what he had been doing when I had first walked in. I reached up and took the bottle and put it in my pocket. I got my keys and we all left there.

We stopped to get them food, took them to the courthouse, and put them on a bench. It was steam heated around the clock. They were warm and satisfied.

I got on the telephone and began bumming money from anyone I could think of. I collected enough money to buy them a one way ticket to where they were going in Florida. Then I took them to the bus station, bought the tickets, and on the back of each one I had stamped "No Refund." We had given them some money and put them on the bus.

No one, no DFCS, no welfare, was involved. That's how it was in those days. People did for one another without a thought about sending the misfortunate to an organization. It was just what you dug out of your own pocket and what you got from someone else. When all was said and done you had the satisfaction you had helped someone.

CHAPTER 28

In 1962 I went to the FBI Academy in Washington. The sheriff of Spalding County knew Senator Herman Talmadge. He called the Senator and Mr. Talmadge invited us to meet him at the Senate Dining Room and have lunch with him. We went over there and he introduced us to a lot of senators.

The one I remember most is Senator Dirkson. We went through the lunch area shaking hands with many men. Jack Flynt was representing the 6th congressional district. I had met Jack the day before and Dwayne said he was going by to see Jack Flynt. I thought, well, I'm going by and see my congressman, Carl Vinson. I went up to his office and he had a lady working in there who probably went to Washington with him. She was very old. She got a pencil out and asked, "Now what did you want to see Mr. Vinson about?" I said, "Ma'am, I don't need to see him about anything. I just want to tell him how much we appreciate all he's done for us in Macon and Warner Robins. We would not even be here if it had not been for him. I just wanted him to know there are a lot of people who would do anything to help him."

She laid her pencil aside and looking at me she said, "Well, he has been down because a man in Dublin is going to run against him." I said, "I saw that in the paper and the people in Dublin don't know that man. He doesn't even have any name recognition. All he's doing is putting his name on the ballot; in case something happens his name will be on the ballot." I kept on, "Don't worry. Tell Mr. Vinson to go about his business. He doesn't have any opposition."

I left and went back to my room. She knew I was in the FBI Academy but she didn't know I lived there. About 7:00 that evening someone hollered up to me I had a call. We didn't have phones in our room. The phone was about three floors down for me. I ran down to answer the phone and when I said hello a voice answered, "Is this Raymond Wilkes?" I replied, "Yes, sir, it is." He said, "The FBI checked on you and while you were in that school they dropped in to see what you were doing at night, if you were doing your studying or if you were writing your notes." I said, "Yes, sir, I am." He said, "I understand you came by my office today?" I answered, "Yes, sir. I didn't want anything. I just wanted to speak to you and tell you how much we appreciate what you've done for us. I didn't want anything." He then asked, "When will you be back?" I had to think for a minute. I said, "Mr. Vinson, I won't be back. They don't have excused absences and I have to be in school." He said, "Well, what time does school start?" I said, "8:30 in the morning." What he said next floored me, "Well, I'm in my office at 6:15. I'll expect to see you in the morning."

I thought, what have I got into? I didn't have any transportation and I was a good mile from the Capitol. I didn't know how I was going to get to his office and back to the Academy that early and not be late for my classes. The next morning when I got up I shaved, took my bath, and dressed, all from 4 to 5 a.m. I then started walking. I walked in the direction I thought the Capitol building to be. I wasn't even sure I could find the Capitol office building, but I did, and found his office.

I tapped lightly on the door and he answered. He's a little short fellow and I'm tall so I towered over him. When he answered the door I shook his hand and introduced myself, "Mr. Vinson, I'm Raymond Wilkes."

He was just as friendly as he could be. He said, "Come on in here, son." So he and I went in his office. No one was in the waiting room, not even the secretary. He offered me a seat and he took his chair behind the desk. We made small talk and then he asked, "What can I do for you?" I was a little taken back. I had told him on the phone I didn't want anything. I answered, "Nothing, Mr. Vinson.

I just wanted to speak to you and tell you people down home in Georgia really appreciate what you're doing."

He started talking and he got real loose. He said, "Mr. Wilkes, do you know what my job is?" I said, "Yes, sir. You're the chairman of the House Appropriations Committee." He slapped the palm of his hand on his desk and he said, "There's not a d--- cent spent by the U.S. Government that doesn't come across this desk. Have you ever seen my committee room?" Well, I had never seen anybody's committee room. He took me in there and showed it to me. Then he asked, "Do you know where I sit?" I said, "Right there at the top at the big desk." He said, "That's right."

We went back to his office and he kept talking. I kept looking at my watch. Time was ticking by rapidly. It was already 9 a.m. and I thought, great Scott, I'm going to be in trouble with them over there for being late. I finally got up enough nerve to say, "Mr. Vinson, I'm going to have to go." He rose and said, "Well, there must be something you would want me to do for you." I said, "No, sir. I don't need anything." He persisted, "Surely there's something." I thought for just a second and then I said, "Well, I've got a little girl. She's nine years old. If you could send her something from Washington or have one of your ladies send her something along with a photograph from Washington I'd like that." He nodded his head and said, "All right. Give me the address."

About this time Mr. Vinson opened the door. I looked and saw a black sleeve belonging to a man in a chair sitting at the door and there were gold stripes starting at his wrist going all the way up to his elbow. I don't know what kind of admiral he was but Mr. Vinson said, "Let me introduce you to Admiral so and so." The admiral stood up and shook hands with me. Then Mr. Vinson said, "I want you to meet Congressman Pilcher."

The four walls of his waiting room were filled with people waiting to see him. Mr. Pilcher shook hands with me and Mr. Vinson just continued around the room introducing people to me and they didn't get any smaller. All those people were important people. I thought, I need a bag over my head. Here I've been sitting here shooting the breeze with Mr. Carl Vinson and all these people are waiting to get just five minutes with him, just five minutes. I thought, I'd better get out of here. Somebody is going to skin me.

I got to the hall and took off. I had to go all the way to the Department of Justice. I'd run a while, walk a while, run a while, walk a while. I finally got over there and ran upstairs to the class where I was supposed to be. When you arrived you were to report in to Mr. Kolson if you were late. He was one of the associate directors.

I went to him and said, "Mr. Kolson, I'm sorry I'm late but Mr. Vinson called me and wanted me to stop by his office this morning. I went by there and time got away from us." He didn't believe a word I said. He said, "Yeah, yeah, yeah. Go in there and sit down," as he was writing his reports.

I entered the room and thankfully, since we were seated alphabetically, I was on the back row. I went in and sat down trying to get down to the business of learning. It wasn't just 15 or 20 minutes when Mr. Kolson opened the door pointing to me and said, "Come out." A lecture was going on so I got up as quietly as I could and went out. I just knew I was on a one-way bus back home. They showed me into the big office and told me to sit down in a chair.

There were a lot of people standing around with nice suits on who were associate directors to J. Edgar Hoover. Mr. Kolson said, "You went over to Mr. Vinson's office this morning I understand?" I gulped, "Yes, sir. He called me last night and wanted me to come by." He said, "Is that Mr. Carl Vinson in the House Appropriations Committee?" I answered, "Yes, sir. He represents our congressional district." He continued with his questions, "You know Mr. Vinson pretty good, huh?" I said, "Yeah, we're good friends."

By this time I had some confidence behind me. I said, "Yes, sir. We're good friends. I know him." He said, "When will you be going back to see Mr. Vinson?" I nonchalantly said, "I don't know. I may go back next week. I just don't know when I'll go back." He paused a moment and then very hesitantly said, "Can we get you to do something for us?" I couldn't believe what I was hearing. I thought I had been brought out of my class to be reprimanded, or maybe even sent home, and here they were, wanting a favor of me. They had a slip of paper with a House Bill on it and a number. It was for the retirement of FBI agents. Mr. Kolson asked, "Will you speak to Mr. Vinson on our behalf?"

After that they treated me with a lot of respect. I never went back but I sure didn't let them know. I kept them thinking I was buddying around with Mr. Vinson on a regular basis.

When the FBI submitted their budget it had to come across Mr. Vinson's desk for the funding. Mr. Hoover would have come down and asked me personally if I would try to get Mr. Vinson to help them if he had to.

Mr. Vinson was a great man but I was probably the only fellow he saw that day who didn't want anything from him. I enjoyed my courses at the FBI Academy immensely. I reported in March and left in June. I stayed in Washington about three months to attend the Academy. It was a good experience for me and one I will always treasure. It helped me an awful lot. I learned many techniques of law enforcement but also how to build an organization. I was only a deputy when I went and I am sure the lessons I learned there were ones which helped me to become sheriff.

CHAPTER 29

I arrived at the FBI Academy in 1962 on a Sunday night. Everyone regardless of where you stayed had to have their housing arrangements approved. They did not have housing quarters for us at that time. Rather, we were given a list of places which had been preapproved by the FBI Academy. I stayed in an extremely clean house owned by a lady named May Pickens. She was approved by the Department of Justice. When we arrived in Washington we had to report to the Department of Justice to check in. After we checked in we were allowed to go to our quarters, then the next day we started our school.

By the end of the first week I had a friend by the name of Tony Demeo. He was from Geneva, New York. Tony said, "Ray, you're going to get to meet Mr. Hoover." I said, "How am I going to meet him?" He continued, "You're a Mason and he holds a reception for all the candidates here in school who are Masons." Mr. Hoover was a 33rd Degree Mason.

Eventually I did meet Mr. Hoover. We had been drilled on how to respond should we get to meet him. We were told Mr. Hoover likes to talk to the men so step up and don't stand back in the crowd. Anything that was going to happen with Mr. Hoover we were prompted on. They didn't want any slip-ups. It was much like the Secret Service. I had an opportunity to speak to Mr. Hoover and I said, "Mr. Hoover, my name is Ray Wilkes and I'm from Macon, Georgia. I want you to know there are a lot of people in Georgia in law enforcement who are a lot more qualified to be here than I am. But there is no one here who appreciates it more than I do." Mr. Hoover said, "No. Don't feel that way. You are here because we want you here."

We talked for a little while and he talked about cases where people use mental illnesses to get away from heinous crimes. He continued and talked about the Leopold and Loeb case, where two college students kidnapped a little boy named Bobby Franks in the '20s just to see if they could commit the perfect crime. These two boys were well-educated, from distinguished families. Clarence Darrow defended the killers. People wanted their necks. They were prosecuted in Chicago where the events occurred. Darrow knew that the best he could even hope for was to save their lives. In talking about the expert witnesses for the prosecution and the defense, Mr. Hoover said: "Here's what I don't understand. You take two men who go through medical school, they go through a residency, then they go to a graduate school of psychiatry. One goes to Harvard, one goes to Yale. They get degrees. One interns at John Hopkins and the other interns at Mayo Clinic. Then they come into court and one testifies they were insane at the time of the crime. The other one testifies they were completely responsible for everything they did. One's in the east and one's in the west. They've got the same education. What kind of education is it that makes you turn 180 degrees away from the other person who has an equal education? It's nothing but opinions." I will never forget Mr. Hoover's words concerning the case. Darrow did save their lives; they were sentenced to life in prison.

Another day we were going to have a class picture taken. The class was on the fifth floor. We were one floor beneath J. Edgar Hoover and one floor above Robert Kennedy who was Attorney General. Everything you did was in a hurry there. They said, "You've got five minutes. Everyone assemble in the courtyard. Go. Go. Go. Go." We didn't use elevators. Everyone hit the stairs and came down. By the time we hit the courtyard an agent was there and someone would say, "You stand here, you stand here." It only took five minutes for us to get in formation. The photographer had two cameras set up. Everyone could be seen in a class picture. Once we were in our positions two men would step into the places held for Mr. Hoover's top agent and Mr. Hoover himself. As Mr. Hoover and his aide were coming into the hall, the courtyard would be closed off and everyone had to be inside. All doors were closed. When he got to the door he would have to take one step to the door and the door would open. He would have bumped his head if the door had not opened. It was timed so that when the agent watching him saw Mr. Hoover arrive, bing, the door opens. He walked to his spot and just as he got to the man filling in for him that man would move ever so discreetly out of the way and Mr. Hoover would step in. One camera man said, "Bam." Then the other camera man said, "Bam." Mr. Hoover had to stand for only a few seconds because everything was timed so perfectly. One of the guys said, "They're taking two pictures. They've got two cameras. They're going to do it twice." Mr. Hoover said, "Yes, he didn't want to go to Alaska."

CHAPTER 30

There was a time when the gypsy population was well and thriving. Then they seemed to dissipate and in their place the spiritual advisors and fortune tellers rose up. There were those in our community who told us they could see our future. Spiritual advisors and fortune tellers are two separate groups. It is hard to make a distinction between these groups and our churches under the laws of the constitution governing the separation of church and state. Anyone can say they are a church and the state must look at them in the context of such.

A fortune teller called Sister Mary was located on Highway 247. Sister Mary was also a spiritual advisor. A guy I will call Gypsy, because I really never knew his name, was married to Sister Mary. He would participate with the carnival part of the year. Sister Mary would be at the home telling fortunes with the Bible on the table. You had to lay your money on the Bible for her to tell what your fortune held. She had a big sign advertising herself and all she was able to do.

Gypsy came in to bring me a big garbage bag full of stuffed animals. They were left over from throwing the ball at the ten pins and other games. He would bring them to us and we would give them out on patrol when we found kids in traumatic situations. If a child's parents had been killed, or the children were in a bad wreck, or they were upset, or they had been molested, we used these animals to help gain their trust. When the children received these stuffed animals it helped them feel more comfortable around us and it helped us with gathering any information we might need from the child.

The animals served a very useful purpose but when Gypsy

came in to talk to you it could sometimes get a little uncomfortable. As I sat in my chair and he sat in his chair he got closer and closer as the conversation progressed. It seemd he wanted to get close because he was afraid somebody in the next room might hear what he had to say.

Gypsy would tell me about the gypsies and their way of life. He told me how they had their own courts and how they disciplined their own people. He would live with the state fair people one part of the year and the other part he worked wrapping steam pipes with asbestos. The asbestos probably killed him. It was like plaster of Paris in that you would take the dry asbestos and mix it with water. You wrapped pipes with it and smoothed it out with your hands. When a fire breaks out the pipes are insulated for so many degrees before they break down.

This particular day he came in, slipped up close to me, and said, "Sheriff, I don't want to worry you but my sister and my brother-in-law, they're gypsies." The gypsies I've known are passionate people. They're easy to upset and they get into arguments fairly regularly. We knew that much. They all have those same characteristics. He continued, "My sister and my brother-in-law got in a fight. The police came by and she's in jail and I want to get her out. If you'll just tell the officer to let them out, we'll handle it. She'll be disciplined. The council of the gypsies will take care of this and there won't be no more trouble." I asked, "What happened?" He replied, "Oh, you know how people will fight and then one will get a gun and then they fight over the gun. They said she shot him." By this time I couldn't believe what I was hearing. I said, "Shot him?" He said, "Yeah. I don't know how the gun went off." I continued with my questions, "How many times was he shot?" "Twice. It went off twice." I then asked, "Where did all this happen?" He said, "It happened just across the line in South Carolina." I shook my head. I said, "Man, are you crazy? That woman is in jail for aggravated assault with a deadly weapon. I can't get her out. I don't even live in South Carolina and nobody else is going to get her out until she has a hearing in front of the judge and the gypsies are not going to solve this!" He asked, "You can't do it?" I responded, "No. I can't do it and nobody else can." I thought to myself, great Scott, what in the world is this guy thinking.

Before long another gypsy showed up in town. Gypsies started showing up all over the place. They were all "spiritual advisors." They got the word we couldn't do anything about them in Bibb County if they were "spiritual advisors." Madam Margo was one of them. She was located on Gray Highway, just out of Bibb County and on the edge of Gray, which was Jones County.

I began to notice signs all over Bibb County advertising these spiritual advisors so I went to Tommy Mann, who was assistant solicitor to Clarence Clay. I said, "Tommy, we've got to stop all this. Isn't there a county ordinance?" He thought about it for just a moment and then said, "There used to be a county ordinance." I knew that. At one time the gypsies couldn't even stop here in Bibb County. They could come through the county but they couldn't spend the night. I kept thinking about the gypsy problem week after week, all the while the gypsies kept springing up all over town.

Finally an idea hit me. I called the Planning and Zoning Commission and I asked, "What are the regulations for putting up a sign advertising a business?" They said, "You have to go through Planning and Zoning to get it zoned for a sign." I continued, "Tell me this, have y'all gotten any applications for spiritual advisors?" They said they had not so I went back to Tommy Mann and told him about the information I had gathered. He said, "Let me do some thinking." He called me back and said, "You're right. What do you want to do?" I said, "Meet me Saturday morning down here. We're going to have a little party."

Saturday morning bright and early we met at the Sheriff's office. I was chief deputy during this time. We got in the car and we started in one end of the county going to all the spiritual advisors. As we entered each establishment I would tell the spiritual advisor who I was and introduce the assistant district attorney of the court. I would then advise them the sign they had put up was illegal and we were giving them official notice it was illegal. If they didn't remove the sign I would be putting them in jail; it was that simple.

I went out the Warner Robins Highway and I informed everyone of the zoning regulations concerning signs. All day we went from one spiritual advisor's establishment to another and the next thing I knew the signs were coming down. Of course, if you took their signs away from them you've also taken their business.

Gypsy had convinced me that the old head of the licensing bureau had given him permission to have a sign. Well, there wasn't any record he *had* given him the permission but there wasn't any record he *hadn't* given him permission. I let Gypsy operate because I couldn't do anything else.

On Highway 247 near Old 41 by the skating rink there was a house where I noticed a sign had been placed in front of it. It was a five-by-eight sign reading "Spiritual advisor" along with some other writing on it. He had taken the sign down—somewhat. Instead of the sign being up in the air it was propped on two cement blocks in the front yard.

I pulled up in the yard and noticed a fellow coming out of the house. I said, "Just a minute. Where have you been?" He answered, "I've been in there to see the doctor." I said, "The doctor! What's wrong with you?" He said, "My stomach's been giving me trouble." I asked, "How much did the doctor charge you?" He said, "Well, you have to lay the money on the Bible and I laid down $5. Then I laid $10. Then I laid another $5. Then he began to tell me all about my stomach, all about my trouble."

About this time the spiritual advisor came walking out of the house. He said, "Excuse me, sir. What's the problem? Is there a problem here?" I answered, "Yeah, we've got one. When did you become a doctor?" He quickly said, "No, no, no. I only pray for people. No, no, no." I said in my most authoritative voice, "I told you in pretty clear English to take that sign down and I see you haven't done it. I'm just trying to decide if I should put you in jail now or put you in jail in the morning." He said, "The sign's down." I shook my head, "You know better than that. Put it behind your house." Within a day he was gone. He left town. No sign, no man. That was the end of him.

When Gypsy died I went over to Crest Lawn Funeral home. The parking lot was filled with trailers and caravans. A Kentucky Fried Chicken restaurant was next door and next to it was some sort of Oriental place. Once again gypsies had rented the chapel. I went over there to view the body. Gypsy was in the front lying in the casket. Someone had placed his hat in the casket with him. His hands were folded over his chest in the traditional manner. When I looked in I saw $20s and $50s. There was money all in the casket. One of the undertakers explained that everyone owing him any money was supposed to pay their debt before Gypsy left this earth, so they were putting the money in the casket.

I also noticed that chicken bones, paper wrappers, all kinds of bottles, and every other kind of trash you can imagine were all over the place. Bill Snow had told me after the last gypsy had been buried he had to bring in a cleaning crew to clean. Parts of the carpet had to be cleaned, while other parts had to be replaced to get the chapel back into its proper condition. He said, "I came out all right but it sure was a mess." This chapel was a mess too.

They left the money in the casket. I didn't stay to see who got it. As far as I could see the money was all up for grabs. Anyone could have taken it home with them. Sister Mary may have gotten it. At any rate, Gypsy was ready to go. He had his hat and he had his money.

CHAPTER 31

I had an unusual encounter one day after I had been elected sheriff. A young fellow came up to the courthouse and walked into the sheriff's office. He said to my secretary, "I'd like to see the sheriff." She called back to my office and told me someone wanted to speak with me so I came to the waiting area to meet him. He was wearing a pair of blue jeans with a very casual shirt and sandals with no socks. He pulled out some identification to hand to me and said, "I'm with the Environmental Protection Agency. We understand that y'all have taken some catalytic converters off of your cars and a complaint has been filed with us. I'm here to do an inspection." I was a little taken back. He was not at all how I would have pictured an agent from the EPA. I very politely said, "All right. I'm busy right now. If you'll go out there and take a seat I'll get with you just as soon as I can."

I went back into my office and picked up the phone to call Ed Sell, who was the county attorney. Whenever we had any problem with an agency we would call and get Ed's input on the situation and how it should be handled. I said, "Ed, there's a man over here from the Environmental Protection Agency. They're checking our catalytic converters. Floyd Busbee ordered them taken off as chairman of the courthouse committee so we could burn 100 test Amoco gasoline. The man's over here and if he comes over and asks me I'm going to have to be honest and tell him, yes. If he asks me who took them off I'm going to tell him the commissioners took them off. That's going to be my story. If you've got a different story you want to tell him you come over here and tell him your story. I'm not going to tell him a lie." Ed always cleared his throat before he spoke. He did his throat clearing sound and said to me, "I don't see anything else you can do."

I returned to the waiting room and invited the man to follow me to my office. After I offered him a chair he said, "I'd like to see this car, this car, this car, and this car." I thought a minute before I responded to him, "The first one you called out is going to take a little bit of time to get here. It's on a surveillance." He said, "Wait a minute. If it's on surveillance I don't need to look at it. Where's this one?" I said, "I can get that one in here but it will take a few minutes to get him off patrol."

The officer on patrol came in and the EPA agent looked at the car and said, "This car is all right." I breathed a sigh of relief and then told him, "Well, it's going to take some time to get the other two cars in. I'm going up to the jail and get some lunch. If you feel like it would compromise your position to go up there and eat a free meal then I'd like you to know now what I'm going to do. You're welcome to join me but if you don't feel comfortable there are three restaurants across the street. You can pick any one of them you want." He said, "No, I'd like to go with you." So he went up to the jail and we sat together enjoying the family style meal being served.

When we returned from lunch he looked at the other two cars and they were both all right. Apparently we had gotten the catalytic converters back on. He said, "Well, I've checked what I was supposed to check and everything is all right. I can send you a report of my findings if you would like." I really didn't want a report of anything that had transpired. I just wanted to be rid of the whole situation. I said, "If you won't write me, I won't write you. I don't want any reports or nothing else." He left and I never heard from him again.

There wasn't much to the situation but it was an experience I'll remember just for the fact I would never have thought a man would be representing the Environmental Protection Agency looking like he had jumped off a turnip truck.

CHAPTER 32

In 1973 Macon made history with the largest snow storm it had ever seen. Flurries had been expected from a cold front coming from the north but the city was not prepared for the accumulation it would actually receive.

As we prepared for bed the snow was lightly falling. I must say it was beautiful. Macon does not see a lot of snow so it was always a novelty of sorts when we did get some of the powdery white fluff. When we awoke the next morning it was to a blanket of white covering the city. Most places had 18 inches of accumulation with drifts several feet high.

We quickly realized we would not be able to work all the wreck scenes. Cars were slipping and sliding into one another everywhere. We posted someone at the phone so when a call about a wreck came in they were told to exchange names and insurance information. There was no way we could cover them all. We had let the air out of the tires of our patrol cars just to be able to drive a short distance. The roads were totally impassable. Calls were fielded so that we only answered emergency situations. The National Guard was called in to help us.

I received a call that mid-morning from a lady saying she really needed a favor. She lived in Macon near the hospital but her son and daughter-in-law lived in Bloomfield. She explained that her daughter-in-law was expecting a baby at any minute but the father was young and had no experience. She pleaded with us to help get her daughter-in-law to her house so that if she went into labor, the lady would be able to take her to the hospital. I could tell she was upset and I told her I would help her.

I got a young National Guardsman driver, and one of the two-

and-a-half ton trucks from the National Guard and slowly made my way to Bloomfield. The roads were a mess. You could only drive a few miles an hour but we finally made it. I turned in Bloomfield and as I did I met a fire truck coming out. We were both trying to give each other room to maneuver. Those two big trucks were sliding sideways all over that road. It was one time I was glad there was not a Bibb County Sheriff sign on the side of the truck. We finally got ourselves straightened out and proceeded to find the house.

The truck was warm as we got the girl settled into the cab. She was great with child so we had to help her quite a bit to get in because the cab was so high. I told the father to climb in beside her and I would ride in the back, which was open to the elements. He insisted I ride in the cab and he would ride in the back. I said, no, no, you ride in the cab. We went round and round with that a few times before we both sat in the back of the truck. It was cold as the mischief from Bloomfield to her home near the hospital in the back of that National Guard truck but we finally made it. We got her situated in her mother-in-law's home and I went back to work. After several days life was back to a normal routine.

This morning, November 28, 2007, I was reading the "Macon Telegraph." I noticed the accolades given to head football coach, Chris Hatcher, at Georgia Southern in Statesboro. Rumor has it Georgia Tech wants to recruit him for a position as coach at their school but he loves Georgia Southern and will remain there. Chris is the baby born to the mother I helped take from Bloomfield to her mother-in-law's home on that famous snowy day in 1973.

CHAPTER 33

Sometimes events happen in your life that really knock your feet out from under you. One such time was when I was informed by the U.S. Attorney that my friend, Sheriff Jimmy Bloodworth, was under investigation. He had also been informed by the same office of his alleged crime. Supposedly he had taken some money from people we had convicted with gambling. I was really just beside myself because I did not believe it. I told the U.S. Attorney, "It really makes me sick these people can break the law, go in prison, and come up with a cock and bull story, and then we're under investigation." He said, "I agree with you. We've sent agents over to interview them and they're going to put them on the box," which was the lie detector.

I was angry. I said, "Let them accuse me of taking money." The U.S. Attorney said, "Ray, we've already asked them that. They said you won't take money." I knew it was the truth. In a way I was glad to hear those words spoken of me but it also scared me the U.S. Attorney felt it necessary to ask them. At least I knew I was not under an investigation.

This particular circumstance involved gambling of some important people. It involved the Elks Club, Moose Club, and the Eagles Club because they had slot machines in them. For years I was instructed you couldn't go into a private club as a sheriff and search the premises. It had the same protection as a private home. You could not enter the building to search it without probable cause. These places ran pretty much free. The gambling was confined mostly to those places. The gambling supported them.

Later, Sheriff Bloodworth entered a plea of guilty of taking money other than his lawful fees. He was given a very minimum sentence and he had to resign his office. Well, I thought the whole world had fallen on me then. I had nothing to do with it. It was one of those things that had happened and I was right in the middle of it. I had to make a choice to either try to make a deal with someone running for the office of sheriff or to run myself. I had a daughter in college at the time and my son was preparing to enter college soon. I knew if I ran with someone and they lost I would no longer have a job so I decided to run.

There were a lot of people in the community who thought a lot of me and encouraged me to run for sheriff. Frank Jones came to me one day and asked me to run. He was a Phi Beta Kappa lawyer. I had judges come and ask me to run. Mr. William Fickling asked me to run. Win Stewart, the owner of the Budweiser Distributing, wanted me to run. Soon after, those people got together to help me and I announced I would run for the office of sheriff. I first went to the probate judge, Kay Stanley, and I said to the Judge, "I'm the best qualified person to fill this term for Jimmy Bloodworth. I've been his chief deputy for 12 years and I feel like I have actually been running the office myself these last 12 years. But before you do anything to me I want you to go to the FBI and talk to them and see if there's a blemish on my record and then you can make your own decision."

A few days later he called me and said, "I did what you told me to. I did go to the FBI and they gave you a blemish-free record. I'm going to appoint you sheriff." I was sworn in and I was appointed sheriff to fill the vacancy. Then I started running to be elected full time. It was in the dead of the winter when I started my campaign.

It was cold and gray the day we began our campaign. The sky was cold. My friend Jack Caldwell was with me. My son-in-law, Danny Pittman, and Bub Lister wanted to put signs up. They had the big signs made to advertise I was running. Tommy Bates had a crew working with us. John Comer gave us a place on Pio Nono Avenue to use as a headquarters for the campaign. R.L. "Bubber"

Greenway, a good friend, stayed with me every day until the election was over.

James Wood was an opponent. He served eight years as sheriff and gave me my first job in law enforcement. He encouraged me to come in with him. There I was running against him or he was running against me. Don Arnett was also running. Don was a deputy working for me. I actually gave him a leave of absence to run against me. Ronnie Thompson, the former mayor of Macon, was running for sheriff also. You did not have to declare your party affiliation. My whole team ran hard to put me in the office.

One of the most unusual things I did to help with my campaign was to keep three pictures on my dash board. They were pictures of Ronnie Thompson, Don Arnett, and Jim Wood. They each had their best smile on. Sometimes it was those pictures keeping me focused on my campaign.

I was driving home one night and I passed Sambo's Restaurant. Sambo's eventually went broke and they put a used car lot right there on Key Street and Eisenhower where it was formerly located. Anyway, as I passed Sambo's I said to myself, there are a lot of people in there and I should go in there and speak them. Then I thought, no, I'm tired. Great day, I'm tired. I've been going since 6 o'clock this morning. It was then I looked down at the dashboard to see my three opponents smiling back at me. Their pictures seemed to be saying to me, go on in. My body said, 'you're tired. You've had a full day.' The smiling men got the best of me and I turned around and went back.

When I started in the door a black fellow was coming out. I stopped him and said, "Excuse me. Can I speak to you for a minute?" He said, "Yes." I continued, "I'm Ray Wilkes. I'm running for sheriff and I sure would appreciate it if you would vote for me." I handed him a card and I thanked him and he walked away. I never stopped anybody from eating. I just said, "I'm Ray Wilkes. I'm running for sheriff. I'd like to leave a card." and I moved on. I went all the way to the back of the restaurant to the dishwasher and then I came back out.

As I was going out the black fellow was still standing there. He asked, "Have you got a minute?" I said, "Yes, I have." He said, "I was in Tom's Food Store in Lizella when your opponent came in and he put some political material on Tom's counter. Then he shook hands with Tom and he shook hands with another white man and another one and then another one. He walked past me and then walked on out the door and he left." He continued, "I thought, I wonder if he thinks I don't know how to vote." Then he said, "I'd like to tell you who I am. I'm a charter member of the Armstrong Cork Union. I'm a shop steward and I handle all the complaints. I've been there 18 years. My wife works for Allied Chemical. There are 3000 people working there and she's the shop steward in charge of her union there. I belong to a club in Lizella that has 20 members and on each election day we've got 25 people assigned to us that we have to get to the polls. We do that every year." He said, "I'm going to work for you and I'm going to get my friends out there and declare the word for you and I'm going to do all I can and my wife is too."

I thought to myself, great day, you never know who you will meet and what power of influence they will have. I still recall his name to this day. It was Leander Mayes. I was not a respecter of persons. My campaign was for all the people of Bibb County, not just the people with money or political power.

During my time in the sheriff's office James Avera, Harry A. Harris, Raymond Purvis, Carl Barker, and myself all bonded together. We were all idealistic in building a sheriff's office that would be effective, honest, and serve the people. We had no authority to make any changes when we first started out in law enforcement. It would be years later before we would be able to implement our goals and values to the department. Harry Harris became Chief of Investigation. James Avera was promoted Chief of the Patrol division and later served as my chief deputy. Raymond became a captain in Investigation. Carl Barker was sheriff of the Civil Court, and I became sheriff. Through those men and many others we were able to build the organization we had dreamed of years earlier.

CHAPTER 34

L eander would come to see me any time he had a problem or other issue he needed help with. One day Leander had some trouble with another man, another black, and they got in some form of a fight. Leander was in jail and then out on bond before I ever knew what had transpired. I was walking down the hall and I happened to see him standing next to the heater at the courthouse waiting for a ride. I already knew he had been arrested and had been released.

This same day Sam Nunn had come to me and asked me to take him through the courthouse to introduce him to different people. Of course, I was a staunch supporter of Sam Nunn. Sam and I were walking down the hall and Leander was still standing there when I stopped Sam and said, "Sam, hold on a minute. I want to tell you a quick story." I quickly briefed him on how Leander and I met at Sambo's and how he had helped me earlier in my campaign. When I was done we continued our walk until we approached the place Leander was standing. I said, "I want to introduce you to Leander." Leander was still standing against the heater in the hall. We stopped in front of him and I said, "Leander, I want to introduce you to Senator Sam Nunn." I looked at Leander and his nostrils swelled. I knew he was smiling. Sam Nunn said, "Leander, the sheriff told me how much you helped him and I sure would appreciate it if you would help me." He said, "Yes, sir, Senator Nunn. I'll do everything I can." He was smiling all over.

About that time someone touched Sam on the shoulder and he turned away from Leander. I cupped my hand over my mouth and said to Leander, "I'm not going to tell him you just got out of the can." He begged, "No, no, no. Don't do that." We always laughed about that.

I always wondered if my opponent really understood the opportunity he had missed. He could have been the person to meet Leander and say a kind word to him. Leander would have probably said the same thing to him he had said to me and my opponent would have had the office of the sheriff. I tried to never miss an opportunity to speak to someone. I always stopped and spoke to everybody.

CHAPTER 35

One of my favorite stops for coffee was the Sizzler on Riverside Drive. They had good coffee and good food too. One day I had just come out of the Sizzler after drinking coffee with a friend. There wasn't anyone around so I drove out the little alley between WBML and the Sizzler. Just as I started out I heard a call from the radio, "He's run from the courtroom. He's now on Second Street and someone said he may be running towards Riverside Drive."

I stopped my car and got out so I could assess the situation. As I looked down Riverside Drive I saw a big man running down the street toward me. He was huffing and puffing as he picked his feet up and put them down. I leaned against the building and waited a few more seconds. I pulled my gun out and about the time I leaned forward he was in front of me. I said, "I think you've run just about enough." He stopped so suddenly I thought I had scared him to death. He must have thought, now I've got two years for escape to add to my sentence. I put handcuffs on him and took him back to the jail. Here I was just goofing off enjoying my cup of coffee and the escapee ran right into me. That was a situation of being at the right place at the right time.

=========== CHAPTER 36 ===========

I learned early in my career the job of sheriff did not end when I took my uniform off at the end of each day. One Saturday Pearl and I had taken our daughter and the little girl who lived next door to do some errands. I had just bought the first new car I had ever owned in my life. It was a 1953 Chevrolet 210 Series. I paid $1980 for it and boy, was I proud of that car.

As we were driving I heard a siren so I pulled over and told the girls, "Y'all watch and you'll see the patrol car when it drives by." I was sitting almost in front of the old filling station before you get to Burton Avenue going west on Columbus Drive. I pulled over and got off the road. I saw the patrol car had gotten ahead of a car I knew to be Walt Booker's. Walt Booker was a black fellow and probably one of the best car drivers I've ever seen in my life. I mean, high speed. He was in high speed. He had a Hudson Hornet. They rebuilt all of them. They bought all the pistons and then used oversized pistons to give them more power. Those cars would run.

The patrol car had cut in on him, causing Walt to go partially into a ditch. Both cars were facing Macon. Walt was still sitting in his car. When the officers hit the ground Walt threw his car in reverse. Rocks were flying everywhere. He was going to make a complete U-turn, a bootleg turn, and go the opposite direction. I was kind of like the guy sitting on the sideline and another player had the ball running. He didn't have anyone near him so someone comes off the bench and tackles him. When I saw Walt coming out of that ditch I gave it the gas and rammed my car into the side of his car, knocking it back in the ditch.

Little did I know Walt had 100 gallons of whiskey in the back of his car. The back seat of that car goes all the way to the trunk.

The whole thing was full of whiskey.   We arrested him on several charges and the officers took him back to the station for processing. Well, I looked at my new car and boy had I messed it up. I had a knot in the pit of my stomach. I acted on impulse doing what I knew to be the right thing but in doing so I had damaged and torn up my new car.

The county commissioners found out what I had done and they repaired my car for me. The liquor dealers gave me a bonus for getting the illegal whiskey out of commission. I did the right thing and then was rewarded. Walt was a bad guy. It was a good day when he was taken off the street.

CHAPTER 37

In my early days of law enforcement we had a technique for catching bootleggers. The bootlegger made moonshine using a still. Sometimes it was in his backyard or hidden in a basement. Most of the time they were a little more cautious, hiding their still in the woods. Bootlegging whiskey was a crime to be punished so we treated it as such, trying to put as many of them out of business as possible.

Most of the bootlegging and stills were a one horse operation. The man would take the bottom out of two or three 55 gallon drums and attach them. He would then cut a hole in the enlarged drum so he could fill it with mash. This would make a 150 gallon still. He used one pound of sugar for every one gallon of water using a total of 150 pounds of sugar. After this he would put in a hog feed called Hops. Hops is what they made beer out of because it's easy to ferment. To this mixture was added a little yeast. In the summer time the fermentation process would only take about three or four days because of the hot weather.

I have seen revenue agents who could stick their finger into the mix and tell when the mash was going to run. The elasticity the mix had between their fingers let them know when it was going to run. I was never able to do that but some could.

That was the small bootlegger. The big bootlegger would be the fellow with an organization operating a still of maybe 1000 gallons. With a 1000-gallon still the bootlegger would make one gallon of 125 or 150 proof alcohol, moonshine liquor with ten gallons of mash. He could easily turn out 300 gallons a week with a still that large. In those days it cost him 70 cents a gallon to make the moonshine and he could sell it at the still for about $3 to $4 a gallon. That man would in turn take it to the bootleggers who were picking it up. He paid $4 for it and sold it for $7. This man poured it into quart jars and sold it for $4 a quart. That was a bootlegger.

We received information about a big still operating. Federal Agents were called in but I was the one with the information on the still. I've never walked so much in all my life as I did that day with the Federal Agents.

We started on Estes Road. We began on a pig path walking it until it went no further. We continued on through the woods in the general direction I thought the still was located and eventually we found the still. When we found the still it was ready to run. The moonshine was ready and waiting to be bottled and sold so we knew it was time. We couldn't leave. We had to stay there and wait for the bootlegger to show up to put out the finished product.

Wally Williams, who was a Federal agent, said, "We're going to have to eat out of the tub today." I said, "Tub?" I didn't know what in the world he was talking about. I thought about the people over there in the Far East and how everybody sticks their fingers into one large bowl and gets something out. I couldn't imagine what he meant. I asked, "Tub. What's the tub?" One of the agents walked to the back of the car and opened the trunk of the car then lifted a tin tub from it. When he brought it out I saw pork and beans, spaghetti, Vienna sausage, potted meat, and all sorts of other food items. There was some cheese in the tub as well as saltine crackers. Anything that wouldn't spoil right away was in the tub. Everyone eagerly went to the back of the car and chose a can. We all ate lunch out of the tub.

It was later explained to me every time they went to a still they always found food there. When the agents finished demolishing the still they confiscated the food and put in a tub. Then when they got tied up on a case the tub fed them.

I had never seen a still blown. On this particular still the agent was going to blow the still with TNT. He loved to blow stills. He took ten sticks of dynamite. He then took a plastic tool and pushed it into the side of the dynamite, putting a fuse on it in the side of each of the TNT sticks. When he pushed it in there it acted as a fire cracker setting off the dynamite. That's how it worked. He started off with long fuses, then he began cutting the fuses down, getting them shorter and shorter.

The agent had a big cigar in his mouth. He'd puff that thing a cherry red. He went over to the longest fuse, lighting it and pitching over into a barrel. Then he took the next one, lit it, and put it in there. While those were still burning he lit a third one and tossed it into the barrel. All three of them were burning now. He lit another one and put it over in there. What he was trying to do was make the blast go off simultaneously. When I realized what he was doing I thought to myself, no, not me. I'm gone. I took off running to a big open field. When the still blew it blew just about like he thought it would. When he dropped the last one into the barrel he had to take off running because it had a shorter fuse. I was sitting there in the field and I watched as the bottom out of a 55 gallon drum was up in the air just whirling like a big saw at a saw mill. I looked at that thing and I said, that thing's too close. It's going to hit me. I began running and when I looked back up it was still on top of me. I ran another direction and when I looked back this time it was like the "Uncle Sam Wants You" poster with his finger pointing at you. Every way I ran that thing looked like it was going to run right into me. It finally hit the ground and I got out of the way of it.

I walked down where the still had been to see the destruction to the still or what was left of it. It was all blown to pieces. The smoke from the explosion was just hanging over. The smoke contained large amounts of nitrogen. The dynamite and alcohol content had caused fumes. If you inhaled the fumes your head would split open like a migraine headache. That was one lesson I never forgot. I never went back to a still and sniffed the air after it had been blown.

A lot of times the agents would ly on a still or watch it from a distance in hiding places. I heard the story one time about a black fellow who was firing up the still and the agents were lying in position. They were really waiting on the man who owned the still to show up. The black man was whistling and talking to himself and he said, "Well, Mr. Still, today the boss man will be here." The agent whispered, "Everybody stay still. Everybody quiet down and it's going to be payday. I can hardly wait to see him come." The agents always wanted the "big" man to show up.

You could arrest the still worker all day long but unless you got the owner all you were doing is wasting your time. The owner could move his still from location to location in very short order and be back in business in no time. When they said the boss man, he was the one the agents wanted to start with each time. If they knew we were on to them they would walk off into the woods to gather some fire wood to put under the still. Some stills were fired with wood but a lot of bootleggers used propane gas. Each time he would go farther away to get his supplies, then without any warning he would take off running and get away from us.

CHAPTER 38

A man and his wife came into the office to see me. They told me the story of their daughter, who was in Jacksonville, Florida, married to a sailor. This is the story as they told it. The girl came home and stayed with them a few days. After she left a letter arrived at their home for the girl but it was from another sailor. Her mother opened the letter and read the contents. It was a letter written to their daughter telling her how much this sailor loved her. It wasn't her husband doing all the writing. It was another sailor.

They said, "We called down there and have tried to talk to them about finding our daughter. We don't know where she's at." I talked to them a little more, getting as many details as I could then I said, "Let me see if I can work it out." I placed a call to the Jacksonville Naval Base, to Naval Intelligence, and I got a young officer on the phone. I explained to him who I was and what the problem was and how these people were looking for their daughter. He said, "Oh, yes. They called and I've asked him about it and he doesn't know where she's at." I very politely asked the officer, "Will you go back and do another search and talk to him again and I'll call you back?" So he went back and saw him, questioning him a second time. He called me back and said, "Yes, sir, I've talked to him. They don't know where she's at. No one knows."

I was getting a little frustrated by this officer's lack of concern to get to the bottom of the problem. I got a little firmer with him as I said, "Well, this sailor wrote her a letter and said how much he loved her and she has a husband. She's got to be with one or the other of them." He said, "Well, sir, they didn't have any knowledge of it."

By this time I was getting to the end of my patience rope. I put aside all niceties and said in my most authoritative tone of voice,

"Well, let me tell you what they told me. They told me if they didn't get any results they were going to call Uncle Carl. Do you know who Uncle Carl is?" He said, "No, sir." I said, "Well, let me tell you who Uncle Carl Vinson is. Uncle Carl is a senior member of the House of Representatives. He serves on the most powerful committee of appropriations as a chairman. Uncle Carl is not going to come down here and look for her. Uncle Carl is going to call an Admiral over there. When that Admiral comes into his office Uncle Carl is going to tell him he's got a member of his family missing. The Admiral isn't going to go down there. He's going to call the Captain. The Captain is going to hear the story and when he hears it coming from the Admiral I guarantee you the officer who goes down there is going to have enough brass on him to put you in jail and everybody else." I continued, "When this ball quits bouncing you know where it's going to be? In your lap."

When he spoke next he said, "Sir, let me see if I can talk to him again." I told him thank you and hung up the phone. It wasn't but about an hour when I got a call. The young officer said, "Sir, yes, sir, we've got her. She's sitting right here and you can talk to her. Her mother can talk to her right now."

I didn't know Mr. Vinson, or Uncle Carl, until later in my life. It sure did feel good to use his name like he was a personal friend though.

CHAPTER 39

One of the most notable cases I encountered during my career involved Paul John Knowles. Paul John was a very ruthless killer. He is believed to have killed 36 people. Every time he killed somebody he would make a tape recording giving all the details of the murder. For instance, he would say, "I'm traveling down Highway 74. This is Tucker Road. I'm near the intersection of Tucker Road and there's a Southern Baptist Church here. I'm going to pull in behind it. I have a girl in the car. I took her out of the car. She looked like she was 15 or 16 years old. I raped her and killed her then I put her body back to the left corner of the lot and covered her with pine straw." After he completed the recording he would then send the tape to a lawyer in Miami. This person was going to write a book about Paul John Knowles.

Paul John Knowles wanted to be known as the most deadly killer in America. Jack the Ripper never killed over five people and Paul John had killed 36. He was being sought all over the country.

Paul John was in a car in Florida and a man from Delaware had been stopped by a highway patrol. The patrolman's name was Campbell. Campbell had the Delaware man in handcuffs sitting in the back of his car when he picked up Paul John on radar. He pulled Paul John over onto the side of the road to issue a speeding ticket.

When he handed Paul John Knowles the ticket Paul John pulled a gun on the patrolman. Having the situation now in his own hands he handcuffed the state trooper and the man from Delaware together so they couldn't move, then he started driving back north.

Well, the trooper had called in reporting he was making a stop but the dispatch didn't hear any more from him. Later that same afternoon they found the trooper's car on the side of the road and in it was a pad listing every car he had stopped with the tag number. He had checked off each car when he had gotten back in. Because of the list Georgia State Patrol was able to determine the tag number of the car he had used in abducting this patrolman. The tag was stolen and the car was stolen.

The search began. Everybody was looking for him. The Georgia Bureau of Investigation was gathering all the information they could on Paul John Knowles. They soon found out he had been in Macon prior to the killing. Paul John Knowles had been in a car when he pulled into Mr. Bowdoin's service station on Riverside Drive. It was a convenience store and service station combination. Mr. Bowdoin's wife had placed flower pots between the pumps. It was country from the word go. Paul John Knowles had whipped in there faster than he should have. When he whipped in there he hit one of those flower pots. Mr. Bowden had come running out saying, "Get off this property. I mean, get out of here." He had given Paul John Knowles an earful about entering his service station in that manner and disturbing his wife's flower pots.

About two hours after he had been at Mr. Bowdoin's the GBI went out there and questioned Mr. Bowdoin saying, "We'd like to show you a picture and see if you've seen this guy." They showed him the picture and Mr. Bowdoin said, "Yeah, I've seen him. I started to stomp his a--- out there. I started to beat the snot out of him. He came in here fast and messed up my wife's flower pots. I told him to get out of here." They said, "Mr. Bowdoin, we don't recommend that. He's already killed 35 people." When Mr. Bowdoin heard that he had to sit down.

Later I got a call while I was at my home. I didn't know about all these things that had already transpired. I went to the office and Colonel Beach was there. He was head of the Highway Patrol in Florida. I asked, "Colonel, how long are you going to be here?" He answered, "I'm going to be here until we find Trooper Campbell or we take his body back." He introduced me to the assistant district attorney. He told me he wanted me to go with him to interview Knowles, who by this time had been arrested.

The district attorney and I went to Paul John Knowles' cell. I didn't take him out of the cell because of his track record. We had it documented he would do 100 pushups a day. He would do squat thrusts. He would continually beat his hand on the hard surface of his cell so his hand would be tough on the sides. He did karate chops and all other sorts of exercises to keep himself fit so I didn't let him out of the cell. The district attorney and I went into the cell.

I let the district attorney lead the interview because he knew more about him. He tried his best to get Knowles to talk to him but he wouldn't give him any information. He had served a long time in a prison in Florida and he wouldn't open his mouth to say anything. The district attorney finally said, "Do you want somebody to beg you? I've got to go back and face his wife and three children and I'd rather get on my knees and beg you than face them. If that's what you want I'm on my knees." He got on his knees. "Please," he said, "just tell me if he's alive or dead."

Paul John Knowles still wouldn't say a word. We left and the district attorney asked me, "Will you keep working with him?" I assured him I would so the next day I went back to Paul John's cell. This time I went by myself. I told the jailer, "I'm going in there and I don't know how good he is but I can stay with him a few minutes. Don't y'all be bashful about opening this door and getting some help in here if I have trouble with him." They placed some officers nearby waiting around in the event I needed some help. They had their night sticks out. The Major said, "He may be the karate man and all this but he hasn't got any eyes in the back of his head. We'll knock his brains out if he starts that."

I began talking to him and I noticed a ring on his finger. I decided to ask him about it. "Paul, what's the ring?" He said, "I had it made in prison." I asked him if I could see it. He told me I could as he took it off and handed it to me. It was a gold ring. I asked,

"What is that on it?" He said, "It's a seagull." I knew there must be some significance to a seagull being on his ring so I asked, "Why do you want a seagull on it?" He said, "Have you ever read 'Jonathan Livingston Seagull'? It's the most read book on college campuses today." I said, "No, I've never read it." He continued with his story, "Well, the seagull dared to be different from other seagulls. He flew higher than they flew and he refused to eat garbage thrown off the ships, even fish. The seagull said he rebelled and they put him on trial because he dared to be different."

I began to put the pieces together in my own mind as to why he was doing these heinous crimes. He portrayed himself as a seagull that dared to be different and turned against society. I bought the book and read it from cover to cover. When I finished I started interviewing him again and he stated, "He's dead."

When I heard those words I left him and went downstairs. The bodies of the man from Delaware and Officer Campbell were both found in Houston County. They were handcuffed together at the base of a tree, each having a bullet hole at the base of his head in the back.

Colonel Beach was a stalwart football player for Florida State. He was a man's man. He got on the telephone and called the governor. When he called the governor to tell him Officer Campbell was dead the governor began crying; then Colonel Beach began crying also. Two grown men were crying on the telephone because an officer was dead.

While riding in the back of a car going to find the location of the murder weapon that he had used to kill the highway patrolman and business man, Knowles used a hidden paper clip to free his handcuffs. There was no screen in the car. Knowles grabbed the sheriff's handgun and fired a round through his holster. The detective in the car drew his gun and shot Knowles to death in the back seat. That was the end of Paul John Knowles.

CHAPTER 40

Many times during my career as sheriff when I was called to a scene I had to use skills of psychology. I never knew when I would have to think on my feet to create an answer to a problem or maybe even thwart a potential problem.

I was in my office one day when a call came in from Tommy Mann. He was talking rapidly as he said, "Ray, get to Wesleyan Drive at such and such a number as quick as possible. I've got a client of mine who has caught his wife with another man and I'm afraid he's going to be facing a murder charge."

I jumped in the car and turned my siren on. I was by myself but I gave it all I had to get out there. When I arrived at the house I ran to the door finding it ajar. I went on in and the man was standing there with a pistol in his hand. His wife was on the couch with no clothes on. I didn't see any other man in there.

I started issuing orders to them, "Okay. Hold what you've got now. Lady, get your clothes on. Give me that gun. Go ahead and get dressed." She started getting her clothes on and all of a sudden he blurted, "I'm going to kill her." I said, "No, you're not going to kill her. Give me that gun." I took the gun.

I made him step outside with me so he and I could talk privately. He began to tell me, "I suspected something. My neighbors told me the locksmith had been coming back to fix the locks but we don't have any locks that need fixing. So I got here early today and I hid. I came in and they were on the couch. I had my gun in my hand and when he saw me he jumped up with his clothes in his hand and started running and I started shooting. I was shooting and he got away." I told him to stay where he was while I went back in the house.

I noticed inside they had pine paneling on the walls of the rec room and there were bullet holes everywhere. The locksmith was about ten or twelve inches in front of every bullet hole coming behind him. All I knew was he was one lucky man. An angry husband was shooting blindly and the "other man" had dodged bullets and missed every one.

The husband was bent out of shape. I knew he needed to get away from the situation and cool off. I said, "Let me tell you. Leave everything here and come with me." I put him in my car with me and we went to Shoney's. I ordered two cups of coffee and when I could see he was cooling off I said, "Okay. I know you're hurt and I know you feel betrayed. But before you pass too much judgment I want you to think back to everything you've done. Don't tell me about it. Just think back on some of the things you've done that would be vice versa if she had come in. Think about it but don't tell me. Before you find too much wrong on her you ought to give some thought to it. Y'all have been married a long time. People can get infatuated with somebody. There's a chance that something can go wrong but it doesn't mean it's the end of the world. People can work their problems out."

I spent an hour to an hour and a half talking to him. I drove him back home hoping they would work things out. I didn't hear from him any more until Christmas when I got a call from M&H Restaurant to come pick up a ham. This man had ordered a smoked ham for me. It was good. They gave me a card with both their names on it. They were in Florida. Every Christmas for I don't know how long he sent me a ham.

This husband might have murdered the other man or he may have shot his wife. It could have been accidental or on purpose. Anything could have happened that day. When in a highly unpredictable situation someone must take charge. I wasn't positive how things would turn out. I just used my instinct and tried to put everyone at ease. Thankfully, I was able to talk some sense into the husband and get him to think things through.

I didn't ever check on the locksmith. He might have gone to work on somebody else's wife. He didn't come back to work there. I don't know where he went. He went out of there like a bullet and hit the street naked with his clothes in his hands. I don't know if he got his clothes on or how he got out of there. I'm sure it was not an obstacle for him. He would have done whatever he had to do to get out of that house. I don't ever drive down that street and look at the house without remembering the locksmith.

CHAPTER 41

In the late '50s there was no training program in the Sheriff's Department. The only training we had was called field training. It consisted of a new officer getting in the car with an officer who had been employed for at least a few months. It was complete on the job training. A new officer only hoped to have an experienced officer teach him.

Sometime before 1958 Carl Barker was a brand new officer. Carl was assigned to me. We were riding together one day when we received a call to a juke joint in East Macon located in an area right in the middle the boot legging. It was an area known for shootings and crime. It was one of the worst.

The call came saying there was a problem in a place I knew well. The building was made from half of some barracks from Camp Wheeler. It sat off the ground about three feet. They had a juke box in there on the right side with a bar stretching across the back. The man tending the bar we knew as Red. He was of mixed race but he had kind of light skin. When we arrived the music was wide open. It could be heard loud and clear inside the car with the windows closed. When I opened the door and stepped inside I knew we were in trouble. No one was dancing. Folk were standing against the wall. The people sitting in the booths all had their hands on the table.

Carl was new to the whole situation. He didn't see any danger. I could feel the tenseness in the room and being more experienced I knew trouble was brewing. We had the five cell flashlight which had been issued to us. I walked back to the bar and I didn't even look at Red. I leaned against the bar looking behind me at the room of people as I said, "What's the trouble, Red?" Under his breath he said, "The one sitting in the booth with the blue shirt on and the other tall one. Everybody in here is afraid of him. They've got a bad reputation and I think one of them has a gun. Everybody is scared to death somebody is going to get killed."

About this time one of the trouble makers started casually walking out. I walked forward and told the little one, "Stand up." When he stood he dropped a large size knife in the booth. I heard it hit the wooden seat. I pushed him over to Carl and said, "Put a pair of handcuffs on him!" Carl handcuffed him and I said, "Take him to the car." I looked at the other trouble maker and said, "Stand up!" He didn't stand up. He looked up at me in defiance. I repeated myself, "Stand up!" Well, this time he stood up.

I wasn't quite prepared for the size of this man. When he stood up I saw he was about six foot four or five inches tall. He wasn't that heavy but he was tall. I looked up at him and I said, "Turn around." I began to shake him down and when I did he hit my hand. I knew we were in trouble then. I gave him a shove with my left hand and put my right hand on the stock of my gun. I put three fingers in the middle of his back holding onto the handcuffs with my other hand and shoved him towards the door following close behind him.

I could see the muscles in his back begin to tighten as he started to turn towards me. When he started to turn I pulled my pistol out of my holster and I hit him upside the head with it as hard as I could hit him. I stunned him so bad he dropped to his knees. We were very close to the door by this time so when he dropped to his knees I drew back and kicked him the rest of the way out of the building. He went head over heels to where the car was parked. Once we were outside I stood him on his feet and put my pistol under his nose. I said, "You're fixing to die and you don't even know it. Get your hands on the top of the car." This time I turned him around and shook him down. We put him in the car to take him to the station.

I had to go back into the building to get something. When I started in I could hear people in conversation. Someone said, "That's the way it ought to be. He got what he deserved." All of them were on my side then.

I got what I needed and headed back out to the car. I was thankful we had been able to handle it single handedly because I really didn't think Carl was even aware of our situation.

CHAPTER 42

We had to go to the juvenile home one day to pick up a boy who was causing a lot of trouble. He thought he was tough and liked to be a bully. He was 16 years old, not old enough to be put in jail but we had a court order to do just that. He wasn't 17 yet. He wanted me to handcuff him in front of everyone. He just wanted to look "bad" in front of all the other hooligans there. There was no way I was going to be a party to his little scheme. I said, "Get out!" I made him go into another room with me so his friends couldn't see. I made him put his hands behind him then I put the handcuffs on him. I took him to the car and put him in the back seat and started into town.

As I started toward town I noticed a new Pontiac going extremely fast. I picked up some speed and was able to pull in behind him. He was doing about 70 or 75 miles an hour on Emery Highway. I pulled up to his left, turning on my siren and lights. He made a hard right turn onto Fort Hill Street. Fort Hill Street wasn't paved then. Dust was just flying everywhere. I was chasing him hard but he was outrunning me.

Carl Barker was in the front seat saying, "I can't see anything. I can't see nothing." I had the bully in the back seat with handcuffs on. All I could see were the tail lights on the Pontiac. We proceeded along a little farther down the road then he made another hard right turn. We went by another joint Jim Haywood ran and then on Smith Street he turned right again.

This time when he turned right I was able to get on the left side of his car. He slammed on the brakes and jumped out of the car. I threw my car out of gear, put the brakes on, and jumped out. I ran up to his car with my gun in my hand. I had no idea what I would find or why this person was trying so hard to get away from me. I figured with a new car it had either drugs or whiskey inside or the car was stolen.

When I ran towards the car he was bailing out towards me. I side-stepped him hitting him in the head with my pistol. When I did that the gun fired. "OW!" He fell to the ground and the blood starting running. Carl looked at him in shock and said, "I think you killed him." I thought to myself, oh, Lord, I hope not. Just as I went to give him a little check to make sure he wasn't dead he came up from there. His car was rolling down the street. He was running trying to catch the car. I was running trying to catch him.

We finally got the car stopped. I put handcuffs on him and took him in. We searched the car and there wasn't a thing wrong with it. He had papers, he had a title to it. Everything was legal. He just by chance decided to outrun us. He had a brand new car and on just the spur of the moment decided to do something foolish. That was all it was. I had come close to killing the guy for his stupidity. When he jumped out of the car and I stepped aside I had hit him with the gun. I don't know where the bullet went but the barrel hit his head.

I still had the bully with me in the backseat. When I looked at him he was white as a sheet. I'm telling you, if there was ever reform that was going to happen it happened that day. He didn't say a word. He was sitting back there and he couldn't even hold on because his hands were handcuffed behind him. He went from one side of the car to the other side on that high speed chase. I've never heard from him again. I've often wondered what happened to him. If there is repentance, there was repentance that day. He saw first hand what could have happened by making a foolish mistake.

CHAPTER 43

Some of the events occurring during my law enforcement career ended up being humorous even though they didn't start out in such a manner. Many years ago while out on patrol in East Macon about 2 a.m. a call came over the radio stating there was a car theft in progress on Millerfield Road. The dispatcher informed us a man's car had been stolen and he was all upset. We hurried over there and when I arrived I saw a car in the middle of the road.

As I walked up to the house I saw the old fellow in his underwear with his wife standing behind him. The man began his story, "We were asleep. Ethyl woke me up and said they're stealing our car. I keep a shotgun right there and I grabbed my shotgun and ran out to the front and they were pushing it down the road and I heard them talking and I hollered, stop! Stop right where you are. Bam, bam." He continued on, "They started flying." There was a long pause. I looked at him a minute and then I looked back at the car and he said "you know, that car looked just like my car." This man had shot at a group of students coming home from a holiday. They had run out of gas and they were trying to push the car to the service station. The lady heard the kids out there and thought they were stealing their car. While he was shooting at them she was on the phone hysterical.

I searched but I couldn't find the boys anywhere. They were long gone. They just left the car sitting in the road. Those boys didn't ask any questions. The only thing on their mind was getting out from the way of the bullets. The man's only explanation was the car looked just like his. He didn't have any regrets. The funny thing is I never heard from any students calling to say they had been shot while trying to get their car to a gas station.

CHAPTER 44

A nother humorous case I was involved with started with a call saying the First National Bank on Gray Highway had been robbed. I jumped in the car and tried to cut off the traffic coming on Spring Street bridge. The robber had already abandoned the car on the bridge and he was hiding under a house. We searched the neighborhood thoroughly, continuing until we found this boy who had robbed the bank hiding under a house. We brought him to the station so we could question him.

Ned Myers, who was an FBI agent, was always full of jokes. I got him in there during the questioning and in the first few minutes we realized this boy's home was Milledgeville State Hospital. The gun he had used was a toy gun. Well, the people at the bank hadn't questioned the gun. They had just thrown the money in the bag. They had also thrown a bomb disguised as a stack of money into the bag. Five minutes after it is planted it will explode. The boy had thrown the bag into the car and right on schedule the bomb blew.

During the interview Ned was picking at him a little bit and the boy said his name was Floyd. Ned said, "Gee, you've really got a real name sake. Pretty Boy Floyd. He was a notorious gangster." The boy puffed up his chest and said, "Yeah, that's me. Pretty Boy Floyd."

This boy had red dye over his whole body from the exploding money. The dye coming from those bombs is there to stay until it wears off your skin. It doesn't wash out of cloths. The money had blown all over the car.

Ned continued interviewing the boy and baiting him along. The boy finished telling us his story, "I robbed the bank and I got in the car and I started and I was trying to get to town and I was coming across the bridge." He paused for a minute and then said, "I'm going to tell you something. Those d--- bombs you put in those bags are going to get somebody hurt. I nearly ran into a car when that thing went off." The longer we talked to him we realized what a nut case he was. Ned kidded the boy some about the bomb in the car but it was right funny to me.

CHAPTER 45

Everything is not serious. Most issues of life have some humor in them when you're dealing with the public. I had one of the biggest business men in Macon, Georgia, come into my office to see me. He was a big fellow and he was in the early stages of Alzheimers. His family had gotten a black man to stay with him to help with his care. Well, he told me the black man came to his house and helped him get ready for bed every night and give him his medicine. He said, "I think after I get in the bed at night and fall asleep he slips out and he's gone all night carousing and he doesn't come back until the next morning." He wanted me to open a case file to find the black fellow who was supposed to be at his home watching him.

I knew he was getting along with his Alzheimers and I didn't want to seem as if I didn't care. I had a long session with him and took down all his concerns. I then said, "I don't know of any law he's violating." That seemed to placate him and he eventually left my office. If I were to call his name you would know right off who it was. It was humorous because of the problem.

══════ CHAPTER 46 ══════

I had another one I thought was right funny. A guy who was in jail was a trustee—a black fellow who was a part time preacher. He was in jail because he had been drunk. He came back and forth to jail quite often. When he got out and raised a little money he would go on WIBB radio to preach. They would ask people to send in money so he could stay on the air. He would preach for a while then eventually he would be back in jail again. He was a nice guy. He was as friendly as he could be when he was sober.

I had been to a reception earlier in the week and I had brought some left over ham to the officers' dining room. I told the chef to put it in there so the guys on the night shift could make a sandwich if the kitchen was closed. He said okay and put it in the refrigerator for me. The next day or two he said, "The ham is going down and I don't believe the officers are eating it." I pondered his statement for a moment then asked, "What do you think is happening to it?" He said, "I don't know but Major Mitchum and I are working on it."

The next day he came to me and said, "We found out who is stealing the ham." I asked, "Who is it?" He said, "It's Rev. We've been shaking down all the inmates and there isn't anything on them. We shake them down every day and we don't find anything on them when they come in from duty." I wasn't following his reasoning so I asked, "Well, how did you catch him?" He said, "Well, we felt like it was Rev and we really got to shaking him down and we found two ham sandwiches on him." I asked where they had found the sandwiches and he said, "One was under one armpit and the other one was under the other armpit. He was selling them in the jail for $3 apiece." I couldn't believe my ears. I could believe he would try to sell them. I couldn't believe anyone would buy one.

I'm sure they wouldn't have if they knew where they had been. I chuckled, "They probably had a mild aroma when they got to where they were going."

CHAPTER 47

I had my debut into the bright lights of Hollywood during my years as a sheriff. John Huston came to Macon to make the movie "Wise Blood." The people financing the movie were related to the Kennedys from Massachusetts. The mother of the men financing the movie went to Mexico to talk to John Huston about directing it. She was a great admirer of Flannery O'Connor. When it came out in the paper that "Wise Blood" would be filmed in Macon I didn't think too much about it. It just passed on by me.

Tom Shaw came into Macon with E.G. Sherrill, a friend of mine who had been a fighter pilot in World War II. He had been shot down over Guadalcanal, and had been saved by the pilots of two planes who said, "Don't worry. We're going to take you home." He lost an eye and he was almost blind in the other eye. The pilots directed him back to the base and set him on the ground. I was a great admirer of E.G. Sherrill.

He came into my office with Tom Shaw. Tom Shaw, from Hollywood, was the man responsible for choosing the right location for the different scenes in the movie. He had chosen the front of the Rescue Mission for the beginning of the movie. If the middle part was going to be shot somewhere else and the third part back at the Rescue Mission, they would shoot all three scenes at the one location out of sequence. They arranged it so they did not have to move their equipment any more than necessary. His job was to couple the scenes at the same location to keep down the cost of the movie.

Tom Shaw, who was the associate director, came in and talked to me for a good while. I had assured him we would cooperate any way we could to eliminate any possible problems in Macon. He also asked me if I would furnish some officers to work as extras. I told him I would do that. As he started to leave he stopped and looked back at me saying, "I've talked to you a long time, more than I should have, and I apologize for taking up your time." Well, it didn't bother me. He was an important man and I had enjoyed our conversation. I thought the movie was important and I wanted to see it done in Macon. He then said to me, "I think there's a part in this movie for a law enforcement officer and I think you can do it. Have you ever been in a movie?"

This was a shock. I had not even remotely thought of being in a movie. He continued to tell me, "John Huston is the only one who can give away parts." We went through anything in the way of acting I had ever done. As a child in school I had shied away from any plays. I stayed away from anything on stage. As I got older I liked the Macon Little Theatre although I had never been in any productions. I did sit there at times waiting to jump onto the stage if I was ever called upon. I never got the call so I had never spoken in any of the plays.

Tom Shaw said, "I want you to meet Mr. Huston." We continued on with a few more parting words and said our goodbyes. I didn't think anything else about it until one day my wife got a call asking me to call the Hilton Hotel. John Huston was trying to locate me. I placed a call to the hotel at the number they had left. I asked to speak to Mr. Huston and he said, "This is John Huston." I said, "Yes, sir, Mr. Huston. I've heard a lot about you." I told him Ray Wilkes was returning his call and he said, "I'd like to meet you. Would you come to my suite tomorrow at 11 o'clock?" I said, "No, sir. I can't come tomorrow." I think I'm the only person who said they couldn't come to meet John Huston. I didn't realize there were people standing in line to meet him. He asked, "Where will you be?" I said, "I'll be in church tomorrow."

My wife and I always went to church on Sunday. He paused a moment and then asked, "How long does this church last?" I said,

"Well, it's a Baptist church and a Baptist preacher so if nobody joins we will be out about 12:30. But if somebody joins, it might run a little bit over. How about we meet at two?" He said, "That will be even better."

At 2 p.m. I went to his suite. Everybody in there was talking film to him. When I entered he didn't have to say anything. They knew he wanted to talk to me privately so they all quietly left the room. I introduced myself and we shook hands. He said, "Tell me a little about yourself." We started talking. I told him where I had been raised and all about my family. I didn't have any airs to put on. I told him my people were cotton mill people and I had been raised in a mill village. I went through my story and then I told him how I had gotten in law enforcement and how I didn't really intend to enter that particular career field but had done so at the request of a friend.

He then asked me, "Are you married?" I answered, "Yes, sir." Then he said, "How long have you been married?" I was Sheriff at this time and I said, "I've been married 30 years." He looked at me incredulously and said, "30 years?" He couldn't believe I had been married for 30 years. Of course, I looked a little better in those days than I do now.

I think John Huston had been married three or four times. His first wife got all his artwork when they divorced, which I later learned really floored him.

We talked for a while longer and then he said, "Let's see how you do with the lines." He had some people come in to give me a script. I had never seen a script before. I did a lousy job of trying to read it. I thought they had given me the wrong script because the character I was reading was named Hazel and he was a man. I thought, I had never heard of a man named Hazel. Then Mr. Huston very kindly said, "Let's do this. Have you ever read the book?" I told him I hadn't and he said, "I'd like you to take the script home and read the whole thing. I think by reading it you'll get a feel for it."

I took the script home and read it in its entirety. Then I studied my lines backwards and forwards and upside down. I read for him once again and he wanted me to do the part.

The day came when I was to be there for the actual filming of the movie. I had on a sheriff's uniform and hat with a big gun belt. I went into the actors' trailer where I had been directed to go to use the restroom. In the trailer a buffet had been set up for all the actors and actresses. There were strawberries and powdered sugar, cheese, salami, baked salmon, different kinds of crackers and chips, everything you could think of.

As I went in Brad Dourif, who played the lead character, Hazel Motes, came out. He was dressed for his part. I said, "Today is the day."

"Yes. Do you know your lines?" he asked.

I said, "Yes. Do you want to run through them?" He responded, "Yes, I do." So we proceeded to go through the lines. I gave him the first line and he picked up the next one. I gave him mine and he picked up the next one. We went through our section of the script together. He then looked at me and said, "You do that good out there and you're home free." That was about the only conversation I had with him.

That particular day we were doing a scene with the patrol car. I was to be on a hill in a car further down the hill. John Huston was in front of our car sitting on the back of a pick-up truck wearing a heavy coat. It was cool that morning. He had a camera in the truck with him. In the car a man was scrunched up in the floor board with a portable camera. He was filming me at the door. There was one more camera being used to film from another angle. In my car was a kind of walkie talkie, only it was a radio with everyone on the same frequency. In the Secret Service these radios are called Charlie sets.

John Huston said, "Okay. Let's roll them." We started down the hill. He called, "All right, Sheriff, blue lights. Now your siren." So I started the siren and stopped it. I got out of my car then, went up to the other car, and began my lines. They were rolling the cameras all through that time. Then Mr. Huston said, "It's a take. Everybody back to the hill." I went back to get in my car and Tony Huston, Mr. John Huston's son, came up to me. He had a strong British accent, being raised in England. He said in his most proper English accent, "Oh, Sheriff, I can't begin to tell you how most unusual it is when a person who's never been in movies is in the movies and the first scene is a take. I can't begin to tell you how unusual it is."

I really didn't know how to respond. I thanked him and continued with the work I was supposed to be doing. We went back to the top of the hill to do our other scenes working for several hours. The last scene that I was to do was where I push the car into the water. That is a scene everybody remembers in the movie. When John Huston died a tribute with his memoirs was aired on television and a lot of scenes from his movies were shown. One of the scenes played from "Wild Blood" is the scene I was in, pushing the car into the water.

People ask me the location of the lake I pushed the car into. It was in Jones County; E. G. Sherrill found it for us. It had the elevation we were looking for.

Mr. Huston and I went through part of the lines and I said, "There's one thing I think we should do." He said, "What is that, Sheriff?" I said, "Well, you don't push a car in gear off the road or down a hill. You have to put the car out of gear to be able to move it." He said, "Put it out of gear." I walked up to the car and the line was, "Where is your driver's license?" The other actor said, "I don't have a driver's license." Then I said, "He that don't have a driver's license don't need no car." I then walked to the back of the car after I got it out of gear and put my foot on the rear bumper. They had a rope underneath that would pull it, so as I would give it a shove it would go down that hill right into the water. But the line was, "if you don't have a driver's license you don't need a car."

Tom Shaw's son was a baby at the time. They needed a baby in the movie so Tom Shaw's son was in the movie. Tom Shaw was the person who planned the scenes in each movie so all the scenes done in a certain location were done at the same time.

Before we shot the last scene we had some down time and Mr. Huston invited me to have lunch with him. We went to the dining room of the Hilton Hotel and there wasn't anyone in there except us. I was expecting some of the cast to be present. I don't think they moved unless he gave the word. He said, "I want you to try this onion soup, Sheriff. It's superb." Then we began to talk about a lot of things. He began to tell me about his father. He really didn't have a lot of communication with him. He said his father pretty well let him do what he wanted to do. He tried out boxing. John Huston was a prize fighter for a while. His father did not pave the way for him to get into the movies but he got a job and began to work his way up. He became one of the best directors Hollywood has ever had.

We talked about different characters in his movies. I must have seen the "African Queen" about five times. I never get tired of seeing it. I could see it every year. He told me when they were filming the "African Queen" the first living quarters they were shown were terrible. The African government gave them some lousy quarters to live in and he said, "No, we're not going to do that." He said they side-stepped the government and found more suitable living conditions during the making of the movie.

He told me how they were shooting a scene in some real thick jungle and on a river with the crocodiles. Humphrey Bogart was in the front of the boat letting the leading lady, Katharine Hepburn, steer it. Mr. Huston said when they were shooting the scene they had a man positioned above the boat with a high powered rifle and another man with a gun. If the crocodiles got too close they would shoot to kill. Nothing ever happened to make the men have to shoot the crocodiles. I often wondered how Humphrey Bogart was able to act during the river scene. I would have been so intent on watching the crocodiles I wouldn't have been able to say any lines or do any acting.

He talked about that movie and he talked about his father and his other actors. His father played all kinds of roles. John Huston's father left him with stocks and bonds. I said, "I'm convinced that stocks are a good way to invest money." And he said, "My father gave me some stocks and they were worth little more than when he first got them." They were in utility stocks, not in growth stocks. The only thing they did was pay dividends.

John Huston was just as natural a person as you and I. His father was just as superb. He should have gotten an Academy Award for at least some of the parts he played in movies. John Huston in his career probably didn't save any money. He made a lot of money but I think he spent it. He did things he wanted to do.

He told me many stories of his life before "Wise Blood." He lived in Ireland 20 years after his divorce. He had placed a lot of money in art and his first wife got all of it. I think that was the breaking point of him. He spent his future. He lived in Ireland and people would come from the states to stay with him. He said he could take a billfold full of money, drop it in the streets of Ireland, and bet those people who had come from the states the wallet would be returned to him before the sun went down. He said somebody would find it and think Mr. Huston had lost it and would return it to him. The Irish were the most honest people he had ever met. He had never met anyone like them.

He married a very young Mexican girl and they built a house down on the coast of the Iguana. There was a piece of land having very few people living on it and he persuaded the government to lease him a piece of property. He built a very nice home there and made the film "The Night of the Iguana." When the movie was released the town began to grow. It wasn't long before 100,000 people lived there. He told me about the town and living there. People traveled from Hollywood down to Mexico to see him about all sorts of things. Then they came from Massachusetts, asking him to direct "Wise Blood."

He was a very colorful character but he didn't exert any of it. He just exemplified it. Just to be with him was interesting. He was one of the most delightful people I've ever been with in my life. He told me, "I've got one more movie I want to make. It's never been made right. I want to make that movie." He made several more before he died, but I don't know if one of those was the one he wanted to make.

John Huston also told me the story of making the movie "African Queen." He loved Katharine Hepburn and Humphrey Bogart. He told me that Katharine Hepburn played the part of Rose in this particular movie. Rose was the spinster sister of the minister. The minister was a straight-laced Englishman of the Anglican Church. Rose was a piano player and loved to play music. They went to Africa as missionaries. She played opposite a rough-and-ready Humphrey Bogart. At one point, Katharine Hepburn asked John, "Mr. Huston, how do you think I should play this role?" He said, "As if you were speaking like Ms. Roosevelt." Ms. Roosevelt was very distinct, very little foolishness, authoritative, straightforward, and educated. He said the part was played in exactly that manner. He told me when they arrived at the location where the movie was to be filmed they had trouble finding quarters adequate for the film crew and actors and actresses. He said it was a lousy place to make a movie and all of them complained every day. He admitted the quarters were lousy and the food was terrible. One person would bring in fresh game and dress it out. He informed me it was a tremendous help until everybody found out the man was a cannibal.

In the conversation he told me about another movie he directed and how everyone on the set was turning against each other. He said, "I got on the phone and I called someone I knew, and they helped me take care of it. One day I had 12 of them in the cast. I had a box. I opened the box up and gave each one of them a loaded

.38 pistol. That stopped the arguing. After they were handed their pistol they all got along."

When we shot the last scene of "Wise Blood" my son-in-law, Dan, and I were standing there when they gave the word that everything was complete. They said, "It's a wrap," or something to that effect, and it was over with. Everybody immediately started getting their things together. It was night and I looked around and John Huston came up to me. He brought me two autographed manuscripts. On the first one he wrote, "I will always remember you not as the Sheriff but as the actor."

After the night John Huston went back to Mexico, my son-in-law, Danny, said, "You're going to see him again. He's going to come get you to do something else." It never happened but I enjoyed it while it lasted.

I had to eventually join the actors' union. The first movie they let it pass, but the second I had to pay because I had been in two movies. It was the theatrical guild. They ran it on the computer and someone had not put the first one on the computer so I got by with that one. Patrick O'Neal directed the second movie I was in and Burgess Meredith was the star. It wasn't a big movie. It was a television movie called "Mr. Griffin and Me."

I got a call once again from someone at the Hilton. They wanted to talk to me. I went to the Hilton and was told, "Mr. O'Neal wants to speak to you. There he is now." I turned around and he said, "Are you the Sheriff?" I said, "Yes. That's me. I'm Ray Wilkes."

It turned out they would be filming another movie in Macon and Burgess Meredith and Joan Fontaine were in it. Mr. O'Neal said to me, "I've got a part in this movie I want you to do for me. There are 12 people wanting to read for me. I met John Huston last Christmas in New York and we had dinner together. John Huston told me about you and I've seen 'Wise Blood' and I want you to do this part for me." I was flabbergasted. After picking my chin up off the ground I said, "All right."

It came time for me to do the scene. It was a bar scene where Burgess Meredith had run a race and won, kind of like a marathon. My part involved presenting a plaque to him. I was getting ready to go on and I had the script. He asked me, "Do you know your lines?" I replied to Mr. O'Neal, "Yes. But this is not the way Southern people talk. I've never heard anybody say 'sleazy old hotel'. They don't use that kind of language here." They call them a "hot sheet factory" or something else but not sleazy. He said, "Well, let me ask you something. If you were going to do a presentation like this in real life how would you do it?" Then he yelled, "Quiet on the set. Everybody quiet on the set." He wanted everyone to hear. He turned back to me and said, "All right, Sheriff, go ahead."

It was so quiet you could have heard a pin drop as I walked up to the podium. I began my award presentation, "All right. Knock it off. Let's quiet this thing down. We've got something important to do tonight." I said, "One of our own has got a distinguished accomplishment and we're going to give him this award." I continued on with a bunch of words and then finished my part. When I got through it hadn't been filmed. Mr. O'Neal said, "Do you think you can do that again?" I said, "I think so." I was ad-libbing the lines, not sticking to any manuscript. I did it again. He liked my contribution to his film. I was paid $500 for my part in his film—a lot of money back then. After he left Macon I never heard from him again.

The man in charge of doing the make-up during the movie approached me one day. I really didn't know him well. I spoke to him and he said, "Sheriff, I want to ask you something. Have you ever considered making a career out of acting?" I said, "No, I haven't." He said, "Well, I've seen a lot of them come and go and I think you'll make it." I admitted to him, "Well, I had a wrinkle in my stomach for a long time. I got elected Sheriff and I got that wrinkle out. I'm not interested in any more of them." Then another fellow came up who was in charge of the electrical system or the power. He told me the same thing. They thought I could have made a career out of it.

John Huston was kind of a loner. No one went after John Huston. He never stayed in a crowd talking. When he sat in there he was watching the camera and nobody really talked to him. But he was personable. He was extremely kind and extremely considerate but he wasn't an extrovert at all.

John Huston once told me a story about Errol Flynn. John was not a party to the situation but he knew about it. He said there was a director in Hollywood who died. Errol Flynn, who stayed on alcohol an awful lot, was whining and crying saying he didn't get to say good-bye to the director and it was all too sudden and if he could have just seen this man one more time he would have felt better about it. Some people who drank with Errol Flynn took him to a producer's house one evening to pick up something there. They were still drinking and they went into a drawing room where the director was sitting directly across from them in his suit. Errol Flynn almost went to pieces. They finally got him calmed down. These people had gone to the undertaker and given him a bribe to bring the body of the dead director back to this house after the funeral home closed that night. They sat him in the chair so he looked like he had come back to life. It had scared Errol Flynn so badly he almost passed out. After it was over they immediately took the body back to the funeral home and put him back in the casket. That was John Huston's story and he laughed about it.

John Huston was also a good friend of Clark Gable. In 1961 he produced a film called "The Misfits," starring Marilyn Monroe and Clark Gable. It was the last movie for both of the stars. John Huston made several more films, including "Wise Blood," before his death in 1987.

I was in two movies, "Wise Blood," and "Mr. Griffin and Me." They called and offered me a part in "The King." I was asked to play the part of a lieutenant in Birmingham, Alabama, where the bombing took place. The part I was playing was anti-law enforcement and red-neck. I said for everything I believe in I don't think so. I could not play a part in a movie when the character went against all I believed in. I turned them down for the part and ended my career in the movies.

When John Huston died I was in Norway. I noticed his picture on the front page of the paper so I approached the desk clerk and asked if he could translate the article about John Huston to me in English. In one of our conversations John Huston said, "I wish I had realized the damage of smoking and alcohol and had realized the taste of good wine in my early life. I didn't do it." He showed great interest in me and the things I did, including a bank robbery that I'd told him about; he always wanted the whole story.

CHAPTER 48

There was a fellow at the Mulberry Market who told me a very amusing story. Each night one of the brothers of the man who owned the market stood at the door as the hired help went home for the evening and checked their bags. He would open their bag and he would say, "Thank you, very much. Thank you, very much. Betsy, that's fine."

One evening a man came through and he said, "Thank you, Willy B. Willy B? Willy B! Come back! Willy B, what have you got under your coat?" Well, Willy B. had taken a fish out of the market that did not belong to him. He had tied one end of a string around the fish's tail and tied the other end to his belt. When he came out his coat lacked about an inch and a half of covering the fish. The man said, "Willy B., I am so disappointed in you. I will see you in the morning but next time you steal a fish you either get a shorter fish or a longer coat."

CHAPTER 49

This is a story of an event happening in the jail that took on a more serious note. One summer we had so many people coming in to visit the inmates at the jail we really couldn't control them. We instituted a new system whereby each prisoner filled out a card with the names of three people he would like to see. He could only put down three names. Some inmates had six or eight visitors coming in at one time. We made them put down the names of three people and any of the three could come.

The inmates were to put the names down in the preference they wanted the visitors. At that time we had the Federal prisoners and the State prisoners locked up together. We really didn't know anything about the Federal prisoners. The Marshall put them in the jail and picked them up the next day. We did not receive any information on them.

I was at home when I got a call from the jail saying, "You better get down here in a hurry. We've got a riot in the jail." I went to the jail as fast as I could and before I could even get out of the car I saw the fire department was there. They had two ladders up to the windows of the jail and the men had hoses. They were ready to go. Jerry Modena, who later became the sheriff, was there. Modena headed the SWAT team at that time. The SWAT team members were some of the best officers we had.

The prisoners had started a fire in the cells, burning the mattresses, linens, and pillows. They were throwing the burning stuff in the middle of the jail. They had also torn up some of the church benches we had sitting in the building. They split off pieces of wood so they were sharp like spears. The inmates had them between the bars and when someone passed by they would push it towards them. It was as dangerous as a knife.

I took in all the information trying to evaluate the situation when Shaffer, who was the fire chief, said to Sheriff Jimmy Bloodworth and me, "I think we ought to turn the water on them. We've locked them out of their cells and the water will get them." I said, "Wait a minute. Before you turn the water on them you better understand. There are nine drains in this jail. Eight of them are stopped up. When you start throwing water in there you're going to find the ceilings on four floors start falling out. Water is going to go all the way down and the ceilings are Celetex and all of it will be falling. I don't know how much money we're going to lose."

They dropped that idea. Ronnie Thompson, who was the mayor of the city at that time said, "I think we ought to shoot tear gas in there, Sheriff." I was chief deputy. I said, "Sheriff, tear gas is made to dispense crowds, not to shoot at people who have no way to get out. There are people in there with respiratory problems and there are some old people in there with emphysema. If you shoot tear gas and they can't get out of the way of it we're going to have some people going to the hospital." So we stopped that.

I went to Jerry Modena and began talking to him. I said, "Modena, open the door. Get the doors open. I'm going to go in there." He said, "No, sir, you can't do that. We went in there while ago and I didn't think I would be able to get the SWAT team out. This riot is about two Federal prisoners. When the cards for visitation came down the line they seized them and hid them. The cards didn't get collected and taken to the office. When the inmates went downstairs today no one had any cards and the officers wouldn't let any visitors in. That's what is causing the riot, this new system we tried to put in today."

I thought about the problem for a minute then said, "Well, open the door." This time he reluctantly opened it and I went in there to see if I could get the situation under control. We had one of the biggest trouble makers in there and he was cussing at everything.

He started cussing me so I walked straight to him and put my foot on the cross bar at the bottom of the cell door. I then put my arm on my knee so I would be face-to-face with him. I started listening to him. Well, he started going over the grievances and he was just raising Cain. I didn't say a thing. He continued with his rantings and I still didn't say anything.

About the third or fourth time of him repeating himself even the prisoners were getting tired of hearing it. So then I said, "Okay. I've listened to you. Some of your complaints are valid. Some of the things we can't help but we'll look into the problems and see what can be done. Now, I've got a slew of officers out there and they're armed with the latest technique for controlling riots. Some of you are going to get hurt. The people who are going to be hurt are most likely going to be charged with this crime and they're going to be here a long time. I'm going to try to separate the ones who don't want to be involved with this. They've got less time than they thought they were going to get. Their wives have promised to stay with them. They've almost made their time. I'm going to open the cell doors. When I open the cell doors anybody in here who doesn't want to be a part of the riot simply go into their cell. The ones who remain outside will be identified as the trouble-makers. We're going to open the doors and deal with them. You've got 30 seconds. Open the door."

The trouble maker said, "Wait a minute. Wait a minute. We ain't going nowhere. We ain't going to do that." I said, "You've got 20 seconds." Some of them began to get in the cells. I said, "You've got ten seconds. You've got five." When I said five it cleared them out. When I said, "Close the doors," he almost jumped in there. He was the last one in and we locked it down.

After we locked it down I got a crew in there and had the prisoners clean up the mess they had created. We got the fires out and the firemen left. Everybody was locked down the next morning when I had a group of pastors who had come to the jail from the black churches. They informed me, "We're with the NAACP and we want to see those people who have been accused of having some misbehavior in the jail." I said, "No, I can't do that. I can't let you up there to see them. I'm going to tell you why. We had a riot up there and we had damage up there. There were no misbehavior problems. It was a riot and it's lucky somebody didn't get killed. We've got the jail locked down now. If you come in and start talking to them they're going to get the message all you've got to do is raise Cain and then the jail will be open to people coming in to see about you." I continued, "Not so. I'll show you what the damage was."

I took them in where all the mess remained from the clean up. They looked at all the burned material and stomped plates and broken dishes and all the other debris. One of them said, "We don't have any business down here." And they left.

I didn't think any more about it. We got over the situation and I went about my duties. A few weeks later we had the Shield Club meeting at the country club. Peyton Anderson had put together a forum of 100 men from the community who gave $100 each to raise $10,000 and formed the Shield Club, which provided college scholarships for city and county policemen and women, firefighters and their immediate families. The Shield Club has a big banquet every year, with top officers bringing guests with them from the department, usually privates. It's a very formal affair. Hines Causey of House of Hines always furnished the tuxedos for us.

At the banquet that year, E. Raymond Smith, who partially organized the event, rose and began talking about the riot. He said, "My wife and I came out of the Green Jacket and as soon as we walked out I heard noise like I have never heard before coming from the top floor of the jail and all the fire trucks were there. I just figured I would like to get on out of here now." About that time they called me to the front and Raymond said, "Here's the man that went in there and calmed it down." Mr. R.C. Cropper presented me with a large silver bowl. It says, "For outstanding and courageous service. The Shield Club. 1972." That was 36 years ago.

I received another bowl by a group of people in memory of Jim Hicks. They present a bowl every once in a while to a sheriff for outstanding service. Jim Hicks served for 38 years, longer than any other Bibb County Sheriff. He started in 1904. I didn't know Jim Hicks. I began in the department when Julian Peacock was the sheriff. Mr. Hicks had already died when I started. There is a club, a group of men, who still honor his memory. I didn't know anything about them until one day when they walked in wanting to see me and made the presentation.

CHAPTER 50

It has been said a dog is a man's best friend. I don't know who said it but I had the opportunity to find the saying true. I was not in the market for a dog nor was I looking for one the night I was to be gifted with my new pal.

I was speaking to the Cross Keys Men's Club at Cross Keys Methodist Church one night. I got there a little early and was speaking with a few of the men outside when a dog came up. The dog was a pretty dog, but he was just a dog. He had some features of a Rottweiller, but his tail was wagging. I asked the men standing around, "Who's dog is that?" One of the men said, "He's been hanging around here in the garbage can hunting food." I noticed the dog was holding up one of his legs. I knelt down feeling his leg and I said, "His leg is broken."

I picked up the dog and carried him back to my car. I called a patrol car and told them my location asking them to come. I didn't have the dog tied up but he just stayed where I put him. I think he instinctively knew he was my new best friend.

When the patrol car got there I told the officers I wanted them to take the dog to the office and ask the cook to come up with some food. I told them to go into the laundry and come up with whatever they could to make him a bed with some old blankets and then I would take care of him the next morning.

Well, the next morning they had the dog down there just like I had asked them to. I took him to the vet and had his leg set. It was broken. I made the dog comfortable and he began staying with us. I called my new friend "Buddy." He loved everybody. He was a fine dog and everybody knew how much I liked the dog.

One day someone accidentally let him out. He was in the fenced area by the new jail. No one told me he had gotten out. There were men running all up and down Second Street and Orange Street, and around Tabernacle Baptist Church. A passerby stopped one of the officers who was slowing down and asked, "What have you got? A robbery? An escapee?" The officer replied, "No. We're looking for the Sheriff's dog."

I didn't know there were so many people involved in the search and I surely didn't know they didn't want to lose the dog. I got the dog back and later the dog got out again. Someone put him on a pick-up truck and when they slammed the tailgate closed they slammed the door on his tail. It took all the hide off. He came back hurt. I took him back to the vet and he had to have surgery.— it cost me $200. But he was my pal and I would do anything to take care of him.

When I got ready to retire I told the sheriff coming in if he had any plans of doing away with the dog to tell me now and I would take him. I didn't have a place for him but I would find a place. So the dog stayed there at the sheriff's office until Cathy Candler retired. Cathy started out as my secretary and I promoted her to _____. She is an avid animal lover. She took the dog home with her and kept him until he died. He lived a full life as the official dog of the sheriff's office.

I still have pictures of my dog and me. He was a fine dog. When I found him he was hurt, hungry, and alone and no one was concerned. That was the sad part, that no one was concerned. A dog always meant more to me than that. I was always glad I had taken the time to care for the poor creature. He brought me and many others much joy and pleasure through my years at the sheriff's office.

CHAPTER 51

From time to time there would be fights in the jail. Usually they were innocent little scuffles which tended to work themselves out. One day I was in the jail when a fight occurred.

The dining room would seat 40 people. The tables were constructed of stainless steel with the chairs attached. When you stood the chair would automatically return to it's position under the table. One of our black officers was walking down the hall when he saw a fight breaking out. He called for help to get the fight stopped, then we got to the bottom of it. One of the fellows in the fight was a short black man. The other fellow was a large black man.

As we were to find out, the big man had walked over to the table where the little fellow was sitting and said, "Get up. That's my seat." The short fellow responded, "Man, go away. We don't have seats here. Ever who comes sits here." The big man did not like that. He said in a stronger voice, "I said, get up!" and the struggle began.

My officer told me as he was coming down the hall he looked through the window and the only thing he saw was the big fellow going through the air. The officer said the big man hit the floor like a ton of bricks and the little man landed on top of him. The little man reached down and bit a chunk of cheek out of the big man. One had a mouth full of left cheek and the other was screaming at the top of his voice. Of course, blood was coming out profusely. They got them separated and another inmate walking by said, "Man, he sure has bit you bad. I hope he ain't got none of them AIDS." That big man on the floor hollered, "Get me a shot! Get me a shot!" Someone told him, "There's no shot. If he's got AIDS, you do too."

CHAPTER 52

Another time I was called to go back to the jail for a fight in the dining room but this time it was on the women's side. You haven't heard anything until you've heard a bunch of angry women yelling and hollering and raising Cain. I hurried to find out what the problem was and how it could be solved before it got out of hand.

It seems they had a serving line for the women to get their dinner. Each woman had a tray. When they came through the line, the men prisoners put food on the tray and gave it to them. One of the men serving was sweet on one of the lady inmates. He had been eyeing her over the counter while he was serving. For dessert that day we had banana pudding. As the ladies were coming through the line, he served the lady in front of the one he liked, he served the lady he liked, and he served the lady behind her.

By the time I was called to the scene those three were in a big fight. When I got down to the bottom of the matter to see what the argument was about I found out the lady in front got one vanilla wafer in her banana pudding. The lady in the back got one vanilla wafer in her banana pudding. But the lady he had been eyeing got three vanilla wafers in her banana pudding. Three grown women were fighting about how many vanilla wafers they had received in their banana pudding. They didn't like that at all.

CHAPTER 53

I had a situation happen I always thought was unusual. We had located a large drug operation growing marijuana in a south Georgia county. I forget how much they were growing but the weight of it amounted to a million dollars. We had been talking with an undercover agent and they were interested in selling the operation but they weren't interested enough until they saw some money.

Major Terry Singleton came to me one day and said, "We've got to get some money they can see. It won't leave the bank. We're going to make them come to the bank." I thought about it and then I went to the bank and said, "We're going to need a million dollars of show money." They said, "Ray, there ain't no way in the world we can do it. Something may happen and if it does we're going to all be in the wind."

So I went back to talk to Emory Greene, the chairman of the county commission. The bank told me if I got the commission chairman to issue a check for a million dollars they would put the million dollars in a safe deposit box but we would have to be responsible because a million dollar check is going to cover it. I talked to Emory and finally persuaded him to go along with the plan.

We had planned to meet with them that afternoon. I told Emory everything was going to be all right. I received a call from him about an hour before the meeting and he still had apprehension and nervousness in his voice. He said, "Mr. Sheriff, we're not going to lose our million dollars, are we?" I assured him, "No. We're not going to lose it. It's not even going to leave the bank. Don't worry about it." He said, "I'll be glad when it's all over with."

We took the growers to the safe deposit boxes where we had agents and officers. Then we showed them the money. They demanded to count it so we allowed them to start counting the money. The money was put into an old Air Force brief case. We put the money in there and said, "When we get the dope you'll get this money." That was the deal. There were two identical brief cases under the table.

One of the brief cases contained telephone books and the other had the money in it. When we left, the one brief case with the money was left in the safe deposit boxes. The one with the telephone books is the one we let go out. The other one went back to the bank. We walked out and they saw the brief case and thought that was the one the money had been put in, but there were two of them.

The officers had to go down to Milan, Georgia. That is some tough country down there, McCrae, Milan, that part of the state. They went out into a field. We had a U-haul trailer that was closed and had a SWAT team in the U-haul. When they opened the door to deliver the dope the SWAT team was coming out to arrest them and we were going to seize the marijuana. When we got down there the SWAT team was sitting there in the dark. One SWAT team member said, "Did you hear what that man said? He said if something goes wrong we're going to kill some d--- body." They were just sitting there waiting until the doors were opened. They were filled with apprehension too. When the drug dealers opened those doors the SWAT team came out of the U-Haul and grabbed them. One of the drug dealers tried to use a gun but we made the arrest.

Dodge County Sheriff Jackson Jones was there. We made a press release and I said, "When the doors came open, shezam, the officers were all over them." One of the reporters said, "Shezam? What's that?" I responded, "That's something that happens. Don't you ever read Batman?" So I thought it was right funny.

They put my statement in the paper, "Shezam. Don't you ever read Batman?" I was glad we were able to accomplish our task with no serious consequences. The whole scene played out just as we would have hoped it would. The money didn't leave the bank and we were able to seize the marijuana, taking it out of the hands of the population.

═══════ CHAPTER 54 ═══════

In law enforcement you learn very quickly to be cautious of every call you respond to. Even a traffic ticket can be a dangerous situation. You never know who you will encounter when you arrive at the scene of a crime. Many times the situation is easily remedied and there is no threat. Other times the situation is extremely dangerous and could potentially be life threatening. One such event happened to us.

A bank robbery occurred at a bank located on Napier Avenue. One of the robbers was carrying a sawed-off shotgun and the other two were carrying .38 revolvers. The series of events would show they were well trained in bank robberies because they knew exactly what to do. They got the money and put it in a bag; when they came out they jumped in a car. I don't know whether they went down Pio Nono Avenue or Napier Avenue but Jerry Modena and I were at Mercer University when we heard the traffic over the radio describing the three black males who had robbed the bank and the car they were driving.

Modena and I took off across town in the direction of the perpetrators. Some of our city police officers were traveling on Interstate 75 south coming back from a meeting in Atlanta. They had spent the night in Atlanta and since the city is so notorious for theft, the officers had locked their guns in the trunk of the car. As they returned to Macon they still had their equipment in the trunk. They heard the radio traffic and were able to identify the car going north on I-75 at a high rate of speed. The officers crossed the median of the interstate and began a pursuit.

The bank robbers hung out the windows of the car and began shooting at the officers. The officers' guns were still in the trunk so they had to fall back in the pursuit. We were coming up behind them so the pressure was on the robbers. The patrol was coming the other way and they ran the robbers' car off the road onto a flat area and jumped out of the car.

The catalytic converter on the bank robbers' car was so hot it set all the brush underneath it on fire and then set the woods on fire. The fire was burning everywhere. I had called a good many deputies to the scene for backup and when I arrived I said, "Everybody hold what you got until we get organized and let's get this in teams of four. In every team I want to make sure we've got communications."

Terry Singleton and I were in the first group that went in the woods to see if we would be able to arrest them. We had organized to cover that particular area because there was a fire break past the highway on the other side of a thick pine area. A Georgia State Patrol helicopter was flying over the right of way, which had electric lines everywhere. He radioed to us he had seen two men and they were headed back north.

Terry and I were moving along when the pilot radioed us again saying they were going across a creek. I had on a nice, green, Jack Nicklaus coat with dress pants and a nice pair of shoes. It was the most expensive coat I have ever bought in my life. We started walking and we came to an area where beavers had built a dam and the water began to run in over our shoes. Terry and I both continued walking, crossing over the beaver dam. Then we had to get our wallets out of our pocket and guns out of the holster because the water was beginning to come up almost to our waist. We crossed there and cold, man it was cold. We kept in pursuit of them.

In our pursuit one of them gave up. We still had two of them at large but we were able to apprehend the one. We continued the search into the night. As we worked more police, deputies, and dogs were brought in. We were able to put up a perimeter of law enforcement officers. The dogs were in the middle of the perimeter. Every farmer in the area who heard a noise in his yard had been instructed to contact us with the information. Dogs were immediately taken and if they picked up a scent the dogs would follow it.

Patrol cars were parked around the perimeter with loud speakers calling for the criminals to come out of the swamp, walk to the road, and drop their firearms.

We had previously found a military medical bag filled with ammunition. Due to the weight of the bag we surmised the criminals had to abandon it. About 2 a.m. our efforts paid off. The men were arrested on the roadside with no resistance. From that point on it was an FBI case. Through interrogation and mode of operation the FBI was able to clear four other bank robberies these men had committed. Similarities showed it was the same group of men. After we seized their money we counted it, finding we had ended up with more than the bank had originally lost.

I was dog tired when it was over. I went home, showered, and went to bed. It had been a long day and an even longer night. I was glad it was over.

CHAPTER 55

During my tenure in the sheriff's office I had the privilege of meeting so many interesting people. One of the most memorable was Lord Gordon Parry of England. I first met him in the spring, about the time of year when the annual Cherry Blossom Festival was beginning. The jail was new that year and Carolyn Crayton brought over a couple of people from England. Lord Gordon Parry was one of them.

I introduced myself and we began to talk. I gave them a tour of the building and that sort of thing. After the Cherry Blossom Festival was over and he returned to England we kept in communication with each other. Each year he came here he would always call me. He's been in my home. On one occasion Pearl and I invited Lord Gordon Parry and Lady Glennis to be our guests at Beall's 1842 Restaurant.

Lady Glennis didn't sound much like a lady when I first met her. In fact, I asked her who her daughter had married and Lord Parry said, "She is living with an Irishman in Ireland." Lady Glennis said, "He's a blasted, blooming, bloody Irishman."

We cultivated a true friendship over the years. He called me on one occasion before he was to leave again for England and we went to Cracker Barrel to have breakfast together.

Years later Pearl and I made plans to visit England. I called and told him I was coming to London. We made our trip and sometime after our arrival I telephoned and let him know we were there. Well, the House of Lords was going to be open on a certain day while we were going to be there. He told us we must come and meet him there. On the appointed day we went to the location where Lord Parry had told us to go. I announced to the guard Lord Parry was expecting us. He sent the message forward and Lord Parry came out to meet us. He shook hands with us and was very cordial.

The House was not officially opened yet. It was kind of like the Capitol. There was a lot happening in the halls. He took us into the dining room where we had a cup of coffee and pastries. The dining room of the House of Lords looks over the River Thames. It's a beautiful view. After our coffee he wanted to take us on a tour. He took us to the House of Lords first. I went up and sat in the chair the Queen of England sits in when she addresses Parliament. I said, "I want to sit there." I have, in fact, sat in the chair in Westminster Abbey where William the Conqueror was first crowned in 1065.

We saw all the different sights at the House of Lords. Lord Parry then took us down to a place where Guy Hawkes was planning to blow up the House of Parliament. He was placing kegs of gun powder under there. He showed me where all those events took place. Every year the English still celebrate Guy Hawke's Day by building big fires because he failed in his attempt to blow up Parliament. They do the same thing in Bermuda. It's like a carnival.

We then went to the House of Commons. In the 1600s the king was in trouble. Charles I was the king and Oliver Cromwell was an advocate of throwing him out. Charles I wanted to know where Cromwell was in The House. The Speaker of the House, according to Lord Parry, said, "Your Majesty, my eyes are the eyes of this house, my ears are the ears of this house, and my voice is the voice of this house. If you want to know where Oliver Cromwell is you'll have to ask The House." Oliver Cromwell leaned back and two men in the House of Commons with their robes on leaned forward and he was behind them. Charles I was so upset he turned around and stormed out of there. In the end, Charles I was beheaded, largely because of Cromwell's plotting against him. That's when some of our forefathers came over here.

Lord Parry gave us a wonderful tour and then he brought us back and we ate lunch together. He showed us the dining room of the House of Lords. It had a long table with a bench. He said, "When you enter the dining room you sit next to the last man that sat down." They don't reserve any spaces. The theory is you may fight on the floor of the House of Lords but when you leave there you are still friends.

Then he wanted us to go to the opening of the House of Lords. He led us to the right place and showed us Blackstick, the man who raps the door when you come up. He raps it the first time when the Queen is there and they don't answer the door. They purposely refuse to answer the door because she does not dominate the House of Lords or the House of Commons. She makes the appointments but she does not dominate. When she does come in with her entourage they go in. He showed us all of those proceedings then he took us to the formal opening of the House of Lords. We had been there all day. He sat us in a place where the House members of the Lords were on one side of the rail and we were on the other. He was a wonderful friend, interested in our seeing all the sights of England. I feel so blessed when I think about the son of a mill worker and the daughter of a dirt farmer were there in England with royalty.

Lord Parry became ill and died while in Wales. I have a friend who lives on the lake near the area. He told me a town was set aside to honor Lord Parry. Every year cherry trees are planted there in his remembrance. I have found it to be true that most of the time you are treated like you treat others. Lord Parry certainly treated people with utmost respect and kindness.

CHAPTER 56

England and my English friends are memories I will cherish forever. I have many stories I could tell about my experiences there. I later became acquainted with a fellow who was the former chairman of the United Kingdom Red Cross, who offered to take us to the place where the United States Air Force flew in World War II. This man and I became friends. I didn't know anyone there. Pearl and I had come on the train to meet him and since it was too early to leave he asked us to have tea with him at the Angel Hotel. I said, "I will if you'll let me host it." He told me it would be fine so we went to the hotel to have tea.

The Angel Hotel is where Charles Dickens went to have tea when he was in Borough Saint Edmund. He was living there and it was his routine to have tea there every afternoon. It had beautiful old Victorian furniture. It was what you would expect of an English hotel. This man's counterpart in the United States would have been Barbara Dole at the American Red Cross.

I called over there once to talk to him, and his wife, Catherine, informed me he was out of town. She proceeded to tell me he had gone to Cambridge and he wouldn't be back until the next day. He had been invited to a black tie supper and then they would have breakfast the next morning. She was to pick him up at lunch. When I talked to him I said, "You're the first guy I have ever talked to who graduated from Cambridge. I heard about those two who were spies for Russia." He said, "Yes, I'm afraid they gave us a rather bad name."

Oliver Snow was another friend of mine. Oliver Snow was in conversation with Lord Gordon Parry on one occasion. Oliver was an avid hunter. He loved to hunt. Oliver wasn't always straight up

and down. He would hunt at night and a whole lot of other things.
Anyway, Oliver told Lord Gordon Parry, "Have you ever eaten wild
turkey, not domesticated, but wild?" Lord Parry said, "Oh, yes, yes.
I have eaten it and it's very nice." Oliver told Lord Parry he would
get him a wild turkey one day. Lord Parry said, "That's nice of
you." That was supposed to end the story but it didn't.

Lord Parry was here with his wife, Lady Glennis, for the Cherry
Blossom Festival. They were staying in the Alumni House at
Mercer University. Carolyn Crayton kept them coming and going
the whole time they were here with every activity imaginable. They
had probably been up half of the night when sometime between 5:00
and 6:00 in the morning they were awakened by the doorbell ringing.
Lady Glennis got up and went to the door. As she was telling me
this story in her English accent she said, "There was that bloody
Oliver Snow, that bloody, blasted Oliver Snow standing there with a
bloody turkey, feathers and everything, with its head on the floor for
a gift. I could have shot him."

════════ CHAPTER 57 ════════

Some of the people I have met during my years in office have not only been interesting but famous as well. It has been an honor and a privilege to meet six of the Presidents of the United States of America. When I began working in law enforcement it never crossed my mind I might meet these men. It was certainly a perk of the job I was most pleased to receive. I had the chance to meet President Carter under most unusual circumstances.

I was in the west end of Bibb County with not much going on so I made a radio transmission to the office telling them to pass some traffic on to me. As soon as I quit transmitting to the office another car cut in and very hurriedly said, "Sheriff, this is Buster Williams, Secret Service. We're in a motorcade about five miles south of Bibb County. How about going to the Hartley Bridge Road area and securing a service station until we get there. The president's got to go to the toilet."

The adrenaline started flowing. I was at least four minutes away from Hartley Bridge Road even with the sirens on and lights flashing. I didn't know how in the world I would get to the area, find a service station with no one there, and get it secured for the President of the United States to go to the restroom. I thought, am I going to be the only sheriff to cause the president to mess up his pants? Surely not, I hoped.

I hurried to the area and whipped into a Phillips 66 service station. I jumped out with a badge in my hand and said to the attendant standing there, "Is anybody in the restroom?" The fellow working there had a push broom in his hand, some mineral spirits, and some stuff you sprinkle on grease. He very slowly looked at me and calmly said, "No." I hurried on, "Don't let anybody in." I rushed back to the car and radioed the Secret Service agent saying, "Buster, it's the first filling station to your right. It's a Phillips 66. I'm holding it." He said, "Okay. We'll be there in four minutes."

The man working at the station still went about his business as if nothing was happening. After a minute he said, "What is this all about?" I said, "In three minutes there will be a motorcade of Secret Service and the President of the United States will be here on this lot and he's going in that bathroom." The man looked at me and he said in a most calm manner, "Okay." He went back to his sweeping and a few seconds later he said, "Who did you say was going in that restroom?" I said, "The President of the United States." He thought for a minute and then he went back to sweeping.

He may have been calm but I was afraid. When I got the call I had only a few minutes to get to a station and secure the area. My heart was beating wildly the whole time I was trying to accomplish this task.

The president arrived and went in the restroom. When he came out he approached the man at the grease rack, talked to him, and then he thanked him and left. He was coming from Plains but I'm not sure where he was going. I was reminded that day of just how human a president really is.

CHAPTER 58

When I went to the FBI Academy in 1962 I got along real well with the people from New York. They liked me. They liked to hear me talk. Several people, Michael J. Todd, Looney, and Joe Caren, when we had a break from any of our classes, we were together. After we left the Academy Joe Caren and I kept in contact with one another.

I called Joe one day years later after we had all left school. He was a captain in the New York Police Department, which is a big deal. I said, "Joe, I'm coming to New York and I'm going to need a hotel room. Can you get somebody to pick me up?" He was excited I would be coming to his city and told me he would have someone at the airport for me.

When we arrived he had a detective there waiting for us. The detective was an extremely nice guy. We retrieved our luggage and got settled into the car and the detective said, "Mr. Wilkes, Captain Caren would like you to have lunch with him." He drove us to a big fancy restaurant in the city. Joe was sitting in there with a full uniform on with a gold braid on his hat and a drink in his hand. I chuckled and said, "They'd run you out on a rail in Macon, Georgia for drinking on the job." In New York no one said anything. They all had a drink with their meal. The big city was so different from Macon.

Joe informed me, "Ray, I reserved a room for you on 46th Street. You're close enough to Times Square you can walk down there. You're far enough away you won't get mugged." I knew he was really looking out for me.

Before we left I said, "Joe, I want to go to Greenwich Village. How should I dress?" He replied, "Gee, Ray, let me think. If you go over there with a suit on they're going to think you're a cop. If you open your mouth they're going to know you're not. If you go over there in old clothes you could get in trouble. Go over there like a cop but don't say nothing."

We went to Greenwich Village staying over there pretty late that night. There were people still out and about at midnight. They were moving furniture from one apartment to another one down the street. I learned this was a common practice. When the man goes there to collect his rent the next morning the renters are gone. They move during the night then no one knows where to find them to collect back rent. They can live free for several months by rotating through the different apartment buildings.

I saw some of the hippies sitting in front of the fire station. We were across the street standing on the sidewalk. When we looked up there was a man in the window of the fire station with a large bucket of water in his hand. After carefully aiming he poured it on the hippies. I guess it was the most effective way to move loiterers from the places you did not want them to congregate. Before the Empire State Building closed we rode the elevator to the top. New York was a wonderful experience but my real purpose of going was a matter of business.

I had traveled to New York with Detective Raymond Purvis to bring back to Bibb County a man who had killed his wife. He had cut her body severely, very near Jeneane's Restaurant, in front of the American Federal Building. Harry Thompson's law partner, Milton J. Wallace, had been walking down the street when he came upon this man cutting the woman. The lawyer started kicking him in the face with his shoe. He kicked him off of her but she bled to death before he could get her to the hospital.

The man had fled Macon and was being held in New York. Bibb County District Attorney Fred Hasty had sent us up there to bring him back but he hadn't signed a waiver of extradition. Having an extradition is a must. Without one you can stay for months without an extradition hearing. When I arrived in New York and realized Fred had not signed it, I was sick. I knew Fred should have known better than that. He was new at the time so I let it go but I told Joe Caren we weren't going to be able to get him out of New York because he hadn't signed the extradition.

I told a detective my predicament and he said, "Sheriff, let me handle it." I said, "All right." I had no other choice but to trust him. My hands were tied without the extradition. He told me he would pick me up at a certain time to go to court in Brooklyn. Early the next morning we were on the sidewalk waiting and they picked us up. We got in the car for the ride to the court in Brooklyn.

We were sitting in the courtroom waiting for the case to be called and this detective was with us. They called him out by Willy B. Hill. They stood the man up. The judge said, "Mr. Hill, these gentlemen here are from Georgia. They're here to carry you back. They've got a warrant for murder." Willy B. said, "Yes, sir. I want me a lawyer. I don't want to go back. I want me a lawyer."

The judge continued explaining to Mr. Hill, "Mr. Hill," he said, "There are three elements that constitute an extradition. One of them is a warrant, and they've got one. The other one is a copy of the grand jury indictment and it's properly been documented as being true and accurate. They've got that. And one other thing, the crime you're accused of is on the same law as New York. That's murder."

Mr. Hill cried out, "I want me a lawyer." The judge just kept right on speaking as though had had not heard a word. He said, "Well, you can't settle it here. Okay. Next case." They escorted Mr. Hill out of the court room and the next thing I knew all three of us were in the car heading for the airport. There was no lawyer. There was no extradition. When we arrived at the airport the New York officer pulled up beside the plane we were going to get on said, "If you'll give me your tickets I'll take them inside and get them validated." He got everything taken care of and we boarded our plane.

When we got on the plane Purvis sat next to the window with Willy B. in the middle and I was in the aisle seat. We started to really give Willy B. a fit kidding him. We weren't working the case. The city was working it. Willy B. was all nervous and apprehensive. He began to whine, "I don't like to fly. I don't like to fly." Detective Purvis couldn't let an opportunity to give Willy B. a hard time pass by. He said, "Aw, man, you ever been on a Greyhound bus?" Willy B. responded, "Yeah. I've been on a Greyhound bus." Purvis continued, "Are they concerned about you falling? Look, on this plane they've got a belt on you. They don't want you to fall out of your seat." Purvis just kept making comments, making Willy B. more and more nervous.

The plane began to taxi down the runway. As soon as the wheels of the plane left the ground Purvis said, "See there, we're off the ground." Willy B. began to cry, "I don't like to fly high. I don't like to fly high." He was a nervous wreck the whole way back to Macon.

We brought him all the way back to Macon. If it hadn't been for Joe Caren and the New York Police Department we'd still be sitting up there. Their help was invaluable to us. When they called Willy B.'s name the detective went behind the bench and whispered to the judge and that's all there was to it. We got him. I later called Joe and told him how much I appreciated all he and his men had done for us to help with that situation and all his courtesies extended to us.

Joe called me about two years later. He said, "Hey, Ray. How are you doing?" We exchanged pleasantries with each other and then Joe said, "I've got a favor I want to ask of you." I said, "You know I'll do it if I can." He continued with his request, "I've got a brother-in-law who is an engineer. He's working for the city of Atlanta, Fulton County, on their waste system. He's trying to help them on how to handle it. He went out to dinner and he had a couple or three drinks. He got stopped on the way home and didn't pass the breathalyzer so they got him for DUI. If his company finds out he's booked for DUI he's probably going to lose his job."

I said, "Joe, great Scott. Atlanta is almost 100 miles from here. That's a city outside of everybody." He said, "Please, do something." I assured him I would do my best although at the time I had no idea where to even begin. I started to think about the problem and I remembered a fellow who went to school before I got out. His name was Royal and he was Ivan Allen's driver. I called Royal and told him I needed a favor. I told him the story of Joe Caren helping me with the Willy B. situation in New York and how if it hadn't been for him I would have never gotten him out of New York. Then I told him of the help Joe needed in Atlanta. Royal said, "I'll see what I can do."

Royal called me back about three days later and said, "Tell him to forget about it." I didn't ask any questions. The problem was taken care of and that was all I was concerned about. I called Joe Caren and repeated what Royal said to me and I haven't heard from him since.

CHAPTER 59

Joe and I were big buddies while at the Academy. The dormitories at the Academy had not been built then. We were living in private homes approved by the FBI. Where we lived had to be inspected and have the stamp of approval from the FBI. There was a particular occasion when he was walking down the street in front of the building I was living in. I was at the third floor window with a Confederate flag flying out the window. Tony Demeo was sitting down below on the sidewalk. He was a good fellow but he was a born and bred Yankee through and through. He didn't understand the South or anything about it. When I saw Joe coming down the street I whistled loudly. Joe stopped and I yelled down to him, "Joe, didn't you forget something?" Joe responded, "Ray, I'm so sorry." He then turned around and saluted my Confederate flag. Tony said, "Joe, don't do that. Don't do that." He was appalled anyone would salute the Southern icon. Joe was a Northerner also but I had a good relationship with Joe. We were close friends all throughout our time at the FBI Academy.

CHAPTER 60

Sometimes criminals aren't the sharpest knives in the drawer. I've met all types in my life. I am amazed at the mind of an individual who can pull off the most impossible criminal act and get away with their crime. I am equally amazed at the stupidity of some of those who try and end up failing because of a dumb mistake.

Sometime during the '60s in the month of March we had complaints of a couple of slick guys doing business on the Warner Robins Highway. They were overcharging people and getting mortgages on their houses and the people didn't really know about it. The long and short of it was tax time was quickly approaching and their time was running out.

Tax time in those days was a little different. All I had to do was sign my W-2 form and send it in. I didn't have anything to deduct or anything to claim. I didn't make enough money. Others may have had to do a little more on their taxes but the whole system was still by and far a lot easier than it is today.

These guys were in the aluminum siding business. They went down to Magnolia Court, which was a nice court then, and rented a room so they would be able to work undisturbed. They were in there for a good long time and I think the taxes looked worse than they had originally thought they were going to look. The further they looked into the matter the worse they found their tax situation to be. They knew something had to be done to alleviate their tax woes. They concocted their plan and executed it before leaving to take a break and go to the Chicken House, proposedly, and eat supper.

The Chicken House was a rough establishment. If you wanted some action in those days you went to the Chicken House. There was always plenty of action there.

They hadn't been gone but about 25 minutes when they saw flames coming from the apartment. At the Naval Ordinance plant there was an old Commander Davis there with an old fire truck. Any time anyone needed help he would arrive in full command of his fire truck. He loved to ride that fire truck. He had a big tank of water on it because there weren't any water mains out there at that time. He would hop on the fire truck and call for some Marines to help him and here they would come. It was a short run for them. They whipped the truck down there and Jimmy Sapp joined them with his old fire truck he had gotten from the surplus people.

All these volunteer firemen arrived and doused the room with water. They sprayed water until they had the fire under control. About that time the men with the aluminum business came from their meal at the Chicken House. They said, "Oh, my God. Everything is ruined. All our records are gone." Which is exactly what they wanted, all their records to be destroyed.

One of the new deputies said, "No. It ain't gone. Everything is okay. I got it all in the box and got it right here." They had set the room on fire with all the records inside trying to get out of their income tax problem and the deputy had saved it all. There was no way to set a second fire without being conspicuous. Sometimes you just can't win no matter how hard you try.

CHAPTER 61

S ome of the cases I was involved in were tragedies from the start. I had a particular case in Macon which touched me greatly at the time. I thought it a real tragedy because when the situation began it appeared to be almost nothing. It ended up a completely different way.

A young black man went to the First National Bank on Cherry Street. He approached a teller and he told her he wanted to draw his money out of the bank. He claimed to have $200,000 in the bank and he wanted all of it withdrawn. She pecked on her computer for a few minutes and then said, "I'm sorry but you only have $12 in your account." He said, "No. I know I've got money in the bank." He continued on explaining to her about a dream he had the previous night. In his dream someone had put $200,000 in his account and he was told to go over there and get it.

The teller called the supervisor and explained the situation. The supervisor called the police because by this time the man was becoming vocal and causing a disturbance in the bank. Tom Mitchell and Roscoe Hinson were the two detectives sent down to the bank. These were two seasoned officers. They walked in the bank going straight to the man to ask him what the problem was. He explained the whole story to the officers. One of the officers calmly said, "Well, I'll tell you what to do. Let's go up to City Hall and talk to the Chief and see what he thinks we ought to do."

The officers talked the man into getting inside the patrol car. They didn't put their hands on him and they didn't put handcuffs on him. This man was going to City Hall as the victim, as the person who had money and the bank wouldn't give it to him.

They drove up to City Hall and took the man to see the chief.

When they went in the Chief of detectives said, "What have you got there?" The officer responded, "We've got a signal 16." A signal 16 meant a mental case. The chief said, "Book him." When he said "book him" this man pulled a gun out of his left front pocket. He was left-handed so he shot across to his right side. The shot killed Roscoe Hinson with a bullet to his heart. Tom Mitchell tried to grab the gun away from the man. He shot towards the Chief of Detective's office just as the chief was going in and closing the door. An officer by the name of Shorty Simmons was on duty as the desk man and the radio operator. He shot at Shorty. The bullets were flying across the room. Tom was trying to hold the man but he shot Tom through the chest. Tom passed out from his wound.

The man fled the scene. He ran as hard as he could getting out of City Hall and he was on the streets somewhere. When I heard about it the sheriff and I jumped in our car and drove as fast as we could to City Hall. We knew they would need officers to help with the situation. City Hall was in complete chaos. No one was doing anything except screaming how close they came to getting killed. I told Jimmy, "Let's get out of here."

The funeral home picked up Roscoe Hinson. Tom Mitchell was rushed to the hospital. Blood was still everywhere, on the floor and walls and every other imaginable place in the room. Medical personnel were trying to assist people and officers were trying to sort out who should do what. I said once again, "Let's get out of here." We left the building and got into the patrol car. As soon as we got in the car we heard over the radio another patrol car calling in a situation in the south part of Bibb County which we thought might be our suspect. We went there, but it was not the man we were looking for.

We started back toward City Hall and I could hear radio chatter. Everybody was speaking and the whole situation was just so utterly disorganized. I stopped the car and said to Jimmy, "We've got to stop this. This is nothing but a mad house." He said, "What do we do?" I replied, "We're going to set up a command post." He was baffled. "Where?" he said.   I started driving again and then said, "Here." We were at Raines Avenue and Broadway in South Macon. It was a lot Johnny George owned that he used as an auction block to sell used cars. It goes down to Cherokee Brick.

I turned in there very quickly and ran up to Johnny George, who was a friend of mine. I said, "Johnny, we need this building." He said, "You've got it. I heard it on the radio." I thanked him and went into action. I immediately called the office and said, "Direct all personnel that are not engaged in some active call to report to this building. Call the City Hall and tell them to report to this building. All out of town inquiries tell them to report to this building. Anyone that has dogs, bring them here."

We began to bring in people to work this case. Now when they came in they had a place to sit and work and so forth. There were a lot of people coming from out of town, Perry, Fort Valley, Warner Robins, Jeffersonville, Monroe County, and Milledgeville, to help us with manpower.

At that point Cranford and Pierce had been in contact with Washington with a fingerprint. They were working on obtaining all previous addresses of the man. They began giving me the addresses. I told them we couldn't start sending officers from out of town to the addresses without having one or two of our people with them to make sure they found the right place. We began to send them out in threes and fours. We were covering every known stakeout we could where this man had ever met anyone. We had stake-outs and surveillances of houses all over the place. It was a large manhunt with many agencies from many towns involved.

About 10 p.m. B.F. Merritt, who was the mayor, came to me. He said, "What do you need, Ray?" I said to him, "Well, a lot of these men, including me, are now on their sixteenth hour of work. We're going to need some bed rest and we're going to need some hotel rooms so we can give them three or four hours sleep. Then we will be able to rotate them so we can keep people on the line at all times." He said, "I'll handle it. Consider it done." He came back and said, "I've got 25 rooms at Magnolia Court." I said, "Fine. I'm going to check the stakeouts and see what we've got there. Then I'll start rotating the men." I got in my car and went through my list of stakeouts. The first one I went to was Finneydale Drive. When I turned onto the street the first thing I heard was gun fire. When I heard that I gave it the gas and sped in there. I saw the officers running from the house and I saw the man on the ground. They had already fired but I hollered from the window, "Stop shooting. Stop shooting." He was already dead. I guess in the excitement of the situation and the fact this man had fired on them made them continue in their pursuit.

It turned out he had been in that house. There was a black lady with two little boys living in the house. She was a widow living on Social Security and raising those two little boys. When someone had knocked on her door she went to the door and looked out. When she saw the officers she said, "He's on the porch now." The officer said to her, "Go to the back of the house and go in a room and lock the door and remain there."

The man we were after knew this lady because he had lived next to them at one time. Not friends, just next door neighbors. The officers got their firearms in position and they eased open the door next to the one where he was. The house was actually a duplex which had been made into a single family dwelling. Just as they opened the screen they said, "Hold it. You're under arrest." When they said that, he came around with his left hand and fired immediately. The bullet hit about four or five inches behind the head of the officer he was shooting at. The bullet hit right behind him and went into the door facing. The officer was carrying a sawed off shotgun and he just discharged both barrels. When he did, one of the nine bullets hit the assailant's firearm and jammed the gun. He was never able to shoot the gun more than one time. When the gun jammed he jumped from the porch and ran about 30 yards and fell. They were still shooting and pursuing him as he ran.

I didn't want any gunfire on the body so later if someone came and dug up ballistics the officers could be accused of killing him on the ground. I stopped the shooting and radioed in and told them the man had been killed. I told them to get the coroner and get an ambulance out there. Help arrived within a few minutes.

We thanked all the other officers who had given aid to us. No one in the house was hurt. The next day I went back to the house with a ball of twine and some thumb tacks. A photographer and I put the string where the man was standing and the best I could see where the gun had fired out. I let the string out to where it hit the door facing in the line of fire and I put a thumb tack there. Then I found the place on the floor where it had ricocheted and I put a thumb tack there. I then photographed the trajectory of the bullet as it went in and hit the wall of the door facing and then reflected to the floor. That was the first shot. Then I photographed the gun and his hand, showing where it had hit his left hand and shot away his left index finger. He was never able to fire but one shot.

After he was taken to the morgue I went there and the medical examiner did his job and assessed how many shots hit him. I don't remember the number but it was a good many because a shotgun has nine shots.

Hinson had been killed instantly and Tom stayed in the hospital for about two months, then in intensive care a long time. Later he came up to me and said, "Ray, I didn't know anything about it at the time but I was told what you did. I'll never forget you and I want you to know how much I thank you." He never went back to work

City Hall fell in when no one was in charge and I guess I just took charge of it. There was so much confusion up there, which I can understand. If the same thing had happened at the sheriff's office in the main lobby there would be a lot of confusion. Having a clear head and being able to look at the situation from the outside gave me an ability to help.

The officers who were involved in the shootout and the one who was killed had one desire, to get the mentally disturbed man out of a crowded bank. The case started with a person who appeared to be a mental case and in his mind was a victim. No one could have known this man was carrying a gun or what his breaking point would be. Surely it could have had a different outcome. The cost of a life was too high a price to be paid for a Signal 16.

Whenever I had duty to transport a prisoner and had to do so by way of an airplane I always used handcuffs no matter if it was a straight flight or I had to make a connecting flight. I always used them for mental patients also. The reason for this is, one, I can't discharge a gun in an airport. You've got so many people in there you may harm someone. Secondly, in picking up a mental patient I wouldn't shoot him but he might shoot me. You can't shoot a mental patient. He could get your gun and kill you and then be back on the streets. I always felt like I'd rather take a whipping than to get killed with my own gun. That was just my own way of thinking about it.

CHAPTER 62

I was involved in another bank case. In this particular incident a well-dressed man went into the First National Bank on Gray Highway and robbed it. He got a lot of money out of it then he disappeared. We could tell from the scene and the testimony we collected from witnesses this was a person who apparently knew what he was doing. The FBI was covering it. They were looking for all types of MOs to see what type of evidence they had on other cases similar to this one. This was a case with high priority.

Some officers and I had worked a little bit on it but the FBI was really doing the bulk of the investigation and work concerning the case. It ran quiet for about two weeks with no new leads on the case; then one night I got a call. They said, "There is a lady whose children have found some money and they think it came from a bank." Well, I hopped in the car to investigate the lead. The office also called the FBI and Travis Lynch and we met there.

When we arrived at the house we were met with a lady with a Piggly Wiggly sack full of money. She began to tell her story. She and her two little boys lived in this house alone. She was highly respected by me and others because she lived alone and she was trying to make something of the boys. She lived off the money she received from a government check. She continued to tell us how the boys had built a rabbit box and then came to her saying they were going to set the trap on the box. I'm sure they were going to eat the rabbit. There's no question in my mind about that. So they went out to a little plum thicket to set their rabbit box and while digging, trying to level it, this money appeared.

They filled this rabbit box up with bills, lots of them. They took the money in the house and showed it to their mother. The mother told them to go back and see if there was any more. They went back to the same spot and filled the rabbit box with money again. They said they thought they had retrieved all the money so Travis and I took the money and went to the plum thicket. Travis and I, with a few other officers, took flashlights and started digging. We uncovered some more money and we put it in the sack. By this time the money was amounting to about $22,000. We put two guards on the plum thicket site for the night. They kept their post until morning and then we did a third search. This time we dug very deep and in a large circle of the original site. I don't think we found anything else. If we did it was very little but we did make a diligent search of it.

After we had done a thorough search we took the money back to the bank and returned it. I went to the man in charge of the FDIC and told him I thought these kids deserved a reward. He said, "No, law enforcement people were involved from the start and we don't pay a reward. That's an insurance matter." So I went to Tom Green, the president of the bank who I respected a lot, and informed him of my conversation with this other man and then I said, "Tom, this is wrong. These two kids are poverty children. They were out there. They found it and they turned that money in. Their mother could have kept it and spent the money just a little along for the rest of her life. It's wrong to just do nothing for them when everything they did was right." Tom thought a minute and then said, "You're right, Ray." He started raising Cain. Finally the FDIC reported they would give them $2000. I thought they should give them $1100 each but they beat it down to a $1000 check.

I was glad they were getting money but I felt there should be some fanfare to the whole occasion. I wanted a lot of people involved in rewarding these two young boys. I went to the principal of the little school they attended and told her what I wanted to do. She got so excited about the idea she went to the church. Someone with a big pickup truck brought the two big altar chairs with the real high back and carved wood from the pulpit area where the preachers sit, and put them in the school auditorium. It was like a throne. She put one chair on each side of the stage area. I had convinced someone from the FBI to come as an official to speak. I had the mayor come as an official of the City of Macon. I had the chairman of the county commissioners there. I had the school superintendent there. These kids were named kings and we had crowns made for each of them. Then the president of the bank, Tom Green, presented each one with $1000 check. That was a lot of money. The whole school clapped for them and sang for them. All in all it was a big day.

The irony of the whole case was this was the same house where we found the man who killed Roscoe Hinson and shot Tom Mitchell in our previous bank situation. The lady whose boys had found the money was the same lady who had answered the door and told the officers where the killer was hiding. The killer was killed on her front porch. These were two of the biggest events happening in Macon and they happened at the same lady's house. I thought, how ironic would it be for something like that to happen.

The man who robbed the bank was arrested. He was a professional golfer who had come to Macon and robbed the bank, then appeared in a golf tournament. No one had suspected anything from this man except one person, one of our officers who had picked up some information this man was acting strange at the Dempsey Hotel. It was related to the FBI who had photographs of him. He fit the description so they put him in a line up where he was picked out. The FBI interviewed him and were able to solve the bank robbery. The money was returned to the bank, case closed.

The mother of the boys who had returned the money came to my office one day to tell me some of her neighbors were giving her a lot of trouble. It seems her neighbors felt she should not have returned the money but instead given each of them some money to make life a little easier. They were really giving her the devil so I sent some officers to her house. They went door to door asking each neighbor who was giving this lady trouble. When the neighbors found out a deputy sheriff was looking into the situation it cooled off. To the best of my knowledge the mother raised the two boys and there was never any trouble from them.

This lady was one of the most stable people I had ever known, black or white. She lived through two of the most notable events in Macon history and had two boys who were a party to seeing things done right. I often thought, how ironic, with 160,000 people in Bibb County this woman would be in two of the major events.

CHAPTER 63

When Tom Green died Bill Simmons took his place as president of the First National Bank. Bill had previously been chairman of the board there. One day he called me to come down to the bank. I had always had a close relationship with the personnel at the bank and on any investigation they almost invariably called me to come, even though the bank was located in the city. I would work with them and solve most of the cases.

On this particular day Mr. Simmons had a man in his office when I arrived. Bill told the man to tell me what had happened. The fellow said, "I had a fruit jar. I had $12,000 and I put it in the fruit jar. I live at a certain place and I went under my house and while no one was looking I dug a hole and I put the fruit jar in the hole. I had only one door, one lock, and I had the only key. I locked it up. The only man that's ever been under there is the Orkin man. I went back under there yesterday to check my money. It had been under there a long time. It was an annual inspection. I looked in my fruit jar and this is all that was in there. That man squirted some of that juice in my fruit jar and took the rest of my money."

I looked in the jar and there was a wad of something comparable to what you might see at the cow pen or the horse pen. I looked but I didn't do any touching. It was really disgusting looking. I couldn't see too much, just a wad of yuck. I said, "Why would the man squirt the bug fluid in there and not take the money?" The man replied, "I don't know but he's the only one that's been under there and I know he's got it."

I assured the man I would investigate the situation and contact him as soon as I had any information. I told Bill Simmons, "I'll find the Orkin man and interview him. After he gives me his testimony

I'll get back with you." Well, I found the Orkin man and when I told him I wanted to interview him it scared the man to death. He said, "I ain't seen no fruit jar. I ain't seen no hole. All I did was take and put out the chemical. With the schedule I work I don't have any time to dig holes. I have to get in there and get out. I wouldn't take money from nobody." Well, he convinced me.

I went back to the man who owned the fruit jar and told him, "He says, no, that he hasn't done anything." I reported back to Bill Simmons, "I don't know what happened but I don't think the Orkin man had anything to do with it."

The Orkin man, Otto, went on about his business. I told the Orkin man I believed him and there was no problem but he was still scared to death. About three or four weeks later Bill Simmons called me back to the bank and once again the man with the fruit jar was there. Bill said, "Ray, I want to tell you what happened. I sent the fruit jar in to the U.S. Treasury Department and their laboratory has identified $11,007 of that money. What had happened was he had put his fruit jar under there and as the temperature changed condensation set in and molded his money away. He now has only $11,000 where he previously had $12,000."

I couldn't help but look at the man and say, "Do you need another fruit jar?" The man replied, "No, I don't need another fruit jar." Bill Simmons said, "We've already talked about the fruit jar, Ray. He's opening an account and the money is already in the bank." That's the only case I ever had where money just disintegrated.

CHAPTER 64

I was down in South Georgia at one of these little jails. In small towns there is no money for jail expenses. The jails would usually have about six cells in them. The jailer would be some old man, a bachelor, who would stay at the jail overnight with the prisoners and then he would go home the next morning. The jailer would serve the breakfast meal and lunch meal then the dinner meal would be fixed by his wife. Then the next night the jailer would report in again to do his night watch. If a prisoner got sick or tried to get away the jailer could call somebody. If they had a fire they would call the fire department. There was no law enforcement. He was just some bachelor who usually chewed a lot of tobacco and did a night watch.

When morning came the sheriff's jailer would deliver food. The jailer had to get up to the stove and put the breakfast on plates. He had some tin plates he would prepare with breakfast for each prisoner. He put two slices of bread on the tin plate, a dipper full of grits, and then gravy on the grits. He would then slide the plate through to the prisoner.

There were three people in the Cordele jail who had been doing a lot of crime throughout Georgia. Most of it was in flimflamming and passing bad checks and that sort of thing. They were really proficient in the crimes though. State patrol had picked them up and brought them to the nearest county jail. So these prisoners were in the Cordele jail.

Several of the cells had men in them and then down the line separated from the men a little was a lady. Well, the men looked at the food being served and they were used to being served Canadian bacon, eggs on the light, juice, cereal, and all sorts of other good stuff. Here they got those grits and gravy. The jailer got down to the woman and put her food in there. This girl was a nice looking girl. She hesitated and then she said, "I can't help it but I've got to have a Kotex." The old man looked at her like she was a fool and said, "That's the way y'all do. Y'all go out there and create all this crime and make all this money and live high. Then when you get in jail you don't want to eat what the others are eating. You're going to eat these grits and gravy just like the rest of them do." He thought she was talking about some fancy food.

═══ CHAPTER 65 ═══

I was involved in a case helping Major Mincy, the GBI agent in charge of the Milledgeville office He called me and said, "Ray, I need some help." I assured him I would do what I could. He continued, "We've got two stores in Augusta and there were armed robberies in both of them yesterday. Someone came into the store, one was carrying a sawed off shotgun and one was carrying a revolver. They held the store up but the old man running the store didn't move fast enough for them so they discharged the shotgun in there, blowing all the bread off of the counter. Then they took the money and fled. Ten minutes later they went into another store. There they announced a robbery and somehow the owner of the store acted as if he was not going to comply. They started shooting, hitting him four times. They grabbed the money, and as they were running to the car the son of the owner who had been shot grabbed a pistol and started shooting at them as they were running away. He thinks there were three of them. In the first robbery we were only able to identify two of them. We've got a partial identification on them as a probable.

They were here in Milledgeville but now they're gone. They stole a car from the Medical Center of Central Georgia. We feel like they're still in that area. Right now we can only say they are near the Medical Center according to our informant." I told him to give me whatever information he could gather and I would help him in any way I could.

A little later he called me back and said, "Is there an Orange Street in Macon?" I told him there was. He said, "Is there an Orange Terrace?" I confirmed we had an Orange Terrace. He said, "Ray, they're on Orange Terrace. They're in a big house. That's all I

210 **I Didn't Save the President's Life**

can tell you but be careful. Both of them just got out of Reidsville. They're bad news."

I drove up to where I thought the apartment house that had been described was located. Then I looked for a place I thought we could watch it without being seen. You couldn't park a car in that section. It was a dead end. If you parked in front of the house they would see you. If you parked in back they would see you. If you parked down the hill you wouldn't see anything. I went across the street to an upstairs apartment and talked to a fellow about using his apartment. He started rattling and immediately I knew he was not capable of giving an agreement either way so I left. I next called the gas company to see if they would let us have a truck so we could approach the house about a gas leak and try to identify the men and where they were. Well, liability was an issue and they couldn't do that.

When I could see we were running out of options and time was getting away from us, I decided we should just go to the house ourselves and check out the situation. Harry Harris, Ray Stewart, Carl Barker, and I went to the house. Two went to the back door and two went to the front door. I was at the front door. We knocked on the door and no one came.

Eventually a lady came out of the house. As she exited the doorway I eased over to her and showed her a picture we had of the men. She nodded her head. She didn't want to say anything but she indicated they were inside the house. I knocked again and still no one came to the door. The windows of the house were of the old style, coming all the way down to the floor of the porch. As I looked at the apartment windows I noticed they were raised and a little morning spring breeze was blowing the curtains out. I thought, no one would leave the house like that. They had to be in there.

I told Harry I was going around to the other side. I asked Carl if he had heard anything and he said he hadn't. He showed me where there was some broken glass so I stepped up there and was able to get my hand through the broken glass and unlock the door. I had my gun in hand as I opened the door and stepped into a living room. As I did I noticed a baby in a crib. I knew there was no way they would leave a baby in a crib. I was figuring the men may have left but their wives or mothers were still there and the women didn't want to tell us anything so they wouldn't come to the door.

I started walking down a narrow little hall to a big bedroom. There was a bathroom on my right hand side. As I passed the bathroom I thought I saw the shower curtain move. I looked closer and noticed the grid of the window was down. I knew at that point it had not been wind moving the curtain but for sure he was in there. I then saw him in my peripheral vision. I walked up to the shower curtain with my gun in my hand. I pushed the curtain back and there he stood in the bathtub with a gun in his hand. I guess for about ten seconds we had a Mexican standoff. About then I said, "If you try to use it I'll kill you," and I reached in the bathtub and twisted the gun out of his hand. Carl put handcuffs on him and took him out. When Carl patted him down he found another gun in his back pocket.

I walked back into the house and found a little girl in there less than three years of age. I thought to myself, she must be terrified with that gun. I knelt down to her level and said in my calmest, sweetest voice, "Sweetheart, is there anybody else here?" I knew there were at least two in the robbery. She said nothing. She looked like the little fawn of a deer, her eyes were so big. I asked her again, "Is anybody else here?" She didn't say anything but she looked toward a closet and I thought, oh, my. Here we go again.

With my gun in my hand I started walking toward the closet. As I was walking I heard something fall. The other man had dropped that sawed off shot gun and had his hands up. We took him into custody also. I said, "Lock them up. I'm going to wait here in case there is a third one." We still had not eliminated a third suspect. When I was first told about the case I had asked Major Mincy if they had looked for a fresh grave because the car was burned. There was a lot of blood in the car and if there were fingerprints in the car they would burn it. I said, "If one was here there's a good chance he's buried here." He said, "We've already done that, Ray. We looked all around here and we didn't find anything." At any rate I told my men I was going to wait there so I sat down on the couch. I held the little girl in my lap telling her she didn't need to be afraid. We sat on the couch and waited.

After about 40 minutes to an hour I heard some people coming. It was the suspect's mother and his wife. I told them who I was and we had made an arrest there at the house. I went outside and called Major Mincy in Milledgeville and told him all the details that had transpired. He said, "Ray, that's hard to believe. I know them. I'll be there in a few minutes." He got in his car and was in Macon in no time. He said, "I know those fellows and I know them well. They're two of the most dangerous people I've ever dealt with in my life. I can't believe you all took them down."

They had the men in custody and I didn't think any more about them. After it was over I had the sobering effect of all the events in retrospect. I was thinking one day, you know, I've been in a lot of danger in my life. This was one time I was probably a lot closer to death than I ever realized. When I opened the shower curtain he could have fired very quickly, even accidentally. I feel like I had a guardian angel sitting on my shoulder to help me get the gun from the suspect. Then there was a man in a closet with a sawed off shotgun. He could have shot me any time. Here I was in the living room with the little girl. He had to hear my voice. He could have shot me at several different times, even as I opened the door to the closet or when he dropped the gun. In fifteen minutes time I was in a line of fire with two different suspects and could have been killed by either one.

The whole incident was very thought-provoking to me. I said to myself, you're a Christian. You've made your profession in Jesus Christ. You believe He was born of a virgin. You believe that He died on the cross and He's coming back. Do you really believe that? Yes. If you really believe it how many people have you told about Him? Jesus said, "If you confess Me before men I will confess you before My Father which is in Heaven." That verse hit me like a brick. I had done part of my part but I had never done anything to really profess my faith and to try to lead someone else to the Lord.

Our law enforcement chaplain and my pastor, the Reverend Jimmy Waters, knew of that incident and one day he talked to me about it. I told him how I felt so burdened to tell others about Christ and what He had done for me in salvation. He asked me if I would be willing to share my story and my testimony on the Sunday morning television broadcast that Mabel White Baptist Church hosted. I told him I would do it. The next Sunday morning as the film crew was filming the Sunday morning service Jimmy Waters called me up to the podium and told everyone who I was. I gave my testimony telling the story and how it had impacted my life. I told them the full story of the robbery suspects. I don't know how many thousands of people were listening. After it was over I got a call from Mr. William A. Fickling. He said, "I want to tell I was very proud of what you did this morning."

It's an incident I still think back on and know what could have happened and what didn't happen. I believe angels are on this earth and each of us has a guardian angel.

After it was all over I went about my job. About a month later I was getting ready to go to bed when the phone rang at my house. It was a young patrolman from the Macon Police Department. He said, "We're looking for those two men. They escaped from the Augusta jail. We think we've got them in a place but we don't know them and we were wondering if we could get you to come lead this raid because you had arrested them before?" I said, "Okay. I'll be there in a few minutes." I put my clothes on and went over there. I'll be honest with you, I knew what I was dealing with. We hit the house and searched under it, around it, the attic, everything. We had enough people surrounding the area to make sure they couldn't get out.

When we started searching the area I saw the mother of the suspect was there and the wife and children were there. As they were searching, the mother turned to me and said, "You arrested my boy before on Orange Terrace." I said, "Yes, ma'am. I did." Very spitefully she continued, "I'm going to tell you something. You won't be that lucky again. He's going to kill you."

You know, with no parental guidance and a mother like that it was no wonder the man had turned out like he had. I thought, this is like Frank and Jesse. With a mother like that what do you expect of the children? That was a case that was really a cliff hanger until we got the men in custody. They escaped again in Augusta and I don't know what happened to them after that.

CHAPTER 66

O ne of the hardest cases I ever worked was the Akins murder case. It had so many angles to it. I was in the front yard cutting the grass when my wife came to the door saying I was wanted on the telephone. I went to the phone and was told, "It looks like we've got a double homicide. Quinton Cotton, a pilot, while flying an airplane, has seen a body on the ground and one in a car." I said, "I'll be there in a few minutes." I jumped in the car and took off out there. As I was turning onto Fairmont North a deputy was coming out of the same street. The incident had happened at the very end of the street. He said, "We've got one of them identified. One of them is Ronald Akins. The other one is a woman but we don't know what her name is. We don't know whether it's a wife killing somebody over a husband. We just don't know who it is." I said, "Let me see her picture." They had a picture and they held it up. I said, "Hold on, turn around. I know who they are."

This young couple was from up around Dalton, Georgia. The man had been married before and his ex-wife had gone to Florida. Ironically, I had rented an apartment to the couple at 4251 Napier Avenue, Catherine Arms Apartments. I thought, I've got a key to that apartment. I had so much on the crime scene I said, "Okay. First thing I want to do is find out who is here from the County Engineers?" Bob Fountain had come in. I said, "Bob, we're going to need some maps of this area and I'd like to get some topos if I can to see how this land lays out here. We need to start a search. We need to find a weapon or anything that will tie this to who did this." It looked like it was going to start raining at any time so I called a wrecker service and had them haul the car to dry storage. I gave them instructions, "I don't want you to touch anything on the outside. Nothing. We're going to process but we can't do it right now. Forensic science guys are going to do it but they won't be here until tomorrow and we're going to process it then. Don't touch a thing. Just move the car to dry storage." I put a guard on the car at the storage facility. I didn't want anyone to touch that car so I put a man on it all night.

I knew that this boy who was murdered had worked at Southern Natural Gas. I used my key and entered the apartment. The utensils and food items were out, suggesting they were getting ready to have a sandwich and a bowl of soup. Ronald Akins put up antennas as a side job. He worked on radios for the company. It looked like he had been called away at the last minute. It really just looked like he said "I'll be back in 30 minutes," and she might have said she was going to go too. That cost her her life.

We went through the house and there was nothing that we could find. Then I called Carl Barker. I knew the address of the new manager of Southern Gas because his wife had applied with me for a job. She had worked for Gary O'Tell at the Hilton Hotel but she got sick and had to leave. He was trying to find her a job. He had approached me about a job for her. She was overly qualified in every area of what I wanted in a secretary but one thing. She was married to a man who was going to be transferred. I knew about the time she got the hang of what we were doing in the sheriff's office she would be gone so I didn't hire her. Later I ran into her at a paint store and she told me where this couple had bought a house.

I told Carl and another officer to go there and start knocking on doors on Ridge Avenue until they could find him. When they found him I said, "Tell him I want him and the supervisor of Ronald Akins, closest man to him, to meet me at Hart's." They met me at Hart's Mortuary and they began to unravel the story. It would take a book to tell the story of all the trouble they had had with this man's former wife.

On one occasion, when Ronald was still married to Rebecca, he hadn't come to work, so his supervisor went out to check on him, only to find him lying on a bed, unconscious. The supervisor called an ambulance to come and take the man to the hospital. Rebecca was one of the world's greatest liars. She could lie better than anybody I've ever known. She said, "Oh, my God. He's done it again." The doctor said, "What do you mean?" She said, "I begged and cried. He's got three girls and he won't leave that dope alone." Later in the case we found out she had tricked him: "Do you want a milk shake?" He said, "Yeah. I'd like one." She made one up and filled it full of drugs, knocked him out, then got the three girls, who all believed their mother, to confirm the story. She had convinced the girls the father had molested them. She even convinced them to hold her husband down and try to smother him.

She was our number one suspect. We began to put pieces together and unravel the story. I looked at my watch and I said, "If she was in Macon she hasn't had time to get back to Miami." I got on the phone and started calling. Miami is made up of over 30 municipalities. It's Greater Miami and unless you know which one of those municipalities you need you're just lost. What made it worse was they weren't in the phone book and they weren't in any city directory.

The Assistant District Attorney, Walker Johnson, and Chief Investigator Harry Harris went to Miami. I had told the District Attorney, "I don't need another officer or two more officers going down there. We can get officers. I need a lawyer to be with us because if we start running into any legal entanglements I want a lawyer with us." We were able to get two lawyers to go down there with us. Don Thompson and Walker Johnson went. I had Don Thompson with me and Harry had Walker Johnson with him. So we went to court. Now there is a law that you can be forced to give fingerprints, sputum, semen, hair, or any other samples. They can force you to give them, whether you want to or not. If you refuse you can be held in contempt of court.

I learned later they had been keeping people in contempt of court in New York for I don't know how long by giving them immunity. You couldn't talk about the mob so they stayed in jail. They wouldn't talk. Each time they would carry them in front of a grand jury they wouldn't talk so they were given immunity. They had been in jail two or three years.

Anyway, we got fingerprints, hair, and everything we wanted and sent it all to the lab. I got a call from the lab saying they had identified every fingerprint on the car as being either his or hers. We had a major case of fingerprints on the victims before we buried them. We sent in the prints on Tony Machete and John Maree. I was told, "We did a major fingerprint case on them where we did the whole palm of his hand. Ray, I've got a make on that. It's on the palm of his left hand." With that we had positive identification. John Maree was at the crime scene. They had told us a cock and bull story about being gone on that particular weekend. Tony Machete was married to Ronald Akins' ex-wife, Rebecca, and John Maree was going with the oldest daughter. Rebecca had talked them into killing her former husband and his new wife. It began to come together then.

I first went to the District Attorney who happened to be a Yankee. I showed him the pictures of the scene. There was an awful lot of blood there. This husband was hit from behind with a pistol and knocked to his knees and fell and Tony Machete shot him with the shotgun on surface contact. They put the barrel right at his heart. They blew his heart out. Then he squatted down and held the gun to his left temple firing again. This time it blew tissue and bone fragments from one side of the car to the other side of the wheel.

Juanita Akins was sitting in the front seat of the car trying to use the radio when Tony walked up and said, "I've got it. Move." John Maree moved and Tony stuck that shotgun in about 12 inches of her face and shot her with both barrels. It shot from her top lip, her jaws, and her mouth, and her teeth. He just shot her away.

We got down to Miami to make the arrest and we had the house located. The District Attorney said, "I'm going to send ten guys out there. I don't want no d--- blood bath down here." I said, "I think we can handle it if you'll just send someone with authority." He said, "No. We're going to send ten."

We went out there with officers surrounding the perimeter. Vicki, one of the daughters, came in. (Rebecca had three daughters with names beginning with "V:" Valerie, Vicki, and Vanessa.) When Vicki walked into the house I immediately stepped up to the door to show her my identification. I said, "Don't be afraid, sweetheart. All I want to do is talk to your momma and daddy." She said, "Nobody is supposed to come to the house." I said, "We've got a warrant. The Assistant District Attorney, Don Thompson, and I are coming in." We started searching the house while waiting on Rebecca and her husband, Tony Machete, to come in. They eventually arrived, and we nailed them. We put handcuffs on them and Rebecca started with her wailing, "I don't know anything. We've told them the truth and y'all are still taking my babies and scaring them to death." She was going to pieces.

We arrested Rebecca, John Maree, and Tony Machete and put them in jail. I went to each one of them giving them an opportunity to tell their story and maybe make a plea bargain. They wouldn't tell you the time of day. There was a woman jailer down there who was tough. She could bite a ten penny nail in half. She said, "I'll put her over there in the tower and I guarantee you in less than two weeks she'll be on her knees begging you to come back." I gave my permission for her to do just that. We put the other two in jail and served them warrants.

About four days later I got a call, "Mr. Wilkes, come get me. This is the most terrible place I've ever seen in my whole life. I want to get out of here. I don't want to stay here no more. I waive." So Rebecca waived. My wife, Pearl, and I flew down there. I told Pearl, "Sit anywhere on the plane you want to sit but don't sit next to her. I don't want you to have any conversation with her. I don't want you in court. I'm going to be in court and it will be bad enough."

Tony's real name was John Elton Smith. Rebecca had persuaded him to change his name to a Mafia-sounding one. She convinced him that she knew a lot of the Mafia and if he proved himself on this murder, he could get $50,000 a hit. Boy, I'm telling you, the power of persuasion. She could do it. He changed his name. He went to court and he changed it to Anthony Isador Machete. Considering that Isador was a Jewish name, I thought, Rebecca, you better get brushed up on your Italian. Anyway, we went down to Miami and got Rebecca and brought her back to Georgia. Eventually, Tony and John waived and we went back down there to bring them to Georgia.

Purvis and I went down the second time, by automobile. We put handcuffs and a waist chain on them so they could only move their hands a limited amount. As we were coming back, they were constantly complaining: "A person coming from the north doesn't have a chance with all these rednecks. They're taking charge of everybody," and blah, blah, blah. They were mouthing continually. We stopped the car and I made them get out and stand on the side of the road. John Maree kept looking at me; I knew he was thinking about grabbing my gun. So I said, "John, I'm going to tell you something. You're fixing to make the biggest mistake you've ever made in your life because I'll kill you." He knew what I was thinking about.

We got them back in the car and we started on the road again. Purvis was not a seasoned investigator. He had picked up people for the office a long time but he lacked experience. They kept mouthing so I said, "Pull over and stop the car." Purvis pulled over and stopped and I turned around, putting my knees in the seat and said, "I want y'all to listen to yourself. You know you mouth about justice and you've been talking about northern people getting mistreated. Let me tell you what's going to happen to you. You're going to the electric chair. And the reason you're going is because of the Alday family. Two guys came down here and killed all of them, the whole family. They've been in prison and their lawyers have taken the electric chair to the Supreme Court and the Supreme Court said it's not cruel and unusual punishment so you won't have to worry about that. We've got it cleared. I'm going to tell you where you're going to go. You don't have to say nothing but I'm going to tell you where you're going to go. After the trial you're going to Reidsville. I'll take you there. You won't be in the general population. You're going to be on death row. Death row is at the top of the building. There is a long corridor that has two sets of bars, one on one side and one on the other. You will have plenty of time to meditate because you're not going to see nothing but another person that's going to die sitting across from you. He ain't going to see nothing but you. I'm going to tell you how it will come down one evening. Most of the inmates will be out working and then they will come for you. When they come for you you'll know because they will have already cut your hair. They will have already split the legs of your trousers so they can put the brackets on you down there for the electrode. Then they're going to walk you down that corridor. Then you'll get to see all your buddies going down. Then you're going to make a left turn and the day light will still be there so you look up. There's an iron grill above you. Look up because that's the last time you'll see the sky above you. You'll walk just a few feet and you'll make another left turn and you'll see it sitting there. It's a white electric chair. They'll take you to the chair and in all probability if you want a priest or a preacher there'll be one for you. They're going to sit you in that electric chair and strap your arms to it then they'll strap your legs to it. Then they'll put a big belt around your waist a little bit loose. Then they're going to tell you to lean forward and there's a wedge that goes down behind you that's real tight and that keeps you from falling out of that chair when you go into convulsions. When that juice hits you you're going to go into convulsions. You won't even have to worry about funeral expenses. Right next door is a morgue. They're going to have to do embalming on you quick because blood chills when it goes through that much current and they've got to get that blood out of you and put in the embalming fluid. Then they'll put a tag on the big toe of your right foot and they'll slide you in the refrigeration drawer and you'll stay in cold storage until someone comes after you. If nobody comes for you they'll bury you out here and give you a number."

I painted the whole picture for them. They turned white as ghosts. They just sat there and didn't say another word.

When we got to Kissimmee, Florida, we found a little town that was a lot like Mayberry. We asked the jailer if he could put a couple of guys in jail for us and guarantee the security on them. I informed them, "They're bad. Both of them have been in a double homicide." Some old fellows wearing overalls were sitting there and they took the two men and secured them down. I said, "We'll pick them up early in the morning." As Purvis and I left we heard one of the old men say, "They've got two of them, murderers, murderers."

When we got to the hotel Purvis said to me, "That's about the most d--- foolish thing I've ever seen in my whole life." I was still mad. I said, "What?" He replied, "You telling them about the electric chair and we've got 300 miles to drive tomorrow." I said, "Let me tell you something. I've been working on this case since the start of it, either vertically or horizontally, but they will go back. I want them to know now where I stand. This ain't the brotherhood week. I ain't their buddy. We're not going to be telling each other jokes going back." He didn't say anything else. I was his superior so that was the end of it.

The next morning we retrieved the prisoners and continued on our journey to Macon. This time they were quiet all the way. When we arrived we put them in jail. I moved Becky to Warner Robins to keep her from knowing anything that was going on here. I didn't go up to their cell until the next morning. I figured my best bet was going to be John Maree because his handprint was on the car. We didn't find Tony's prints because he had on gloves.

The next afternoon I figured I had given him enough time to soak. I went up there to get him and when the guard opened the door John said, "Where have you been? I've been calling all day for you. I want to talk to you. I want to talk to you." I took him into a private room. He said, "I don't want to go to no electric chair. I haven't killed nobody." I said, "Let me tell you something. You're the biggest sucker I've ever seen in my life. Tony is not going to talk and Rebecca is not going to talk. The only thing they are going to do is say enough for me to get to the courtroom and this is what they're going to say. They're going to say John Maree did the murder. His handprint was on the car. He was going with Vicki. Vicki would inherit from her father his Social Security. She would also inherit a life insurance policy guaranteeing her and her sisters a college education. They are going to say you and Vicki conspired to kill and did kill those people and they had nothing to do with it." Man, he drained again. He said, "What do you want me to do?" I replied, "I want you to tell me something. I want you to tell me what I don't already know. Let me ask you this, where did you rent the car from?" We had made extensive searches on the car. In my heart I knew it was a rental car. I questioned him again, "Where did you rent it from?" He answered, "Fort Lauderdale." I asked, "Who rented it?" He said, "Tony rented it."

I called Fort Lauderdale and got the captain in the detective bureau. He was still sitting there doing paper work that late in the afternoon and he said, "You're in luck. I can look out my second floor window and see the agency now. You stay right where you are and I'll call you back in ten minutes." He walked across the street and gave them the names of the men. They pulled it up and sure enough, it was the car. I was able to get the mileage off the car. It corresponded to our calculations of what it would take to drive from Miami to Macon, drive around a little bit, then drive back to Miami.

The two had given an alibi they had been trying to find locations for rental houses where you put storage stuff. The location they gave and where they went added up to the same mileage it would have been if they had driven to Macon. We punched holes all through their alibi. There was nothing to it.

The long and short of the story was John Maree spilled his guts. Tony never said anything. Each time I would interview Rebecca she would go to crying. I always interviewed her with a woman sitting in there with me. One of those times I said, "Becky, this must be about the seventh or eighth time I've seen you pull that. You know what it's consistent with? I've never seen a tear. Not one of them. I've never seen a tear."

Then she had an old gentleman named Lawyer Hawkins from Athens, Georgia, come over here to represent her because Becky's mother knew his wife. They talked him into coming over here. He was a kind old gentleman. He called me Mr. Sheriff and I called him Colonel Hawkins. On the day of the court opening he said to me, "Mr. Sheriff, we need to talk." I said, "We do?" He continued, "Yes, we do. We've got a problem." I asked, "What's the problem, Colonel?" He said, "Ms. Machete is pregnant and she was not pregnant when she came in to the jail." I said, "Really?" He said, "That's right." I said, "That means we've got to start watching towards the east." He looked at me like I was crazy and said, "What does that mean?" I said, "That means there will be three wise men riding camels coming this way. Did she tell you she had had a complete hysterectomy?" He said, "No." I said, "Read the Dade County medical records." She knew there was no way she could get out of it when they took her to the hospital, no way, but she could interrupt court for a while.

There were a lot of coincidences in this case. I knew the couple who were killed personally. The apartment they lived in belonged to me. I rented it to them. Another coincidence: Quinton Cotton, the Pan American pilot who had rented a private plane to show his girlfriend a house that his brother was building was a good friend of mine; it was Quinton who discovered the bodies.

After spending about four years in prison, Tony Machete was electrocuted at Jackson, Georgia, where the electric chair was moved. John Maree got a life sentence in prison, having received a smaller sentence for turning state's evidence. Rebecca, who has given so much trouble to everyone in the prison system, is transferred every six or eight months to a different women's prison; she's now in her 30th year.

Looking back over the case, several things came to mind: Rebecca had tried unsuccessfully to kill her husband, Ronald, even before she got a divorce. He was transferred with Southern National Gas and I knew who he was working for and knew the man's wife. The supervisor of Southern Natural Gas appeared to know more about this case than anybody. Within an hour of being notified, he had joined us at the mortuary.

Before the homicide and during the planning of it Rebecca had gone to Miami. She loved money, and she had always heard how the rich men were in Miami, looking for wives. So she went to Miami, and hung around the bar of the Aztec Motel. Tony and John Maree also had heard about women looking for husbands, so they were hanging around. Rebecca told them how much money she had, and they told her how much money they had. She ended up marrying Tony Machete; of course, neither one of them had any money. She always put on airs, acting like a wealthy Southern belle. She wasn't beautiful but she was pretty in her own way.

I took Pearl to Miami when I went to bring Rebecca back to Georgia because I did not go anywhere near that woman without another woman present. I always used Ms. Morris, the matron, when I interviewed her in jail. She was trouble all the way around and I always wanted a female witness to be in my presence with her.

Ronald Akins, the man who was murdered, was older than his

wife. Juanita was not a petite person. She was a big, plain girl but she was a lady. She taught school in Red Bud, Georgia, in the school system. Ronald's brother was school principal and he knew about this girl, now approaching her 30s. Ronald was probably over 40. The brother introduced Ronald and Juanita and they hit it off real well. They married and rented a little apartment from me in the complex my family owns.

Becky had planned another way to murder Ronald and Juanita. She had been working for a doctor and had been trained as a registered nurse. But because she was guilty of plagiarism at Macon College they would not give her a degree. She claimed credit for things she didn't do. While working for the doctor, Becky began to put together drugs like Percodin and Demerol. She then taught Tony how to inject the drugs. When they came here, the first move was to try to kill him and make it look like an accident or a homicide, and not intentional. She thought it would look like drug use, that he had married this young girl and introduced her to dope. They got ropes, needles, and the dope. The plan was to go to the house at 5:00 in the morning and knock on the door. When the door opened, they were going to rush the door and get inside. Then John and Tony would tie them up and inject both of them with lethal doses of drugs so they would die from an overdose. They would wipe the syringe clean then place it in the palm of Ronald's hand so his palm prints would be on it. Then they would very carefully lay it on the table and take the ropes off of them. Ronald and Juanita would be in the bed. The needle would be on his side. Rebecca had already planted false information in a psychiatrist's files that Ronald was on dope. The background was laid; he was taking dope again, he introduced his bride to dope, he gave each one of them a lethal dose, an overdose, and it killed them.

When they got to the house to carry out this plan the paper boy saw both of them so they had to stop. It was another coincidence in this case. If the paper boy had not been there they might have pulled it off. There were many 'ifs' in this case. Ronald and Juanita had only been married about 20 days when they were murdered. I went to their mailbox after this and inside was an envelope containing their wedding pictures—pictures they never saw.

Ray Wilkes, 1953

Ray Wilkes, 1953

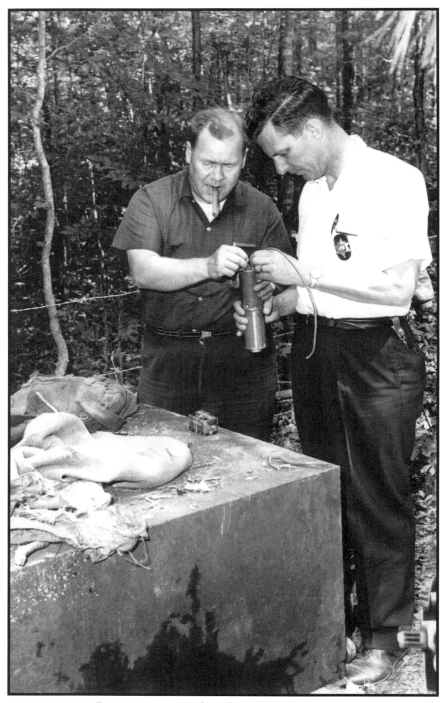

Training session in handling TNT to blow stills.

Arson, used by one who poured five gallons in vehicle.
When he struck a match, it blew. When asked why he used so much gas,
he said he wanted a total loss.

Results of drinking and driving.

A school teacher called me and told me this child couldn't speak or hear. It was winter and I had the pleasure of buying her a new coat.

Terry Singleton, head of the Drug Unit, and me burning seized drugs.

I played the part of a sheriff in "Wise Blood."

Graduation from the University of Southern California
National Sheriff's Institute

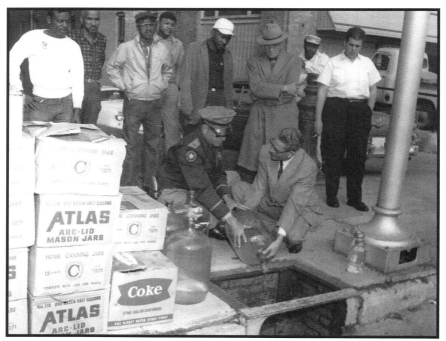

Moonshine whiskey was quite common in the fifties. We made a 100 cases each year for "Violation of the Alcohol & Control Act."

More moonshine going down the sewer drain.

Junior Deputies Annual Picnic Program. I started the Junior Deputy Program in 1962 and it is still running today.

President Carter, me, my son and Phil Walden with him.

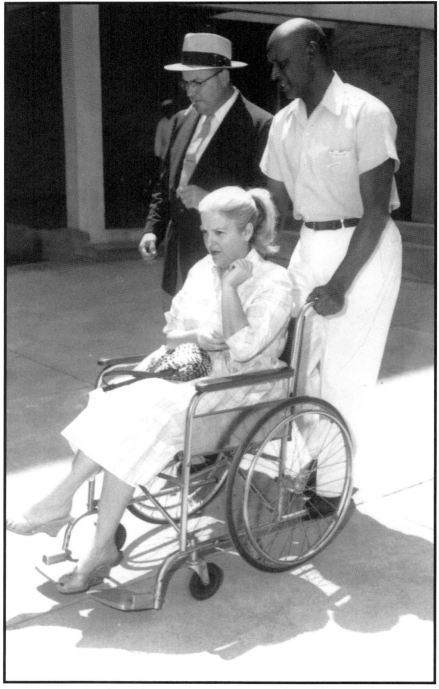

Angett Lyles claimed she was having trouble with her legs –
nothing was diagnosed by medical people.

"Liquor" still

Fruits of their labor

Lawsuit that led to the building a new jail and Law Enforcement Center.

EJ Sherill, Director John Huston and me on the set. The prop man sat a whiskey bottle out as a joke.

Movie "Mr. Griffin and Me". I had a small part in it.
Director Patrick O'Neal and me talking on the scene.

Law Enforcement Center and jail. Inmates are housed here.

Being sworn in as interim sheriff by Judge Kay Stanley, 1976.

Governor Busbee, Pearl and our grandson, Dan, after being sworn in as a member of the Board of Corrections.

When I assumed office we had a total of about forty personnel.
Today it is near 300.

Christmas at the Law Encforcement Center had the biggest tree in Macon.

Buddy

The family of Ray & Pearl: children, in-laws, grandchildren,
& great-grandaughter.

Two heros from World War II, General Robert L. Scott and Col. Earnest Genone
(both retired). General Scott wrote "God is My Co-Pilot" and Earest flew forty-
eight missions over Germany.

LEC Building, named after me December 20, 2005.

Family, 2008

Governor Miller in Senate Chambers with members of
the Board of Corrections.

Picture made for file photo, May 2008.

CHAPTER 67

One night as I was driving on the Warner Robins highway I noticed a car pulled off the side of the road with the engine running and the lights on. Upon further investigation I noticed a drunk was in the car slumped over the wheel. I turned the lights off and took the man out the car and handcuffed him. I went back to the patrol car to call for a wrecker to tow his car.

As I was waiting for the tow truck to arrive I looked into the car with a flashlight. Much to my amazement I saw a pair of shoes belonging to a child. I looked further and found school books, a baby bottle, and several other items belonging to children. I looked at the car and I thought, this is nothing but a poverty guy. He's got a hard life and he's a drunk. He's got kids and probably a wife. I knew I could only give him a fine. If I arrested him and put him in jail his family wasn't going to have anything.

I wanted to know what had happened to cause him to be out on the road slumped over the wheel of his car, drunk. I locked his car and took the keys. He eventually came around and was able to tell me where he lived. He was humble as a dog. I drove to his house, leaving my car parked down the street so it would be out of sight. An officer sat with the man in the car while I went to the house. I knocked on the door and when his wife came to the door I said, "Ms. Johnson, let me speak to Mr. Johnson, please." She said, "He's not here." I asked, "Are you expecting him in soon?" She very meekly said, "To tell you the truth, I don't know." Little kids were hanging all over her. She continued, "He's drinking."

I began to question her, trying to get as much information from her as I could without being accusatory. "He must have knocked you around some before he left here."

"Oh, no!" she said. "No. He never hurts anybody. But he's so ashamed of himself when he's drinking. He won't drink around us. He'll leave and go somewhere else and drink."

The house was just a poor house. It was ramshackled and full of children. I continued asking, "But when he comes back he wants to be ugly about it and hurt you?" She replied, "No. He comes back with his head between his knees. He's deeply sorry and I make him go in there and go to bed and that's the end of it."

I really couldn't believe it. In most cases when a man drinks he usually ends up hitting women and children. I asked, "Are you sure?" She assured me she was fine and the children were fine. He was one of the few men who were sorry for their drinking and would cry. I finally said, "Okay. I've got him out here in the car. I'm going to give you his keys and I'm going to turn him over to you if you'll keep him out of the streets."

She was so grateful. She said, "Okay. Thank you. We really can't afford to pay any fines. You won't have any trouble. I promise."

He wasn't on the road when I found him. I could have made a DUI case out of it but he had enough sense to stop driving and get off the road. In my mind, taking him back to his wife was the best way to handle that situation. Sometimes you have to give people some slack, so that is precisely what I did. She took him inside and I never heard from them again.

CHAPTER 68

All sorts of people end up in jail. I'm sure that those doing surveys of the prison population are shocked at the backgrounds of some of them. People end up homeless and prisoners who at one time may have been rich or famous or just "regular" people like the rest of us.

I remember a time I had a fellow named Roland who was a regular at the jail. He made the best biscuits of anybody who ever walked in the jail. He would come in there drunk, not having shaved in a week. They would lock him up without even looking at him. The officer would make sure he got fed and they would wait on him for about three days. After that time one of the trustees would come to the officer and say, "Roland is straight and he's ready to get going if you'll let him." The officer would tell the trustee, "Okay. Get him to the showers and get him cleaned up and get him some clothes."

Roland would be given some clothes that fit. He had a white coat, white shirt, and a pair of white pants. He would shave and someone would cut his hair. When he left there he looked like he had come out of a band box. He would go to the kitchen about 3:00 a.m. and he'd start working on the biscuits. In the jail kitchen we had industrial size mixers to turn the flour and mix it with the milk and other ingredients. He knew exactly how much to put in. By 6:00 a.m. they were serving those biscuits. They would come out of the oven so nice and brown. Boy, they were good. Everybody loved Roland's biscuits.

One morning as I looked out the window I noticed Roland walking down the street. It was one of those cold winter mornings. I hurriedly went to my car and overtook him. He didn't even have a coat on. He had been in jail for about four or five months and had just recently been released. I put him in the car and I asked him, "Roland, where are you going?"

"I've got to report to my probation officer," he said. I informed him very quickly, "Roland, I'm going to take you down there. Before you leave the probation officer, ask to use his telephone. You call me. I'm going to come pick you up and get you a nice lodging somewhere to stay. Don't go back to drinking."

Usually the regular drinkers will pick up tips working some odd jobs and start drinking again. He said, "Yes, sir." Well, I didn't hear from him again until a few months later when he was back at the jail, locked up. That cycle went on for years and years. When he was sober he would do odd jobs. He could paint really well but he couldn't stay off the whiskey long enough to hold down a regular position.

One morning after he had been in the jail for a good while Major Mitchum called me and said, "Sheriff, we'd like to come talk to you about Roland." I told them to come on up and within a few minutes Major Mitchum and Roland were sitting in my office. "Roland has a request he wants to ask of you. I'll let him tell you about it."

"Sheriff," Roland began, "My wife and I separated 25 years ago. We never got a divorce. We just always stayed away. She couldn't put up with me drinking but now she's in the hospital. She has terminal cancer and there's no place for her to go. She has no relatives and no one to take care of her. What I want you to do is let me leave the jail at 7 in the morning. I'll have the breakfast finished. I'll leave at 7 and go to the hospital and stay with her. I'll be back here at seven at night and I'll be ready to make bread at three the next morning."

It was a very noble thing he was trying to do. As unusual as the request was, I was willing to let him try it. I said, "Roland, I'm going to give you a chance but if you embarrass me by bringing contraband in here or anything else I'm going to have my neck on the line." Roland assured me, "Sheriff, you won't have any trouble."

Well, he went there every day for a month, like he said; then she died. I don't know who buried her but he went to the funeral. He got out of jail but instead of going back to drinking he went into a 28-day program by the state. With the help of the program he was able to quit his alcohol addiction. He attended those classes every day. The program helped him get a place to stay on Cherry Street in a rooming house. Then they helped him get a little job. Roland continued to go to the classes even after he had officially finished them for himself. He became committed to telling other drunks his own experiences and helping them become sober also. That's the way it is, one drunk tries to get the other one off. A person who was once a drunk has more influence over other drunks than anyone else because he has walked in their shoes.

He became a counselor at the program. He was making about $1000 a month as a counselor. He was coming along but that wasn't a whole lot of money.

We built a wing onto the prison building and I knew we were going to have to expand the kitchen staff. The chef in the kitchen came to me and I said, "We're going to have to expand the kitchen staff. Do you have anybody in mind?" He said, "Yes, sir. I'll tell you who I'd like to have. I'd like to have Roland Bloodworth here." I said, "Do you realize how many times Roland Bloodworth has been arrested? The list is longer than my arm. He's been arrested 100 times or more. I've never knowingly hired anyone with a criminal record." My chef said, "Sheriff, Roland wants a job and he's not drinking." I sat there and thought about it.

A few days later Roland came in to see me. He made a plea for the job. He said, "Sheriff, I can do it. You won't have no trouble out of me. I haven't had a drink in so long." I said, "Roland, I'm going to take a chance but my neck will be out to my shoelaces if somebody gets hurt. They're going to put me on the cross and say he had access to all the records, he knew the man personally, and he still hired him. You don't have any arresting powers but you're a part of the staff." He said, "You won't have no trouble, Sheriff." So I put him to work.

When I retired Roland, he kept calling me. He was able to get an early out for retirement and left with a pension. He had worked at the prison kitchen for 17 years and was given three years so he had earned the pension. He even got married. Recently he died. I was glad to have a part in his life. It meant a lot to me that he would always call me and thank me for helping him. He made the best biscuits I ever put in my mouth.

CHAPTER 69

There is a little devilment in all of us and I am no exception. I went out as a fingerprint man in forensics. I found a good footprint at a place of a burglary and there was enough of it to pour a plaster of Paris cast. You have to pour them when the consistency is about like melted ice cream; then you have to wait for it to harden before picking it up.

I poured my cast and while I was waiting I began to fiddle around the area. There was a lot of heavy growth in the location. I looked around and saw a lizard. He was a rather large lizard, about eight inches or so, lying in the sun. I caught the little guy and then thought, what am I going to do with this lizard. I put him in a sack and finished the cast I was making. Instead of going back to the office that particular day I headed back to my house.

I had some pastel colors I used in art work. The pastels are water colors but they're brilliant colors. I got a paint brush out and opened one of my containers of red paint. I painted the lizard's head red like the marking of a scorpion, which will kill you.

I took the lizard to the office, where John Richardson was sitting at a desk. I had played many tricks on him throughout the years. I went over to the desk where John was and I drew him a diagram. The lizard was sitting on my shoulder on my white shirt. I wanted John to look up so I said, "They entered the house here but they had made the preparations here." John looked up and when he did, the lizard was about two inches from his nose. He yelled at the top of his lungs and when he did the lizard jumped from my shoulder over to him. John saw that red head and he shrank back. He was afraid to touch him because he thought the lizard would kill him—so he sat right there. I picked the lizard up and everybody had a good laugh.

I took the lizard outside and turned him loose on a large holly bush and I just forgot all about him. About a month later I went into the courthouse and the whole place was in chaos. People were running around everywhere. There was an employee of the county who thought she was an old aristocrat. She was just a department head but she thought she was the most important person there. Checks were written by the county commissioners. They made the checks out but she put the stamps on them. She took her job very seriously and always acted as if she were the one actually approving and writing checks. If you needed your check in a hurry you could just about eat a ten penny nail as easy as you could get her to give you your check early. She wouldn't let one of the maids in her office because she thought the maid wore her girdle too tight. In other words, she was just a real pain in the neck.

On this particular day that the courthouse was in such an upheaval she had to go into the restroom. The holly bush where I had put my lizard was just outside the window of the women's restroom. The old lady sat down on the commode, looked toward the window, and found herself about eye level with that lizard. She screamed and came running out of the restroom.

She yelled so loud it made everybody started running. They were trying to get her off the floor to get her clothes back up and they couldn't find the lizard. She was telling them it was a scorpion with a red head.   When I heard all that I turned around and went right back out of the building. I stayed out of everybody's way for a while.   I would have been in trouble if she had found out it was me. I don't know why I did that, really. He looked too inviting but I didn't have the slightest idea he would end up there.

CHAPTER 70

Every time I see a certain company I say, thank you. One night we got a call from Cross Keys. There was a good size grocery store located there. Someone had broken the glass on the front of the store and entered the building. I was in the back-up car. When we arrived at the scene there were two other cars already there. The hole in the glass was big enough for a man to step through.

I was told to cover the back entrance in the event the man inside tried to go out the door located in the rear. As I was running to the back with a pistol in my hand I turned the corner and met a man with a shotgun. He scared the heck out of me. I saw the shotgun and then I saw he was barefooted. He lived in the house behind the store. He told me he would cover the back. He was really a very lucky man. I almost shot him because I didn't know anyone was back there.

I returned to the front of the building to find one of the officers had stepped inside the building. That was a totally foolish thing to do. Because he was inside I was compelled to go in; I couldn't let him be in there by himself. I had been taught at the FBI Academy you hold your flashlight in your left hand, arm extended out. In tests that had been done, they found that most people firing a gun shoot to the right. If they are acting on impulse or out of fear and not really aiming, they will shoot further away from you than if the light were in your right hand. I was following all the training. I was holding my gun and a flashlight. It was dead silent in there.

I was taking one aisle at a time. The officer said, "Careful Ray. Last time I saw him he was right there near the meat market." Well, the meat market in the old days had a butcher block. Every night the knives were all stuck into butcher block. Some of those knives were very long. When I thought of all the knives that were sure to be in that place I thought, great Scott, this man has a loaded artillery.

I started to ease down an aisle and it was clean. No one was there. I went down the next aisle still being very careful, holding my light out. All of a sudden something fell behind me and made a big noise. I whirled around and when I did I saw the intruder on the floor sliding. He didn't have a shirt. The first thing I saw were his hands. They were empty so I didn't shoot him.

When we put the pieces together this is what we found: When Nabisco sold cookies, they sold them to the individual store owner. The Nabisco delivery man brought them to the store and stacked the boxes of cookies in the aisle, then the salesman would come back and build the display. This particular deliveryman always stacked his boxes in such a way that they were top-heavy. Sure enough, this night they were just that. The intruder was crawling to attack me from behind when all of a sudden the stack of cookies fell. I came so close to killing him the minute I turned around. I didn't though. I held the gun off him for that split second and was able to see he wasn't armed. He was an escapee from Virginia doing 14 years up there.

CHAPTER 71

In the '60s Governor Maddox appointed me to an organized crime prevention council. There were only five people on the council. I was picked from the law enforcement people in Georgia. They put me on before I consented to go. My picture appeared in the paper with a notation I had been appointed by the Governor. I attended some meetings and then I met a fellow in the legislature in charge of organized crime who had formed a committee. They were preparing a bill that would make professional gambling illegal in Georgia. When the Braves, the Hawks, and the Falcons came to the state, professional gambling would follow. This committee wanted to prevent the Mafia coming in here and taking it over.

We were asked to go to New York and talk to the most knowledgeable people about Mafia operations. Our goal was to learn as much as we could about passing laws that would prevent the Mafia's coming into our state. They wanted me to go to New York, along with one of the legislators and the Assistant District Attorney of Fulton County. So we went, but I didn't know anything about who we were meeting until we arrived.

When the plane landed we got our luggage and a man by the name of William G. Gallenero was waiting for us. Bill Gallenero was an unusual fellow. When we got to his car, the District Attorney from Fulton County asked, "Bill, have you had any more problems with the hit?" Gallenero replied, "Well, it has been a problem. It's caused a marital problem." Then the District Attorney started to tell us the story.

Bill Gallenero was working for Senator Scoop Jackson in a Senate committee investigating organized crime. He took the committee over from Estes Kefauver. Bill Gallenero was involved as a Mafia investigator because of his background with New York Police, the U.S. Marshall Service, and other investigative agencies he had been involved in. Bill was in Albany, New York, to catch a plane. He hadn't read a paper in three or four days so he picked up one to read on the plane. When he opened it he saw his own picture on the front page.

There was a commission in New York called the Knapp Commission. The Knapp Commission was one of the most prestigious commissions in New York. They had formed a committee with power to hire special investigators on organized crime. This was done to circumvent any dishonesty on the New York Police Department and any other existing agency. They were running with a lot of Federal agents and they were using wire taps excessively. One of the wire taps they put on was being played before the Knapp Commission. The Knapp Commission was being covered by the newspaper in New York. There was a known Mafia leader in New York—a godfather—talking to a vice president of Schenley's Whiskey. This vice president had been in the Schenley organization since the end of bootlegging. They went legitimate but the structure of Schenley's at that time was still covered with Mafia people. Anyway, this vice president was talking with a godfather of one of the Mafia families in New York and Bill's name came up. He said, "Bill Gallenero is giving us a lot of trouble." Bill Gallenero had killed three people so Mafia operations were trying to kill him. All of them were armed.

They had a big organization in New York with a guy named Joe Columbo. This guy had organized the Italian Anti-Defamation League and they were trying to stop "The Godfather" from being published and made into a movie. In the conversation the godfather told the vice president of the trouble they were having. It was rumored that the man at Schenley's said 'go ahead and put a quarter of a million hit on Bill Gallenero.' Well, the hit was still alive and active.

Now here I am sitting in this car with Bill Gallenero and they are talking about this like you would talk about the weather on a nice sunny day. We're driving in New York City. He had lived in his neighborhood a long time and knew a lot of his neighbors. They had gotten a petition together to get him to move away from their neighborhood.

Scoop Jackson went to the president and ordered the U.S. Marshall to send Bill's family to Puerto Rico under 24-hour guard. When his kids went to school they had to have a guard with them. Bill was left in New York and the marriage was probably already thin. His wife divorced him but he continued to work mob operations.

So this was how I met Bill Gallenero. He was assigned to us for ten days. He wanted to show us the shady side of New York. We started out one night and went from one joint to another. At one building we started down some steps where, under a building, a guy had built a bar. It was like a pub. There was a lot of granite down there so he just took all the granite and had it embedded in the walls to make granite walls. There was a large television and a bar with a lot of people.

Every so often they would holler, "Police, police, police." I finally asked, "Why do they keep saying that?" He said, "The side they're pulling for has a black running back and every time he gets the ball they holler 'police' to get him to run faster." That was New York.

We went to all kinds of places during our time there. We went to the docks, to the waterfront which was controlled by the Mafia, and we went to the district attorney's office. There was one assistant district attorney still there who had been in office during the Thomas Dewey racket busting days, the only one left from that group. I was able to meet one of the Untouchables. I met the one they called "Wallpaper," so named because when he searched a building he took everything but the wallpaper. Every scrap of fragment, everything was taken but the wallpaper. We even went into a bar about midnight one night. They would all have a drink. I wasn't drinking. Bill Gallenero said to me, "Do you recognize the clock?" I said, "No, sir. I don't." He continued, "Step back and look at the bar. Do you recognize it?" I still did not recognize anything. He said, "Did you see the movie 'The Lost Weekend' with Ray Milland?" I told him I had. He said, "The scene where he traded his typewriter for a bottle was filmed in this bar. This is one of the most popular bars in New York. When Frank Sinatra is in town, the last place he comes for a drink before he turns in for the night is here and he's in town tonight. If he comes here I guarantee and bet you when he walks in and sees me he will immediately turn around and leave." I was curious. "Why?" I said. Bill continued, "Because he knows I know what he knows." Frank did not show up while we were there.

On one occasion we had been going full steam all day, so he took us to dinner, to a place with red and white checked tablecloths. I don't typically eat supper at 10 o'clock at night. I usually eat supper early. The waiters had aprons that went under their arms and tied in the back and over that they wore a black coat and a bow tie with black pants. It was exactly like the movie, "The Godfather." Bill informed us, "This place is one of the most popular hangouts of the Mafia because it has the best Italian food in New York."

Well, I didn't know what to order so he ordered those little Italian sausages for me. I had those, along with a bunch of other stuff. After dinner we started walking and I said, "Isn't that Madison Square Garden there?" They said, "Yeah."

"Isn't our hotel across the street?" Bill said it was. I said, "I'll see you later. I'm going to bed." I wasn't interested in any more sight seeing. It was late and I was full of Italian food and tired. I went up to my hotel room and got in bed. About 2 a.m. I woke up with my stomach and chest on fire. The sausage was talking to me. Man, I was burning. I got up but I didn't have any Maalox, or Tums, or Rolaids. I hit the street in the middle of the night. I stopped by some restaurants but no one sold anything but food. I saw bums on the street. I saw the whole shooting match.

The Penn Central Rail Lines were under Madison Square Garden. I found a little snack bar there. The only thing I could find was a pint of milk, which I bought and drank it down. It helped soothe that sausage down.

When I went down to the rail lines there were bums lying all over the floor of the station. I had to step over them to get in there. Nobody laid a paw on me. I wasn't armed. Then I went back to the hotel and went to sleep.

We stayed in New York ten days, and had many unusual experiences. I had lunch next to the Al Smith Dining Room in the Empire State Building. While we were there we had a bomb scare in the Pennsylvania Rail Station and I was able to go with them on the bomb scare. There must have been 10,000 lockers at the Pennsylvania station. I had never seen a man come in and change his clothes in public. But here I watched a man come down to his underwear; then he pulled some different cloths from the locker to put on. He was changing clothes. He was living out of the locker.

The agent in charge was looking for anything suspicious. I said, "To conduct a search here would do 100 times more damage than if a pipe bomb blew one of these lockers up." He picked up his telephone and said, "Say what you just said again." He called his boss and told him what I said. I said, "If a pipe bomb goes off it isn't going to cause the damage this other one is going to cause." We saw some odd sights there.

We went all over New York and I saw some things that struck me as funny. I noticed a parking place in the garment district across from Macy's. There was a truck there about the size of a UPS truck wanting that parking place but he couldn't get it. In front of the space was a vehicle that took up a little more room than he should have. This guy with the truck started hammering on the bumper of the man's car. He must have done about $1000 worth of damage. It crushed the trunk and the fenders in. He pushed that car into the front space and parked his truck behind it and went into one of the buildings. In Macon, Georgia, they would be hunting him on a hit and run and everything else.

I was exposed to a lot of things there. We picked up a lot of data, bringing it back and enacting a lot of it into law. We really never had anything but the Southern Mafia, which included big car theft rings. We were able to handle most of it. Bill Gallenero and I stayed friends for a long time. While still in office, Scoop Jackson died suddenly in 1971 of an aortic aneurysm. Sam Nunn took over Scoop Jackson's committee. Bill Gallenero was working for Sam Nunn and almost anything I needed I could call Bill Gallenero and get.

When I was in Washington I would always go in to see Bill and we would go out to eat together. He came to the University of Georgia to speak and I met him over there. When he left the University of Georgia he went to Texas. He was working on a Mafia case that involved the purchase of a bank in New York and selling bank money orders. They put them in all the convenience stores. Stores would send the money orders to the bank and the bank would redeem them for a fee. The Mafia waited until it got big and bankrupted the bank so they didn't pay any of the convenience stores. It held all the money up and the Mafia had millions of dollars.

Bill was working the case for the Senate. One night he went into his hotel room but unbeknownst to him someone had gone in there before him and in the dark they beat him almost to death. They thought he was dead when they left. Soon after that, I lost contact with Bill. He survived the beating and next went to Las Vegas, a place where the Mafia operated with impunity. They poured money into casinos in Las Vegas and began to look respectable. Bill was pulling charters from back in the '40s to see who was on them and who succeeded them. Then he went to Texas. He was looking into an operation of a bank the Mafia overtook. They eventually shut it down and went bankrupt.

CHAPTER 72

Macon has had a few famous people. We've had General Scott, Little Richard, and Otis Redding. Little Richard washed dishes at the bus station. Otis Redding carried shingles for a roofer named Willie Andrews. He was trying to develop his music career and get into the music industry. He would frequent Bubba Greenway's station and play blackjack on the pinball machine. His opponents could see his hand every day. The reflection of his cards in the glass helped them know what he was playing every time he laid a card down. Then they would pitch pennies.

J. Calvin Beck and Ernest Sinclair who appeared on 60 Minutes were both from Macon. Calvin Beck went to Virgil Powers School and Ernest Sinclair lived on Hemlock Street. It was Orange Street once you got to the top of the hill. Both of them were smart and both of them were crooked. They always had a scheme going. Calvin Beck, along with some others, had a scheme on Charlie boards. They would sell the Charlie boards and the man who owned the store, and who bought them, didn't know they knew where the winning tickets were. Later a man would come along and punch the lucky number.

One night I was watching "60 Minutes" on CBS and Maconites Calvin Beck and Ernest Sinclair were the subject of two episodes of the show. Calvin was posing as Colonel somebody who could help those trying to develop a talent. Someone brought a boy up and I don't know if he had talent or not but Calvin didn't care. He told the man the boy had talent and he could develop him but it was going to take some money. The man put about $20,000 or more into developing his son's talent.

I don't know whether Calvin made the record but it was either a clandestine studio or one of these phone booths where you make a record. Calvin made a record for him. " 60 Minutes" interviewed Calvin but he denied the story. He said some people came to him who had talent and he could help them and some didn't have talent but you couldn't do it with no money. You had to have some money. I don't think anyone was turned away except the people with no money.

While watching that same "60 Minutes" I saw a segment about Ernest Sinclair on the west coast. He was printing college diplomas. They said, "You charged that man $2000 for a fictitious diploma." He said, "No. No. Wait a minute. You got this all wrong. I've helped a lot of people. That man came to me with tears in his eyes. He had been working at Boeing for 12 years or so and then all of a sudden they wanted to see his diploma from the college because he was an engineer. They're updating their files. The man didn't know what to do and he came to me and I asked him what school he wanted to have gone to. He said Georgia Tech." Ernest got him a diploma with all the seals and signatures from Georgia Tech. The man took it in and they made a Xerox copy of it then gave it back. "The company was happy. The man was happy. I was happy." That was his rationalization of counterfeiting.

Ernest came to Macon and rented a place next to Tucker Realty Company. He was putting all kind of telephone lines into the place. He had an 800 number for runaway kids who could call him and he would help them get back to their parents. It was nothing but a scam. He was setting the scheme up so he could get their bus money which was intended to help them get back home. His probation officer and the court told him that if he did it he would be violating his probation.

He went into the pest control business. He stayed in that business for six or seven months. The next thing I knew he sold his corporation to an employee who lived on Robinson Road who didn't have two nickels to rub together. This man told me he had bought the whole company. All he did was buy the debt and it wasn't collectible.

Eventually Ernest just left. He did those two things then took off. (By the way, R.E. Sinclair was Ernest's brother and a fine person.)

════════ CHAPTER 73 ════════

During my career, I had a very unusual criminal case that I felt was noteworthy. We had fellows who were arrested and put in the Bibb County jail. One was named Jimmy Gleason and the other was Pat Huff. They had been in the penitentiary together, and in the work camp Pat Huff had been a dog boy. A dog boy is the man who handles the dogs when there is a hunt for an escapee. He is hated by every prisoner so they don't even sleep with the rest of the inmates. Somewhere in their time together Jimmy Gleason had befriended Pat Huff. Pat Huff would do anything Jimmy told him.

There was a fellow with a small trucking outfit. He was in the Hilton Hotel drinking at the bar one evening and he and Jimmy Gleason got into an argument. Jimmy asked him to step outside. They walked out on the sidewalk on the First Street side and Jimmy turned to Pat and said, "Shoot him." Pat just started shooting the man. When Jimmy told Pat to do something, Pat obeyed. He shot this man three or four times. The man lived through the ordeal and Jimmy and Pat were arrested and put into our jail. They were bad news anywhere they went. I decided I was going to separate them. I called Monroe County Sheriff Cary Bittick and asked if he would keep Jimmy Gleason for me. He said, "Yeah, bring him on." So I sent Jimmy there and I sent Pat Huff to Dublin where Rock Bussell was sheriff.

Jimmy and Pat had some experiences down there. Pat Huff knew the inside workings of the jail. The Grand Jury would come through the jail and Pat Huff would always know how to handle them. He would say, "Sir, may I speak to you please?" The foreman on the Grand Jury said, "Go ahead." Pat would just start in, "Sir, this place is awful. They don't feed you. The place you sleep is bad." And he would go through a list of complaints with the grievance committee telling them everything wrong with the jail.

When they finished the walk-through the sheriff didn't say anything. The committee left and the Sheriff turned to the jailer and said, "Who is that fellow back there?" The jailer said, "That's Pat Huff, the one that Ray sent down here." The sheriff continued, "I'll tell you what to do. Go back there and take off all the clothes he's got on and everything he's got everywhere else and put them in a sack and bring them to my office and I'll tell you when to give them back to him."

I sent Purvis down there to move him to Reidsville and Pat wasn't wearing anything but a blanket. He had been wearing a blanket for a month. He was naked and had been for a month.

Then Jimmy Gleason sued me and they made me bring him back. Jimmy was going to Reidsville but he didn't want to go back there. He knew there was no escaping the place. So Jimmy was looking for a way to get out of the jail. There was a fellow he didn't even know coming down the steps of the security cell to go to an exercise court. This fellow was from Texas and he refused to waive extradition and go back to Texas. So Jimmy, for reasons known only to him, pulled him by the hair and grabbed his neck back and cut his throat. He didn't say a word to him. He just slit his throat. One of the jailers grabbed the carotid arteries and held them until they got the man to the hospital where he stayed for about a month. When they brought him back to jail he couldn't sign the papers fast enough to get back to Texas. We had to transfer Jimmy to Reidsville. Man, he had all of this he could stand.

I sent Captain Purvis to pick Pat up and take him to Reidsville. Purvis handcuffed him and put him in the car; he had on clothes this time. Pat began right away, "You won't believe how that jail was. I've never been in a jail like that. They don't follow the law. It isn't constitutional. I bet I haven't had any clothes on for a month." He was really pouring his heart out to Purvis. When he got through with all his complaints the old jury foreman said, "Where the h--- do you think you're at? The Holiday Inn?"

CHAPTER 74

Another good friend of mine was Clint Schaffer, who was in charge of the Atlanta Police Detective Bureau. He later became Chief of Police there. We would meet on occasion and one of those times Clint told me about a fellow from a case he had worked. The case involved the family who owned a pest control corporation. Many people believe the son of the founder of the company put his father away in a mental institution. The son was actually running the national pest control company. My friend, Clint, said, "Yeah, we worked a case where an informant came to us and said the owner's son's driver, his body guard, and his right hand man around the house, and security for everywhere he went was looking for someone to kill the husband of the secretary who worked for the son. He had fallen in love with her and he wanted to have her husband killed so he could marry her."

Clint went on to explain it would be a lot of problems if it went to court. The husband might even sue her for alimony or whatever and he didn't want to get into that. Clint thought about a sting operation: "I wonder who I could get to be a professional hit man?" Eventually he remembered this man who was no longer in an office. It was someone he knew who had been in an appointed position. Clint called him and laid out the whole story and plan. The man said he wanted to do it. The fellow had a lot of money but he wanted to stay in law enforcement and he liked playing the hit man.

So he flew from Mississippi to Atlanta to begin his exploits of being a hit man. He talked to the guy's right hand man on the telephone. He told him he would be at the Hilton Hotel at the airport. At the appointed time the body guard went to the hotel in lieu of his boss. He went to the hotel and as he started to knock on the door he noticed it was ajar. He heard a voice say, "Come on in." He didn't know a professional hit man and he really didn't know too much about criminals. But he stepped inside and when he did a man grabbed him by the collar and slammed him against the wall. The hit man put a .45 under his chin and flipped the light on and said, "Who's with you?" It scared the bodyguard to death. The hit man searched him. The bodyguard didn't have a gun on.

He was told, "Sit down and we'll talk." They sat down and arranged a meeting with the pest control CEO. Clint's friend said, "I don't go through nobody." The CEO agreed to see him based on the fact his right-hand man had told him this man was really sharp and mean too. The CEO met with him but the hit man was wired. Clint had put a wire on him so he was transmitting everything that was being said to the police department. Of course, he wasn't a real hit man. He was the former head of the Mississippi Investigation Division.

The CEO and the hit man went through all the details and finally he said, "Okay. Tell me what you want as evidence." They had agreed on $50,000. The CEO thought and finally he said, "I want a picture of him dead and I want his ring where he graduated from college." The hit man, "All right. Consider it done."

He was supposed to begin now. They gave him a layout of where this fellow worked and his schedule and all the other information a hit man might need. At that point they brought this husband into the picture and told him his wife was trying to have him killed. They then went to the Fox Theatre in downtown Atlanta. The man who was the makeup artist there took this husband and poured real blood plasma over him. The makeup artist had created a bullet hole in his chest with blood all over him. The man gave them his college ring and they put blood on it also. They then placed him in the trunk of a car in an awkward position, making him appear dead, and took some Polaroid pictures of him. The Fox Theatre did the whole process, beginning with the blood and ending with the pictures being taken in the trunk.

The so-called hit man took all the evidence back to the CEO and when he looked at it he handed him the $50,000; then they were able to arrest him. Following the arrest, he was brought to trial in Atlanta.

══════ CHAPTER 75 ══════

I got a call from Atlanta from the supervising agent of the Georgia Bureau of Investigation saying they needed my help. He told me they had some drugs which needed to be destroyed and they had permission from the Georgia Power Arkwright branch to destroy them in their furnace. He proceeded to tell me the details, "We've got a convoy coming to Macon with agents in the front of it and agents in the back of it. There will be an enclosed truck and a helicopter. We're bringing a tremendous amount of drugs needing to be destroyed." They had been in the old vault of the C&S Bank but the cases had been disposed of. One of them was a big drop in northwest Georgia where they dropped kilos of heroin and cocaine. He asked, "Can you meet us and give us an escort out there?" I said, "Yeah. I'll meet you."

I made a preliminary search out there to look over the premises and then I talked to the fireman in charge of the big boiler. He made sure it was ready to do the job. We pulled it off without any problems at all. There were GBI agents positioned on the ground with guns and automatic weapons. Then they started bringing the drugs in.

The drugs were packaged in kilos, which is 2.2 pounds, only there were kilos in five pack units. They had loads of marijuana. We started throwing the packs into the furnace until the fireman running the furnace said, "Slow down, boys. That furnace is breathing." The metal on the side was getting so hot it was expanding. We destroyed $500,000,000 street value of narcotics. A half billion dollars of marijuana, cocaine, and hash. I had never seen drugs in that quantity before.

Drugs are pretty bad everywhere. The people using it continue using until they die, or they go down. Crack cocaine is bad and now they're making other drugs. I have seen evidence of someone putting a propane gas tank in the back of a van with a burner and they start cooking that stuff in an enclosed van while the van is moving. To serve a search warrant is almost impossible because the van is moving the whole time they're making this crystal meth. Generally, cocaine and crack cocaine operations are done out of a house.

Crystal meth is made from cold remedy medicines. It's from over-the-counter products. If a person goes into a store wanting to buy all the cold medicine in the store, the store personnel will usually catch on and not sell it to the person or they will notify the police.

I once testified before a Senate drug committee on narcotics. Sam Nunn asked me to speak before them. I guess that's the only time I have been in the Congressional Record. When it was published Senator Nunn sent me a copy of the Congressional Record.

I would give $5000 this afternoon if I could get rid of drugs and bring back moonshine whiskey. The bootleggers and shot houses, they're basically pretty decent folks. When you caught one they generally only wanted one thing, to place a phone call to a bail bondsman. You couldn't hide 40 gallons of whiskey without a trap door or something. With drugs you can hide the kilos by many different methods.

LSD can get into the prison on the back of a stamp. The prisoner takes the stamp off and licks it and he's high. Drug users will do pretty much anything to supply their habit, even sell their kids.

The last speech I made as sheriff was to the Rotary Club. I began to make a list of names of the bootleggers and moonshiners telling them the same thing I have just stated about those guys being pretty decent folks. Afterwards Judge Owens came up to me and said, "As you began to call those names out I began to think of them and you're right. They were pretty decent folks. In fact, I sentenced Prentice Tucker the other day." I said, "Judge, I hope you didn't give Prentice a long sentence." He said, "I didn't. It wasn't bad at all."

CHAPTER 76

We used to have a game here called a bug racket. It died when the lottery was legalized but until that time it was a numbers racket. It was in New York and it was here in Macon, Georgia. A person chose three numbers and if those three numbers were the winners you were paid 500 to one. The hitch was, your chances of hitting those three numbers were 1000 to one. Those were the odds of the game.

People had crazy ways of choosing what three numbers they would play. There were all types of methods out there. Someone might have a dream; if they dreamed of someone dying they played a certain number. With one hit of a dream book everybody in town knew. It was just purely luck but people wanted those dream books.

There was an older man by the name of Will Parks Clay living in the Bellevue area of Macon. He and Prentice Tucker ran the bug racket. He had a big nice automobile, a Packard, I think. Will Parks Clay didn't handle the tickets, only the money. It was extremely hard to catch him because the tickets would go one way and then the money would go the other way. Then some relative they trusted would go through the tickets and see how many hits they had that day. Well, Bellevue had a lot of people who knew Will Parks Clay was in the bug business so they watched him like hawks to see if they could get any money. They never attacked him or hurt him but they were watching him.

There were all kinds of stories about him having his money buried so there was always someone watching his yard. They were watching one night and I was told by an informant that Will Parks Clay came out of the house and dug a hole. Of course it was dark outside and when he finished the hole he went back into the house. When Will Parks Clay went back in the house those watching went over the fence directly to the place he had been. They saw where the ground had been disturbed so they quickly began digging. What they found probably haunted them the rest of their life. They found out nothing had happened except Mr. Clay had a bowel movement in the hole and rightly covered it over. It was all over them before they knew what they had gotten into. I'm sure they thought extremely hard before ever digging after Will Parks Clay again.

Then Prentice got caught with the bug. His brother-in-law, Big Boy Sanford, also got caught with the bug. We went out on a cooperative raid with the FBI. One of the agents went to a friend of Big Boy Sanford. I had informed them before the raid I had information these men were hiding money in the freezer. Then in case of a fire the money would be insulated and thus protected from the fire. The FBI was searching the house so they took everything out of the freezer and broke open the packages to check the contents. One of the agents looked and something caught his attention at the kick plate on the bottom of the freezer. He got on his hands and knees to remove the plate and then began to run his hands under the freezer. He pulled out a big stack of money. Big Boy said, "Okay. That's it. You got it." The officer continued his search and said, "Let me look." So he got his flashlight out and got back down there and pulled out another big stack. Big Boy said, "That's all of it. That's all of it. And would you believe all the taxes have been paid on it?" The officer just shook his head saying, "No, sir. I wouldn't."

═══ CHAPTER 77 ═══

Moonshining was once a big industry. The moonshiner was a decent fellow. I've seen a lot of them in my day. You would never believe all the different type of people who wanted moonshine. Black people, white people, they all wanted it. It was not a respecter of persons. One fellow had a half gallon jug of moonshine. He was going to give another man a quart of it so he held a quart fruit jar there and started to pour it. The guy said, "Wait a minute. Don't pour it there. If it gets on my wife's dresser it will eat the varnish off of it." I thought to myself, that's some powerful stuff. He's worried about it taking the varnish off but not what it's going to do to his stomach.

We've seen a lot of moonshine come into the Sheriff's office. When moonshine came in people would always say, "What you got? How good is it?" They would splash it out on the floor of the assembly room in the sheriff's office, just pour some out on the floor. Then they would strike a match and hold it down. If the moonshine was good a blue flame would just jump on top of it. If the match went out they would say the moonshine was block and tackle.

People have said to me, "If you ever get some moonshine slip me some." You couldn't slip it. I hadn't been there but about a month and we got a still. John Richardson, who was an office deputy, said, "Get two gallons of that liquor and follow me." So I picked up two gallons of the moonshine and put it on the backseat of the car. We drove out to the old folks home. Bibb County had taken over the Camp Wheeler Hospital. It had become an old folks home for people who had nowhere to go. They had white folks and black folks there. Dick Dillard was the man running the place. He was a very articulate and professional man. John Richardson told Dick,

"Dick, I brought you three gallons." Dick responded, "Good. I'm out." I watched them put it in a locker and then I asked, "What's he going to do with that whiskey?" John said, "Every night before they go to bed they start pouring out a shot. They put a little sugar in it and a little water and pass it out to the old folks. It makes them sleep like babies all night long." That was one use for moonshine.

Joe Stribling, the chief jailer, kept some moonshine upstairs in the locker, and he had a key. When someone was brought in who was addicted to the whiskey he would use his own method of detox. Joe Stribling was a big, gawky, tall man. He could sit almost three feet from you and slap you. He had the longest arms on a man I've ever seen in my life. He had a deep voice. After pouring a paper cup or a glass full of whiskey he would call the jailer and say, "Take this up there to that man." The jailer would take the whiskey up there and give it to the man to drink. A little later he would take him some more only this time the whiskey would be reduced. When the man started fussing again he would take him more whiskey reduced even further. The man would start going again and he would reduce it some more. He would give him the whiskey in gradual stages until the man was completely off of it. You can't do it that way in this day and time. Now you can't give them whiskey. You have to take them to detox and they get the people off whiskey. Before detox a drug called paraldehyde was used.

A man was talking to me and the jailer was standing behind him. He said, "Ray, they won't give me any paraldehyde. I'm getting in bad shape and they won't give it to me." The jailer just shrugged his shoulders and held up three fingers.

CHAPTER 78

Inside the courthouse, the jail was a special place. On Sundays, church meetings were held up there. Fletcher was the man who opened the outside door to let the visitors up. Fletcher was really meticulous. He had snow white hair and kept a real neat hair cut. He always wore a clean starched shirt and clean pants and shined shoes. He would open the door and let them in. He was a trustee. One day a very aristocratic lady said, "Where is the old gentleman who lets us in? Has he retired?" She thought he was an employee but he was just a trustee at the jail.

Fletcher would be in jail most of the time for getting drunk. Fletcher would come in drunk and mean. You couldn't do anything with him. One time he cussed one of the officers who had a short fuse. The officer turned around and slapped him. The officer should not have slapped him but he did. Being cussed at and called foul names is not pleasant but still the officer should not have slapped him. When the officer slapped him it caused some head injury from the fall to the floor.

Fletcher really was not that kind of fellow when he was in jail. It was the liquor talking. He stayed in the hospital intensive care unit that dealt with brain damage. We didn't know whether he was going to live or not. During that time everyone was pulling for him but no one could see him. He finally got out of the hospital and his sentence was terminated. His case was dismissed without him even being tried.

One of the officers talked to him about his life and the way he was living and his belief in God and Jesus Christ. The officer told him, "I'll take you to church with me." Fletcher would go every Sunday with Officer Raymond Purvis. He joined the church and was baptized. He had never been baptized although he was getting up in age.

Fletcher's partner was Willie Corbett. Willie was also an alcoholic. He would come up to me in the jail and say, "Mr. Wilkes, would you mind pulling my record and seeing how much it weighs?" He had such a dry sense of humor. He didn't ask how many times he had been arrested. He wanted to know how much his record weighed.

Willie and his wife had been separated 30 years. Neither of them ever remarried. Willie also joined the church and then he went back to his wife. They were living together in the Bowden Homes. I went by to see him a couple of times. Willie was eventually diagnosed with cancer. I kept up with him during the time he had cancer, doing whatever I could to help him until the time of his death.

Willie was christened in the Episcopal Church on Walnut Street because he had been attending church there. I talked to some of the guys in the office. I said, "Willie's not a prisoner and he's not a criminal. I'm going to the funeral." There were seven of us who went to the funeral. Besides the undertaker, we were the only men who attended. No one really knew him. His wife was there so we spoke to her, telling her how we felt about Willie. We really meant it.

Willie and his wife had a son. I'm sure Willie was not a good role model. I found out his son was drinking and messing himself up. He was driving a Gray Cab. His son picked up a passenger by the name of Dan Carpenter. A lot of people called him "Dirty Dan Carpenter." Dan had served in the Army and was working in investigation. When he got out of the Army he was writing bad checks and that sort of thing, going in and out of jail. Dan got Denmark Groover to represent him. He didn't have any money but Denny would represent him most of the time. Denny would talk to him about trying to get himself straight.

Willie's son, Billy Corbett, picked up Dan Carpenter in his cab.

He sat in the front seat with Corbett and they started for the Pendleton Homes. Dan Carpenter put his hand in his pocket and pulled out a pistol. He said, "I'm going to do something that takes a lot of guts to do." He got the cab driver's attention real quick with the gun in his hand. Carpenter continued, "I'm going to tell you what I want you to do, now. I want you to take me home, then I want you to sit right in front of the house in the cab. I'm going inside and you're going to hear the gun fire. When you hear the gun fire you can come on in."

The cab driver was almost ready to break out then. They were getting closer and closer to the house and the man was holding the gun to the his temple. Just as they got to Pendleton Homes he pulled the trigger and killed himself. The bullet went into his temple and through his skull. Corbett abandoned the vehicle and took off running. He got somebody out there. He told me the story ten times before I could write anything down. He was shaking from head to toe. Ironically, I never did see him at the jail any more.

CHAPTER 79

I know beyond a shadow of a doubt the Lord uses us in many ways. Sometimes we are able to see how He uses us. Sometimes it is much later that we see how things pan out and know how He worked. I had occasion to see God work in my life many times. One of those times was just a small matter but it has remained a constant reminder in my life of the goodness of God.

Major Walter Mitchum went to a military sale and brought me back a box of candles made for the Marine Corps and used in the South Pacific where they had no electricity. They were giving them away. So I had a case of candles that I put in my locker downstairs at the sheriff's office and really just forgot about them.

Christmas was approaching and every year Father Healey and some nuns from St. Joseph's Catholic Church would come down to the jail and hold a Christmas service. I always accompanied them. I would participate in singing the Christmas carols and bringing the Christmas story. That particular night just as we were about to get started the lights went out and they couldn't get them back on. There was some problem with the outside current. At that time, everything was manually operated. I ran out and caught the elevator and went downstairs to get my candles. I passed them out to everyone in the service and they started lighting one off the other. We had a candlelight service. It was so meaningful. No one was on their bed; everyone was hanging on the bars of the cells. I saw tears on some of the men's eyes as they thought of better days. They used the candles that night and I thought it was one of the most moving services I have ever attended. The faces of those people were illuminated.

I brought the candles home and put them downstairs in storage. One night my son-in-law, Danny Pittman, came by the house and said, "Mr. Wilkes, our church has a doctor, his wife, and their three kids who have volunteered to go back to Africa as missionaries. They've been buying clothes for the next five years. They've got everything packed in wooden boxes. The only thing they haven't gotten is some candles. All the stores have sold out. Do you know where I can get some candles? I want to help them so badly." It was Christmastime again. I said, "Danny, you could have gone to any house on this street and been denied but you came to the right house." I went downstairs and got the candles which were already in a wooden box and they went with the missionaries. Years later the family came back and visited our church. I had an opportunity to speak to the doctor. I said, "Out of curiosity, my son-in-law gave you a box of candles and I was just wondering if you ever had a need of them?" He said, "I can't tell you how many times the electric generator broke down in the hospital and those candles cast the only light by which we had to work. We used them for years."

Twice I felt like the Lord led me to have those candles—when I was sheriff and had the opportunity to provide them for the Christmas service at the Bibb County jail, and when my son-in-law came, looking for candles for the missionaries. I believe the Lord used me to be a carrier, providing those candles in the time of greatest need.

══════════ CHAPTER 80 ══════════

I had an informant who told me the location of a fellow who was on a most wanted list. The person was in a dense swamp near the river. We didn't know exactly where, but we knew the informant would be going back to see him at a later date. I thought about how to take him without any trouble. I went to my friend, Dr. Campbell, a pathologist, and talked to him about the possibility of taking some drinks, along with the food and other things, that the informant would be taking to him. The fellow was living in a swamp, running a big liquor still. When the informant went to take supplies to him, I wanted to have something in those drinks that would cause him to pass out. Then we could just go in there and pick him up.

Dr. Campbell and I sat in my kitchen with his book, trying to decide how we could do this. He read about a drug called Chloral Hydrate. Chloral Hydrate was used in California to spike a drink. They would give it to sailors to spike their drink and then put them on the ship. When they woke up they were on a slow boat to China. Basically, they were knock-out pills, used on unsuspecting sailors to fill a crew on a rotten ship. By the time they woke up, they were already on the boat.

That seemed to be logical solution but the question was how to get it in there. Dr. Campbell read further about gasses. We found that at a certain temperature the gas in a cold drink solidifies. You can open the stopper on a drink and then close it, and it will still fizz when you reopen the drink because the gasses solidify before you re-close it. I didn't know how to open a bottle without leaving a mark on the cap. The pop valve had not been invented yet. I went to a well known company and talked to them about the problem. I didn't go into any details but I told them I wanted to be able to take six drinks and drug five of them. I told them I needed to be able to tell the difference without a string, without a mark, without anything on it. He said, "I think we've got the answer to it."

They had a discontinued stopper still bearing the company's name, so I brought them home. He gave me the stoppers and let me borrow a portable bottling machine. We put the drinks in my freezer. Dr. Campbell loved this sort of thing. After the temperature dropped to a certain degree he had mixed up a drug with Chloral Hydrate. This was a big risk for Dr. Campbell; I'm not sure about the jail sentence for doing this sort of thing.

He had this drug mixed up and we put five identical caps on there, and one that was different; they all said the same thing, it looked like the same drink. My informant got his groceries and other supplies together to take to the swamp. I had an ambulance and Dr. Campbell standing by. He had all his equipment out there in case anything went wrong—he would have the equipment to give him oxygen to bring him around. We got in position and then it was a wait and see. The informant went in with all the goodies. We waited and waited and waited. Several hours went by and I was wondering whether the informant was dead or if he was just out for a while.

The informant had been hot for the deal when we started. Dr. Campbell was sitting on a couch with him in my home when the informant had asked how long it would take after the man drank the soda before he became unconscious? Dr. Campbell said, "About 15 minutes. Maybe 20 but he will go under in 15 or 20 minutes." I think the informant got to thinking about them sitting there face to face for that length of time and the suspect saying to him: "What the h--- did you give me?" All he could think about was getting killed down there in the swamp. I think the informant threw all the drinks away before he got in there.

Well, he finally came out and he said, "He drank it and nothing happened." Dr. Campbell said, "Not so. I put enough in there you could operate with." The informant did confirm that the man was in there, so we got into place to go in to the swamp and get him. It seems they brought a woman down there periodically; we found him in the back seat with her. When we drove up he came out of the car. Now in those days, people cut their hair real short. He hadn't had a hair cut in about six months and his hair was waving in the wind. He looked like a deer flying as he disappeared into the thick of the swamp. We had dogs, and I had an old warden there from some of the public work camps. The warden didn't want to go, so he sent a dog boy—a man who was serving life. The dog boy was wearing a prison uniform but he was also wearing a six-shooter, hanging in a big holster. The warden said, "I ain't sending my boys anywhere to get killed. If they're going to do any shooting we're going to shoot too."

I had the dog boy with me and he had the shooter. As we got deeper into the swamp, water began to cover our shoes. It was summer time so it was hot. Then the water was up to our knees. The hound was pushing on. Then I looked up into the sky but there was no sky to be seen. The trees covered everything. I said, "We've got to get out of here. Do you know how to get out of here?" I was so disoriented, I wasn't sure how we had come into the swamp. He called me Captain and said, "Yes, sir, Captain. I think I can do it." He called to his dog and then said to me, "Joe is give out." Joe was a big hound with big ears. I always admired that boy. He picked up the dog—the animal must have weighed 60 pounds—and started carrying him.

We started out of the swamp, with me in the lead. He said, "Hold on Captain. Hold where you are. There's one about 12 inches high." I said, "What is it?" He said, "There's a moccasin right there coiled." Man, I looked over there and sure enough there was a moccasin ready to strike. We didn't shoot or anything. We took off, and I was looking at the water every step and then he said again, "Hold it, Captain. You've got another one on the left." He could spot those snakes. I thought we never would get out of there. We finally left the swamp behind and he took off to take care of his dog.

Federal Revenue officers were working with us when another

crew found the still. We went in that direction, but came to a creek that could only be crossed on a log. I crossed the log and got across. Another crossed, then another, and another one. Then Dr. Campbell followed, and about half way across, he fell in the creek. His head went out of sight. But we got him out and continued on to the still. The Federal officers were carrying explosives and they immediately blew the still, so we left to return to our vehicles. I crossed the log, then another officer came across, and then Dr. Campbell was coming. I said, "Doc, you'll be all right now. Just feel your way and you'll be fine." Well, this other officer was full of devilment and he said, "Yeah, Doc. You're doing good. The only thing you want to do is watch that place about a foot in front of you. It's real slick." And over Dr. Campbell went again. He went out of sight. I felt like killing that officer. We rescued Dr. Campbell one more time, and the still had been destroyed, but we didn't have Rocky.

We were trying to close the case when Wally Williams said, "We've got to go back out there. There's a bunch of half gallon fruit jars we've got to break up." That was the law. You couldn't leave anything usable at the site of a destroyed still. As they approached the general area where the fugitive had been, they noticed a faint trace of smoke coming from under a bridge. They stopped the car and one man went down the left side of the bridge while another went down on the right. There they found Rocky. A fight broke out among the three of them. Guns came out, and there were some mis-firings, but they finally shot him, wounding him in the shoulder or a leg. They were able to take him down and cuff him.

We took Rocky to the hospital. Rocky had some associates who found out about all the happenings and they came to the hospital to see about him. Some of them were ladies. When they all got to the hospital, another fight started and we had to lock some of them up.

Eventually he was released from the hospital. I called Reidsville and told them he would be coming back there in an ambulance. I had a patrol car following them all the way. Years and years later

I ran into Rocky and we talked. We never were enemies. He was just on one side and I was on the other. In the end, he turned out to be a decent fellow. He did his time in Reidsville, and then he was gainfully employed and never got into any more trouble. I haven't seen him in a long time.

CHAPTER 81

At one time we had an inmate name named Gerald Pancake. Gerald served on a mine sweeper running the engine room, while serving in the Navy during World War II. He worked with the maintenance man. Gerald would often come in drunk. Nobody bothered him for about three days; then he sobered up and went to maintenance. He would stay there the entire time of his sentence. He never was locked down. If the heating system failed in the middle of the night, no one called the maintenance engineer. Gerald was on premises, and nine out of ten times he would get it back to running. He was invaluable.

Gerald's time for release was up. I always took him to be a friend, so one day I called him into my office and I said, "Gerald, I worry about you. You're about to get out and you don't have any money. If you go back to drinking you don't have a place to stay. If you get out and you don't have a place to stay, I don't want to find you dead in a doorway somewhere of exposure. You come back here and I'm going to leave word at the front desk to put you up. You come on in until you get ready to leave and we'll get you out of here in the next couple of days until you get back on your feet." He said, "Thank you." Gerald was very kind and polite. I didn't hear anything from him but three or four days later they came up here and told me Pancake had come in the previous night. He was drunk and wanting to fight so they locked him up. I said, "Well, I'm not even going to see him today."

I left him back there, but the next day I told them to bring him to me. I said, "Gerald, I told you you could come back here but not to come back drunk. I've got a jail full of drunks. I don't need any more drunks. I can't have you coming in here drunk like we have revolving doors. I don't have any other choice but to charge you with drunkenness in a public place and send you to court."

Gerald looked at me and said, "Sheriff, please don't do that. Judge Phillips hates my guts and he'll give me six months. Please don't do that." I responded, "Gerald, you come in and out, in and out, and you don't learn nothing. What would you have me do?" He said, "Let me just come in here and work with Mr. John." Mr. John was the maintenance engineer. I said, "Gerald, if you're in here and you died in jail and you're name isn't on the book with a charge they would wonder why I was holding somebody without a charge and they had been in here for three months and was dead." He said, "I ain't going to die." I said, "Gerald, great Scott. Just get out of here. Just go away."

So he went down and stayed with our maintenance man, John. I had never used a prisoner to do anything for me. I had a house on New Street that a college boy was renting. The pipes had burst, and water was running from underneath the house all the way down the hill. All I could think about was somebody coming over the hill and touching the brakes. The water was freezing on the hill and they wouldn't stop sliding until they got to Oglethorpe Street.

I went down to maintenance and asked, "Have you got a water cut-off?" Gerald answered, "Yes, sir. I've got one right here. I just finished making it. Sheriff, do you want me to go with you?" I said, "No. Wait a minute. Are you a prisoner or are you an invited guest?" He said, "I'm an invited guest." I said, "Come on." So he went with me and went under the house and found the leak. I asked him, "Can you fix it?" He said, "Yes, sir. I can take care of it." He fixed it and I gave him $25. When the time came he left.

Gerald was a fellow that could do anything. He was always pleasant and would never violate any trust you had. As long as he was in some form of supervision he never broke it. But as soon as he got out of prison he fell in the barrel. He came to me one day and said, "Sheriff, if it's okay I'd like to go see my mother. She's in a nursing home out at Goodwill." It was Easter and I said, "Gerald, yes. That's all right." He was in jail serving time but he was a trustee. I said, "Gerald, what time do you want to go? I'll take you out there in the car." He said, "Well, Sheriff, I can walk out there or ride the bus." I said, "No. Come on. I'll take you out there." So I took him, but before leaving the office, I noticed that someone had sent me two or three Easter lilies. I said, "Pick one of those lilies out and carry it to your mother. He picked one, and we proceeded to the nursing home. I said, "I'll come back and get you." He said, "No. I'll just catch the bus. I'll be back before 7:00."

He came back before 7:00. He never broke a trust. He loved his mother. He wanted to go see her. I understood that people have feelings regardless of their circumstances. That was one of the things I always admired about Gerald. Unfortunately, he died an early death. I don't know whether it was sclerosis of the liver or something else, but he died before I knew it. It's unusual how those things work.

CHAPTER 82

I was involved in a situation one time out near old Camp Wheeler where a field had burned. Skeletal remains were found at the burn site so I went out there. I had just come home from the FBI Academy laboratory and I had been taught how to handle evidence of this type. I took bags and ties to the site and began by placing the bones of the left hand into a bag and identified them. I proceeded with the left arm, left leg, lower part of the body, and so forth. I went through all the remains, labeling each part. Once I got it all labeled I put it in a box. I then sent the box to Washington to the FBI laboratories. The FBI had contractual agreements with the Smithsonian Institute. They handled all the cases involving bones.

I received a lengthy report back from the Smithsonian, which I think I still have in some of my boxes. In the first paragraph of the letter that the curator wrote, he said, "I want you to know this is the best described evidence I have ever received. It's more detailed and it's thorough and it doesn't appear that anything was left." He went on to say this was a black female, approximately 35 years old. This female had a left deformed hand. She had given birth to a child that in all probability suffered from cerebral palsy. They determined this by the fact the pelvis didn't open wide enough for a child's head. That's where cerebral palsy comes in. He went through all of the data he had found on the bones, giving the approximate length of time he thought she had been there. We researched the missing persons files and I found the person missing—she had a left hand that was deformed. I found where her parents lived and found two children living there, both of whom had cerebral palsy. I re-traced her steps and found the man she was with on the day she disappeared. He confessed to the crime and I solved the case. In law enforcement there is sometimes one small clue that helps you solve the crime.

CHAPTER 83

One day a fellow called me to come to the Laundromat where he was trying to do his laundry, and boy, he was fighting mad. I asked him what was going on. The machines were coin operated and the Laundromat provided a changer that made change for the customers. He said someone had come through there with some coins from Mexico—worth about a penny a piece. They loaded the machines with some of those and had taken every quarter in there. He was dead broke. He was very mad and gave them a cussing.

CHAPTER 84

Two fellows who were friends of mine, Jim Reed and Fagan Fargason, were on patrol together. Jim could inherit more problems and get his foot in his mouth more than anyone I had ever seen. Jim was getting a new car so he was giving the instructions of how to break it in. He said only so many miles at 25 miles an hour and so many miles at 100 and so forth. Fagan was riding with him and he said, "I don't pay any attention to those d--- things. Let me show you how to handle it." He slammed the car in gear and wheels were spinning and rubber was spinning and the microphone was open. Everybody in the office was listening to him. Some of them were trying to get on the air and tell him to get off the air. He was saying, "Do you hear that? Do you hear that?" He was talking up a storm. Well, Chief Avery heard it too so Jim had to face the music. He could get in more trouble accidentally than most people can do on purpose.

Jim and Fagan were driving out Riverside Drive one night and a pole cat with three kittens was crossing the road. Fagan was sitting on the passenger side and Jim said, "Get out Fagan, quick, quick. Catch one of the kittens." Fagan caught one of them by the tail and put him in the car. He was a little bitty fellow. Fagan said, "You can have my part of the polecat. I don't want him." Jim said, "It's a nice little cat. It will be all right. It will be domesticated." So Jim took him home and fed him and it ran around the house like a house cat.

Jim had an old goofy dog who didn't like that cat at all. Jim was a deep sleeper—he slept like someone who had had a drink of Chloral Hydrate. On this particular night, he had worked the night shift, so he came in and went straight to bed. Someone let that goofy dog come into the house and then left, closing the dog inside. Jim was in a deep sleep, with the air condition running.

The dog decided to go after the polecat. The cat had now been with Jim about a month, and was growing every day. After a chase, the dog cornered the cat under the bed, whereupon the cat hiked his leg and gave the dog a full spray. This caused the dog to vomit all over the floor. Jim heard the disturbance and tried to wake up but he couldn't get his breath. The odor knocked him down. He finally staggered outside where he could get some fresh air into his lungs and clear his head. I don't know how they got the cat out of the house.

Jim's wife came in and hit the ceiling. Jim had to take the mattress and box springs to the dump. He had to take all the curtains down, and he had to take the rug up. He never could get the air conditioner to run without producing an odor, so he had to replace it. After that episode, the cat—now a full-grown skunk with a well-developed spray—was no longer a pet.

CHAPTER 85

On another occasion Jim went on a call where a man was shooting a gun inside a house. The officers approached cautiously. Jim took the front door but he was very overweight so he was hugging the corner, trying to keep out of the line of fire. He was standing there with his gun up, while the other officers covered the back door. No one was rushing the house. They had been trying, for about an hour, to talk to the man with the gun, who was still inside the house. The officers were trying to get him to put down the gun, when a drunk appeared on the scene. Somehow he had gotten through the police line. The drunk came up the steps saying, "I know him. I'll get him." The drunk opened the door and went inside. Sure enough, in a few minutes he came outside with the guy. Jim said, "All right. Come on. I've got him." But the drunk guy objected: "Wait a minute. I'm the one that got him out of the house." The drunk wanted to be the one to make the arrest.

══════ CHAPTER 86 ══════

One night I was going out Emery Highway and there wasn't anyone on duty but my partner, Taylor Enscoe, and I. At that time there weren't any other cars in the county. Taylor looked across from the steak house at Rainbow Drive-In and said, "They're fighting." I said, "Let them fight." There wasn't anyone but him and me and there was a big crowd over there. A few minutes later, at the overpass, we received a call, "Fight at the Rainbow Drive-In."

I turned the car around to go back there and gave it more gas. When I got there I almost slid in sideways. I didn't have to break up anything. They were running for their lives. As we jumped out I saw Hawkeye in there, along with some other locals who were con men. There were also some rednecks from the kaolin mines there. There was even one woman in the fight. I looked at her and almost fainted; she looked like a lady wrestler who had been hit by an airplane propeller. I thought, of all things. I've got two of the worst crowds I've ever seen and I've got a lady wrestler.

I called the city and asked them to bring out the wagon and I hauled them to jail. I ended up turning them all loose, one group to go one way and one group to go the other.

In those days the officer had to handcuff the person and then the officer would go to a call box to call in the arrest. Finally, radios were installed in the cars but they were such strong battery takers that it was impossible to keep the car running along with the radio. Someone finally came up with an idea. Using telephone wires, they then put a big bell at the top of the telephone pole. The officer sat under the bell until he got his call. When you got a call in your district the bell rang and they would tell you where to go, and you took off.

That seemed to be working, somewhat. One night the bell went off and when the officers arrived, a man met them there, cussing them for all they were worth. He said, "Ever since they put that d--- bell in I haven't slept a wink." He lived down the street where a bell was on top of the telephone pole at Napier and Pio Nono. It was a fire bell that could be heard on the other side of Cherokee Baptist Church. They had to get rid of those bells. Everyone on the block was tired of them.

CHAPTER 87

hillip Mann had been shot and it had been in all the papers. We had worked the case and it was all over but he was still in some form of recovery. I was in my office one day when one of the girls said, "Mr. McArthur is here to see you." Mr. McArthur, who worked at the YMCA for many years, was a little fellow. I told them to have him come on in. He came in my office wearing a big black overcoat, a black hat, and black gloves. Mr. McArthur took his coat off and he walked around my desk to where I was sitting.

Before I knew it he hit me in the jaw. BAM! I saw stars. I said, "What's wrong with you?" He said, "Now, if Phillip Mann had had one of these gloves he could have knocked the man out that punched him." Mr. McArthur was wearing a pair of leather gloves with lead in the fingers. He was going to demonstrate them to me so he popped me in the chin. I talked to him for a few minutes and finally he left. I worked on getting my jaw unhinged. That was the last I saw of the glove.

Later, Mr. McArthur wanted to see me again. Well, this time I stood up. I was watching him this time. He came in carrying a ladies' handbag that featured a flap on one side and something on the other. He had an unloaded gun in a pocket on one side, and there was space for a dagger on the other so you could carry two weapons. Another part of the bag held mace. He wanted to get this handbag manufactured. I thought, Lord, help us. If you get all those knives in there, and the mace, I don't know what we'll do. We talked a while, but I didn't hear any more about the handbag.

Later, he came back to me and he said, "I figured out about these bank robberies, how to stop them." I went with him to look at a model he had built. It was a building not quite as big as an outhouse, and it had portholes. You put a man in there on a stool with a shotgun. If he's not in there the shotgun barrel is still sticking out.

Dick Hughes was an FBI agent and a Yankee. I said, "Dick, have y'all heard from Mr. McArthur out there?" He said, "No. Sheriff, what is it?" I told him about the little building and he said, "Gee, you blow away the deposits and the withdrawals at the same lick, don't you?" That was Mr. McArthur. He invited a group of bankers to meet with him and see his little building. They all went to see it, but I never heard any more about it.

CHAPTER 88

Clyde Martin was the pastor of Tabernacle Baptist Church, and was highly visible in the community. We became friends and he would come by to see me. He had a television show that aired on Saturday morning. He had a format like The Johnny Carson Show's 'Here Comes Johnny.' There was a platform with a sitting arrangement that consisted of a desk and sofa. He would sit at the desk and have his notes in front of him. The guest would come in and sit on the sofa in the seat nearest him. The camera people were in front taking the video.

He had come to me and asked me to appear on his show. I had agreed, so on the appointed day I was standing in the wing when he came on the air. He introduced himself by saying, "Good morning. This is Dr. Clyde Martin of the Tabernacle Baptist Church inviting you to stay tuned." He would do all his opening remarks then he said, "As our guest speaker today we have Chief Deputy Sheriff, Ray Wilkes. Come on in, Ray." Well, there was a little applause from the people present as I walked onto the platform. When I sat down on the sofa, all you could see were my feet going up into the air. The sofa was on the platform with nothing behind it. I did a back flip and went all the way over. There was nothing there to keep the couch from falling off the platform. Video tape had just started in those days so they were able to back it up and redo it. Someone came out and put a little strip behind the sofa so it wouldn't happen again. I never will forget, when I sat down the only thing I saw was the ceiling as I was going backwards. My debut into television was a real experience.

CHAPTER 89

In the days of moonshine and stills we would work with the State Revenue agents because we were so limited on manpower. If we found evidence of a still or the location they would go out and lay out on the still or whatever it took but we didn't have manpower like that. Everyone wanted a friend in high places; a lot of judges and lawyers would say "when you run across some good moonshine whiskey save me a gallon of it."

There was a young officer who wanted to get promoted. They had run across a still with a lot of copper and it would run about 150 proof alcohol with a blue flame that would sit on it like a Bunsen burner. They said it was good stuff. He thought, I'm going to be in good shape. He went down to Peeler's Hardware and bought a 25-gallon charred keg. He put it up in his attic and filled it with the whiskey. He laid it on the rafters so he could roll it. While it was up there he would roll it and let it set a while, then roll it again when it settled. His wife didn't have anything to do with it.

This officer lived in the Shurlington area of Macon during the time the neighborhood was being developed. One day she said, "I want you to get that thing out of the attic. I'm telling you, I can smell it." He got his dander up and said, ""You just know it's up there and every time you think about it, you think you're smelling it. You can't smell it. It's in a keg. It's locked in there with a bone hole. It's locked up. You can't smell that."

A few weeks later she came in and said, "The women from the church had a meeting here today and they were sniffing. I know they could smell it. I could tell by looking at their noses." The officer got all riled up again, "There you go again. You're doing the same thing." He still wouldn't move it out. He was waiting for

Christmas; the moonshine would have a little taint to it by then.

One day he came in and she was all over him. She said, "I guess you'll get it out now." He looked up and saw a collapsed ceiling. The Celetex had been soaking up the whiskey. He had not filled the whiskey keg up with water to swell the wooden spindles to prevent leakage. It had been leaking and going into the Celetex until it got so heavy the ceiling collapsed. He not only got it out but he had to replace the ceiling too.

CHAPTER 90

Another unusual situation focused on a fugitive who was a wanted felon in Georgia. This fellow had absconded with a church's money. He was the treasurer of the church and he had taken every dime of their money and left with it, and no one knew where he was. Usually when we don't know whether a fugitive has left the state we put what we call a 'stop' on him with the FBI. In the event he was ever fingerprinted somewhere there would be a red tag on his file.

So I put a red tag on his file and we got a hit. He was in Albany, New York, in jail. I talked to the authorities and they had talked him into waiving extradition and coming back. Well, I flew to Albany to pick him up. I was there for a couple of days staying in a hotel, and I had visited a friend I had been in school with up there.

It was cold as the mischief. In those days if you had air line reservations all of them were stamped "Check your reservation 24 hours prior to departure." I looked at my watch and I thought, it's time to check that. So I checked my ticket and it was 24 hours before departure.

Well, he was in jail and the detectives had told me they were going to take him out to the house to get a suit of clothes. They were going to let him change and then bring him back. They assured me I would have plenty of time to make the flight. I checked with Delta and they didn't even know who I was. I wasn't on the list for the flight. I said, "I've got tickets." The agent on the telephone said, "You're not on the manifest. You're not there." I asked what I could do and the agent said, "We can get you to Newark and then you can catch a flight out of Newark back to Atlanta with a better chance than you can out of Albany. But it's going to be standby." I said, "Okay. We're going to be there in just a few minutes."

I turned to the fugitive and said, "Let's go." Well, he was wearing the same clothes he was wearing when he was tearing down a building. He had on a dirty old pair of overalls with the knee out of them, a rough looking coat. He had about a half-inch beard on his face. He said, "Where's my suit?" I said, "Forget the suit. We've got to go. We have to catch this plane."

The detectives rushed me to the airport and we got there in time to make the flight. Everybody gave me a look over. He didn't have any handcuffs on him because there wasn't anywhere he could go up there. I knew I could handle him. We boarded our plane from Albany to Newark, me and the ragman. When we got to Newark I went to the ticket counter and said, "I want a flight to Georgia." The agent said, "We're filled up. What part of Georgia are you from?" I told him and he said he was, too. I said, "What can I do?" He said, "Well, we've got two seats in the first class section. It will cost you a little more but I can give them to you." I said, "Give them to me." So we boarded the plane, sitting in first class. On his seat was a "Wall Street Journal." He picked it up and started looking at it.

There he sat in the first class section, like an eccentric millionaire. I had on a coat and a tie. The flight attendant came by and asked if we wanted cocktails. He said, "Yeah." I said, "No. We don't need any cocktails." She came back later and laid a napkin on his chest so he wouldn't spill any food on his clothes. I said, "You haven't got a sheet, do you?" I thought, if people only knew. Here I sat in first class with a fugitive who was being treated like royalty.

I brought him back to Georgia. It had been his own fault he had gotten caught. Later I learned he was in a rooming house where one man had killed another. He had been drinking, and watched the whole thing. When the police officer asked what happened, he responded, "I'm not saying nothing." The police officer said, "You were there." He said again, "I'm not saying nothing." So they said, "All right. Come on. You're going with us." When they took him to the jail and ran his fingerprints, the red flag on his file came up and that is how we caught him.

CHAPTER 91

I flew out to California with an officer named Joe Brown to pick up a felon. This guy had been in Reidsville for 12 or 13 years. At the time we went to get him a handcuff law had just gone into effect with airlines. The law stated you had to put manacles on the prisoner, then you get a car and drive him. You were not allowed to put him on an airline with other people. If he had to have handcuffs he was not going on the flight.

We started to the airport with him. He had gotten a clean shirt and clean pants and he had just shaved. He said, "This is the first chance I've had to shave since I've been in jail. They gave me and a Mexican who had a beard like a grizzly bear a razor between us and I looked at him and told him to give me that razor. I wasn't about to share a disposable razor with him. I got mine off and gave it to him and he worked on his."

We got to the airport and I started conning him a little bit. I said, "You don't look to be a bad fellow. I tell you what, you know there isn't much difference between you and me. I'm wearing a tie and that's the only difference. You look nice the way you are. If you'll give me your word you won't give me any trouble I won't embarrass you with a pair of handcuffs." He looked at me incredulously and said, "You've got my word." It was kind of like honor between thieves. We were scheduled to fly from Sacramento to Los Angeles, and from there to Atlanta. There were no flights straight through. Our plane got diverted and we flew into a small town in Texas between Dallas and Fort Worth.

When we arrived we were told there was no way to get out until the next morning. The guy said, "I hate to ask y'all but these jails here are pretty rough with you. I'll give you anything for you to not put me in jail. I'll stay with you and go on back and not cause any trouble." I thought about what he said, knowing by the time we got him in jail the first night, found a hotel for ourselves, then went back to the jail the next morning to retrieve him, and continued to the airport to catch our flight, we would have about three hours of sleep. I talked to Joe saying, "Joe, we're really not going to have time to do anything about getting him to a jail and then getting back to the airport. We'll take him up on it." So we did. We drank coffee that night at a Waffle House until 6:30 or 7:00 the next morning, then we headed to the airport. We had no problems with him.

We finally arrived home and put him in jail. Ten days later he had sawed through two bars. He had all the opportunity in our travels back from California to escape. He waited until we got home. His word was worth more than the word of most of the people I know. I thought, there *is* honor among thieves. He sawed through two bars and picked up all the shavings, mixing them with soap to fill the bars back in. He was ready to get out of there.

CHAPTER 92

Leland Harvey was a local boy who made good in the robbery business. Aubrey Smith would help him rob small grocery stores. The custom in those days was to locate small stores within walking distance of the population so people could walk to the store and carry their groceries home with them. There were three such stores in Macon during this time—the Roger's store, the Piggly Wiggly store, and the A&P store. Later development saw very large stores where masses of people shopped. Buses were running so people could come and buy their groceries, saving money in the big stores.

The first of these large stores was a Big Star, followed by an A&P store located in the old Green Jacket restaurant site. It was near the old train station, and was in sight of the old jail where they hung people in the old days.

Leland Harvey and Aubrey Smith were notorious for robbing stores. They went into the Piggly Store that was on Broadway near Ell Street. They announced that this was an armed robbery and told people to put their money in the bag. There was a man standing in the check-out line who had his money on the counter. He shot both hands in the air. He didn't want to interfere with that gun at all. He put his hands in the air as did everyone else except the woman getting money out of the cash register. Leland looked back at the man and said, "Mister, is that your money?" The man answered, "Yes, sir. It is." Leland told him to put it back in his pocket. He didn't want anything but Piggly Wiggly money.

Leland would get long sentences and be sent to Reidsville State Prison. At one time he had over 100 years. Eugene Talmadge ordered him brought to Atlanta. He sat in his office and talked with him, Aubrey Smith, and D.C. Black. He gave the three of them a pardon and let them out.

At one time Leland robbed a store on Mulberry Street. They messed up and ended up right back in jail.

D.C. Black was being questioned by a police officer in Atlanta, Georgia. He was just getting ready to steal a car in front of him. The police officer approached and asked him what he was doing there and Black told him he was getting ready to cross the street. Then the officer asked, "What is your name, anyway?" Black looked down at the car and saw 'D.C. Black Auto Agency' so he quickly said, "D.C. Black." The police officer wrote the name down and let him go. The D.C. Black stuck and he continued to use the name.

Leland had been in jail a long time. The prison at Reidsville had gotten tougher and tougher, making it extremely hard to get out. There was a prisoner in there with a case in Bibb County. Leland took him aside and told the guy he could make a demand for trial. They had a hold on him. Leland said, "Make a demand for trial and they'll have to give you a trial under law. Then subpoena me as a witness." Leland had been in jail all that time and there was no way he could have humanly been a witness to any crime.

The guy made a demand for trial and I had to go get Leland. I knew the only thing Leland wanted was an opportunity to escape. One second and he would be gone. I brought Leland back to Macon and I put him in a good cell. I put the word out, giving all my officers warnings to watch him. Then I went to see Judge Morgan.

The case was coming up the next day in court. I said, "Judge, the only reason he's coming here is to escape because he couldn't have been a witness. The crime was committed while he was in prison at Reidsville. He's only coming here to escape. I've got a plan I think will foil him." Judge Morgan said, "Okay. What is your plan?" I continued to tell him, "I want to bring about 15 deputies into the court in plain clothes. I want to scatter them around all the doors so they are close to where he is sitting. They won't look any different than anyone else and no one will know who they are. None of them have been sworn in for this term of court to act as a bailiff. You will have them all rise when a jury is beginning to be picked. I think we'll have it in the bag."

The day of court Leland was sitting there waiting to be called as a witness and the case was getting underway to put the jury in the box. The judge said, "At this time I'll swear in the bailiffs who have not been sworn in for this term of court. All bailiffs rise and raise your right hand." When they all started standing up around the courtroom I think Leland did a 180 degrees with his neck. He looked all around where the doors were and I knew he said to himself the jig was all up. They had a recess and he immediately went to talk to the boy. The boy pled guilty and they both went back to Reidsville.

CHAPTER 93

One morning I was at Shoney's with General Robert Scott and I saw Jack Caldwell there with Oliver Snow. I introduced my friend, Jack, to General Scott then Oliver said he wanted to meet him also. General Scott was going to have lunch with me so I invited Jack and Oliver to join us and a few others who were going down to the jail and eat lunch. Jack told Oliver to go by his house so they could go together. It is one of the most visible houses in Macon; most everybody knows where Jack Caldwell lives. Oliver looked at Jack with the strangest look and said, "Where's your house at?" They had been friends all those years and with the house so renowned it was incredible Oliver didn't know where the house was.

General Scott had someone with him taking pictures and we all stood together and had our picture taken that morning.

While we were there Oliver went through his normal routine. He said, "Ray, how about putting me and Jack back there in one of the cells next to each other and I'll be James Cagney and he can be Humphrey Bogart. Give us a cup so we can rattle on the bars." I said, "Oliver, you're nuts. You're nuts." But that was Oliver. He was a real character. When he met General Scott he said, "Will you be here a few minutes?" When General Scott assured him that he would, Oliver got in his car and ran home to get a lithograph of one of his paintings. It was in a tube and well done. Oliver presented it to General Scott who was extremely gracious in his comments.

Oliver was a colorful character, as everyone knew. At one time he drove a GTO. He told everyone it was the best car ever made. In fact, it was an old rattle trap GTO Pontiac. On one occasion he and I were having coffee and Oliver said to me, "Ray, where are you going when you leave here?" I answered, "I'm going home." He said, "Would you mind following me over to the service station? I'm running a little low on gas."

I told him I would do that for him so I followed him out to the car, intending to follow him to the service station. Oliver looked at the traffic and it hadn't started rolling yet. Oliver let the car start rolling at Shoney's on the hill and down to Riverside Drive. He crossed the northbound lane and got in the south bound lane and rolled into the service station up to the pump. I thought, great Scott. He didn't have enough to crank his car.

I went in the restaurant one day and Oliver was sitting at the counter, smoking and drinking a cup of coffee. We exchanged pleasantries and I ordered coffee for myself. Georgia was one of the waitresses that everybody knew. Georgia said, "Ray, make Oliver give me a tip. He doesn't ever give me a tip." I didn't know where I fit into all this but when I looked at Oliver he said, "Ray, listen. I come to Shoney's five times a day. They charge me $.35 a cup for coffee. That's $1.75. She wants me to give her a quarter. That's another $1.25. That's $3.00 a day. For 365 days it would cost me a thousand and some odd dollars to come down here. I can't afford it." How do you respond to something like that? I couldn't believe he wouldn't give the waitress a tip for his coffee.

Oliver was extremely talented; in addition to being an artist, he also wrote poetry. Someone in Washington who knew Oliver convinced him to contact President Carter to see if he would accept one of Oliver's paintings for the White House. President Carter had been buying Butler Brown originals. Oliver wanted to get on the wagon where one of his paintings would be hanging in the White House. Oliver had to go to Washington but he hadn't owned a suit of clothes in years. He went to Joseph N. Neel's and bought a gray suit and then he got someone to do an $18 haircut on him. He shaved and put on a tie and flew to Washington. He made the presentation to President Carter and the President gratefully accepted it. They shook hands and that was the end of it. He never got any real licks out of it.

The painting stayed there. As I understand it, there are thousands of paintings that have been given to the White House but have never been hung. Since President Carter was from Georgia I thought he might have hung it somewhere. He went to Washington and met the President and that was the end of it.

CHAPTER 94

I have seen a lot of criminals go through the system and I've never been mad at them. If they hurt someone, murdered someone, or molested someone they didn't even come in my ball park. The fellow who committed a crime against property or was a safe cracker, I always considered them a little more artistic.

I've seen many different ways to get in a safe. A safe cracker I brought back from California told me the story of an old round safe. He said, "I never have done it but there's a guy in Reidsville that swore it could be done." It was an old fashioned round safe that you would place in a barrel or a drum. Then you steal enough carbon dioxide and start freezing the safe until the temperature goes to around zero. Your partner would then have a 20-pound sledge hammer, and he would hit the safe while it was frozen solid. The safe will crack and bust wide open. I've never seen anyone do it but he said it could be done.

Bill Carr and Grady Sinclair were two of the first safe burglars in Georgia I knew who could use nitroglycerin. There was an art in using it. Nitroglycerin in a bottle dropped out of your hand would blow up an entire house. Bill and Grady would steal dynamite from a construction site and take it out of the paper. They would conceal the dynamite with a gel of sawdust mixed with the nitroglycerin. A fuse was inserted into the side of the dynamite conglomeration.

The time of the explosion would depend on the length of the fuse chosen. If the fuse is going to be discharged by an explosion before the nitroglycerin goes off there is an electric blasting cap. The blasting cap can ignite ten sticks of dynamite with a nine volt battery. The red wire is connected to the red wire, and the black wire is connected to the black wire. Then a square battery is posted and screwed down so when you touch it the blasting cap is ignited and in turn the dynamite is ignited.

These guys were boiling the dynamite. They would put it in a wash pan and as the dynamite began to turn the nitroglycerin loose, it would produce a slick oil-like substance. They would skim it off the top and put it into a container. They had to go to a lot of trouble to get it. After all this they would then drill a hole near the release of the combination on the safe. The hole was then packed with cotton.

To make sure nothing fell they would build a trough under the hole with soap. Then they used an eye dropper to put it in ther, gradually soaking the cotton with nitroglycerin. Then they would seal the hole with cotton. A soaking wet blanket was placed over the safe and the plan was then to strike the safe with a sledge hammer and the concussion would set off the nitroglycerin.

Well, it works. The only question is how much nitro have you got in there. Have you got enough to blow it or have you got too much? Bill Carr and Grady Sinclair were at Harvey Bloodworth's loan company over Young's Drugstore at the corner of Second and Mulberry streets. Windows went all the way around.

They had everything in order and when they hit the safe with the sledge hammer it blew the doors off. It blew the windows out, knocking them down. Needless to say, they didn't stay around for the money. Fire trucks, sirens—everything was there. They took off as fast as they could.

Bill Carr told me he retired. He said he got out of the safe business. It seems a couple of guys had come to him and wanted him to blow the safe in a church. This particular church had a building fund. People in those days didn't write checks; they gave cash and the cash was put in the safe. Bill said, "No. When it comes to messing with the Lord's money, I'm not going to do that." He told me that everyone who went in there got caught. He retired and was going into playing poker.

Grady decided he was going to train some young guys on how to blow a safe. There was a big grocery store in Warner Robins, and one night someone who lived near the store heard something hitting and knocking. They called the police and told them that they heard this knocking. They believed it was the sound of a sledge hammer. So the police came into the parking lot from both sides with their lights off. Grady and his new boys were standing there. Grady had gotten old and he was letting the new boys swing the sledge hammer.

The watchman was on the roof with a Coca-Cola and two packages of cheese crackers. After his little snack he dozed off. Before that, everything on the walkie talkies had been okay. When the police came in, they started hollering and turning their lights on; then they started shooting. They got the two boys but Grady got away. The police were looking for Grady the next day. They found him later hiding under a house. A bullet had nicked his ear and he had a heart attack and died from that. So that ended the Grady Carr team.

Billy Doolittle and I always had, down deep, a grudging admiration of him. This came from a time when Billy was a young man, working for a fellow who had an ambulance service housed in the ground floor of the Persons' Building. They had two or three ambulances there and if someone needed an ambulance they would call the service and they'd send an ambulance.

Billy got a job with them so he slept down there every night and went to school the next day. If he didn't have to go out, he was able to get a little sleep and did fine. But if a call came in, he had to go out and work and still go to school the next day. I always admired him for being able to do the job. Later he worked for the telephone company.

I don't know how he and a guy named Will got tied together. I had to arrest Will. Will went into a little tavern and found his girlfriend sitting there with another man. He went bananas. He came out of there with the rubber flying just as I was going by, so I took off right behind him. I dropped in behind him and ran him down Emery Highway, not catching him until I got to the 5th Street bridge on the other side. He was really going fast. So I arrested him. I think I made arrangements for him to go to court and get it taken care of. I liked Will. I didn't have anything against him.

They eventually got together and went into the booking business. Then they got established in Las Vegas. Of all the places they could have picked to set up their business, the one they picked was right behind a Federal Building on the corner of Third Street and Mulberry Street here in Macon. I went to the sheriff, telling him I had an informant who told me Will and Billy were running a booking operation there and they were betting out of Las Vegas. Sheriff Jimmy Bloodworth was naïve and he didn't want to upset the city police so they said they would look into it. He came back and said there was nothing to it.

My informant had come back to me again and I said to Jimmy, "Well, I've got this. The informant has come back to me saying he heard someone ask these guys how they got away with running a booking agency right here by the Federal Building and the sheriff's office. Billy touched his pocketbook and said he had them both right here."

Jimmy said emphatically, "That's a lie!" I was exasperated with the lack of caring and I informed him, "Well, you won't ever make anybody believe that, with us sitting a block away from them." Jimmy considered this and said, "What do you think we ought to do?" I said, "Hit them." Well, we hit Billy and Will that night. We got all the paraphernalia in the building there and arrested them. I still wasn't angry at Will. When I saw him on the street I always chatted with him.

Billy had a deal with borrowing money on loan sharking rates. He would borrow it on Monday and pay it back the following Monday. The Justice Department decided not to pursue the situation. Billy's phone was tapped so he went to a pay telephone on the corner of Third Street right there where he was running his operations. He had gotten big and fat by this time.

FBI agent Ned Meyers and I were sitting across the street on Mulberry Street with a pair of field glasses. Ned was watching while I started the timer when he walked into the booth and then stopped it when he came out. We didn't have a tap on the pay phone but there was a pin graph on the phone of the bookie in Las Vegas he had out there. No one was listening to the conversation on that line. As you dialed the number a pin graph would punch holes in the tape so you could read where the call had been sent. The tape ran through another machine and they could read every telephone number and where it was coming from all over the United States.

We arrested Billy on a Federal charge. We could prove Billy was in the phone booth at the time the pin graph was in operation in Las Vegas calling the pin number out on the line he was on. Billy got out and it wasn't long before he and Will were going at it again. One time they went before Judge Owens. Will had thinning hair and it got longer and longer. Judge Owens was a very immaculate fellow. Will's lawyer told Will, "We're going to be going before the judge and I think you should get a suit of clothes and get your hair cut real nice." Will said, "H--- with that judge. I don't care about him. I'm not going to cut my hair." He went before the judge and he got time in the penitentiary. I thought, Will, you are nuts. Your hair will grow back if you cut it but he wouldn't give it up.

I was at home on the Sunday night of Super Bowl when I got a phone call. Billy and Will had stopped taking bets at a certain time. The call was about the apartments off Vineville. I went by there and I checked some tags. A fellow I knew was there with Billy where the gambling was being checked.

I went back and I wrote a search warrant up; then I had to find Judge Carlisle. The judge was eating supper with a lady friend at Shoney's. (Judge Carlisle was on the bench until he was 92.) I found Judge Carlisle and told him what I had and he gave me a search warrant. I rounded up Ray Stewart, Harry Harris, and a patrol unit and we went over there and hit the apartment. There wasn't but about $300 there but the bets were there. I seized all the bets. Then when the bank opened the next morning I took them to the bank and put them in a safe deposit box. I then went to the District Attorney's office.

Jack Gautier had had a stroke and Denmark Groover was on the case right and left. Billy had him on a retainer. He put a fee on this one. Billy didn't know who owed him nor who he owed. It had messed up the whole shebang. Denny convinced Jack Gautier under the right of discovery he had a right to see those tickets or a right to make microfilm or a right to make copies of them. I refused to do it. I said I wasn't going to give them up without a court order.

Denny went to Judge Carlisle, who by this time was an old judge, and Denny convinced him; he was a very convincing lawyer. In the meantime I went to Judge Morgan. I said, "Judge, is there any law in the book that forces law enforcement to become a part of a gambling operation?" He thought about it for a moment then he said, "I've never heard of one." I said, "That's what they're trying to do." I went over the whole story with him. He then asked, "Where are the tickets now?" I replied, "They're in a safe deposit box over at the bank." We had a box they let us use. Judge Morgan continued, "Those tickets are to stay in that box. If anybody else comes to you tell them to come see me." He was the Senior Superior Court judge.

Then I went to IRS. The IRS came up and put a machine in one of those rooms to microfilm every ticket in that box. I don't know what they did with them. I think the court finally gave me the right to destroy those tickets. It messed up a great deal.

I suspect that day there was a quarter of a million dollars in the Super Bowl. He was laying the bets so he still came out okay. Along about the time the city was clamping down on slot machines and some people who were involved in slot machines were being arrested, one of the big operators in Macon pulled all his machines out. Law enforcement was taking a licking for being involved in it. No machines could be found anywhere because under the new law that had been established the slot machine had been classified as prima facie evidence. In other words, if you can see it you can seize it. You didn't have to get a warrant. If you saw a slot machine you could seize it.

It's like moonshine whiskey. If you see it you don't have to go and ask anyone if you can arrest them. At that time Meyer Siegel and I were good friends and he was foreman of the grand jury. He came to me saying he had some information about where slot machines were stored. He said, "I want to go there and I want to see if they are." I said, "All right. I'll go with you."

I was chief deputy. I wasn't sheriff but I went with Meyer and we took some investigators and a couple of patrolmen over there. I knocked the lock off a building and great Scott, there were slot machines everywhere. I got a ton and a half truck over there and we started loading them up. We brought them in to a part of the building that later became the county engineers on the fourth floor. They had built an annex and we had a sealed room where we started putting them under lock and key.

A slot machine was very valuable. The value was because it was already in Georgia. If they could prove you got parts across the state line it was a Federal offense, unless you were in Nevada where the law permitted you to gamble.

I saw one of the old heads from city hall talking with Jimmy Bloodworth, who was sheriff at that time. My office was across from his. I knew the man from city hall had the power of persuasion so when he left I walked over to the sheriff and I said, "I'm not going to try to tell you what to do but I am going to tell you, you better be careful with him." I found out what he wanted to do. He was a policeman who knew the law. He wanted to bring someone in to take just one spring off the machines so they could say none of them were operational. Jimmy told me what the officer wanted. I told Jimmy he better stay clear of him.

We stayed clear and then the case was ordered. I was ordered to take those machines and destroy them. Denny came to me and said, "Ray, I know you've got to destroy them but my client wants to buy the salvage from them. Once you beat them with the sledge hammer, how about just letting us buy them because the parts will be there." You can't get the parts across the state line. It's just like a slot machine. I said, "Denny, I've got a court order that says destroy them. I don't mean half-way destroy them, but to destroy them."

We hauled them down to Macon Iron and Paper. They took a big pile of the wood ones off and stood them up. Then they sloshed them down with diesel fuel. Mr. Koplin said, "That's as far as I'm going. I'm not sticking a match to anything. They're not going to make me pay for those five years later." I took the matches from his hand and said, "Give me the match." I lit a piece of paper and caught them all on fire.

The slot machines were all metal so he took me into a place with a machine that held a screw. This was not your ordinary screw. It looked like a giant cork screw of about 15 inches in diameter made out of thick steel. I said, "I don't want any hereafter about this. I want them destroyed." Mr. Koplin said, "I've got a machine here." When you throw those things on top it was like a big meat grinder. He took his help out there, most of them black Americans. He said, "When you get off we're going to run those slot machines. As they run, if you throw the copper in one pile and the glass in the other I'll buy it back from you. If any coins come out of them you keep them."

Those workers turned the conveyor belt on and it was probably the slowest moving belt I've ever seen in my life. They were picking up coins and putting them in their pockets. They were throwing machines on the conveyer belt; it might have quarters or dimes and nickels coming out. I could care less. I was only ordered to destroy them. There wasn't a spring or a screw left of those machines when I was through with them.

All three of them did time for the slot machines. Dike Hawk's wife called me and she was crying. I very kindly told her, "This is nothing personal. This was something that at one time was acceptable and it was no longer acceptable." They got out of prison and Dike got short term. They were model prisoners. They weren't causing anyone any trouble. That was really white collar crime. When they got out Dike Hawks came to me and told me thank you for being nice to his wife while he was in prison.

Then I got a call from a banker who had been talking to Dike Hawks and another bank. This other bank had been border-line financing him and gambling. They were scared to death they were going to be indicted by the Federal Government. The banker called me and said, "Mr. Hawks is here and he wants to start banking with us. I want to let him bank with us but you will be the deciding factor." I said, "Well, you know his background. I think his background is over with. I don't think you'll have any more trouble out of him. If it was me and I was in your place I'd let him have it." He banked with that bank from then on. He always appreciated it.

CHAPTER 95

There were three men in jail who had been arrested: Mudcat Smith, Kenneth Dawson, and Wimp Adkins robbed the convenience store on Second Street at Ell Street. The police arrested Wimp and Mudcat inside the store. Kenneth Dawson got in a car and got away. They were in hot pursuit of him when he wrecked it. He was in intensive care for a long time and later died from complications of his wounds.

We had Mudcat and Wimp in jail. Mudcat had been in jail on another occasion. He had been named in Reidsville. All the old prisoners from Reidsville knew him. This time he was in the old jail. I isolated him from the other prisoners and put him under surveillance. One day he called the jailer over to the bars. When the jailer approached, Mudcat said, "I've swallowed a coat hanger." This shocked the jailer. He said, "Really?" Mudcat was adamant, "Yeah. I've swallowed a coat hanger. You can't get it with forceps. You're going to have to operate on me."

The jail called me and informed me of the situation so I took him to the hospital. They took an x-ray, put it on the frosted glass, and there it was. He had broken up the hanger into pieces about 12 inches long. He then bent it, wrapped it in toilet tissue and wet the toilet tissue. He leaned his head way back and swallowed it.

The coat hanger and the tissue were in the upper part of his stomach. There's a way of getting in there with forceps and going down his throat with a fluoroscope and fish it out. He waited to tell us until it went further down so it could not be retrieved in that manner. He wanted to have the surgery. He wanted to be in the hospital on white sheets being served orange juice and he was looking for a way to go. I took him to the hospital and put a guard on the door.

The resident doctor saw him. He gave a little foul language because he had to operate on him. I saw Mudcat the next day. He was in pretty bad shape but he was able to tell me, "That d--- doctor you gave me thinks he's a smart a---. He operated on me and he didn't put me to sleep." I don't know whether the doctor used a local anesthetic, but he didn't put him to sleep. That doctor wasn't about to let this guy get the best of him.

The doctor told me later, "There's so much scar tissue in his stomach it's going to kill him." He had been swallowing hangers for so long that he was well-known at the hospital.

Wimp went bad. He was a deserter and I caught him. The Army paid $50 for deserters. That was a big lump to me. He begged me to turn him loose and let him go back on his own. For kindness sake I did let him go and he kept going. The Army eventually caught him and then he went through a lot. He was out of the Army and he was in jail.

By that time we had moved the jail over to Oglethorpe Street. Judge Balloon's wife was also a lawyer. He was Judge of Municipal Court. She came to me and said, "I understand you know Mr. Wimp Adkins?" I said, "Yes, ma'am, I do." She said, "I've got him the best deal he'll get. It's nine years and they will give him credit for the jail time he's already spent, which is over a year." After he made one third of his time they would release him. I told her I would talk to him.

They brought Wimp to my office and I shook hands with him and told him to sit down. I told him the lawyer had cut a deal for him for nine years and he wouldn't have to do but another year and a half or so and he would be released. He said, "I can't do that." I said, "Listen, Wimp. You've been in jail long enough. There's nothing pleasing about a jail. If they gave you steak, you'd want chicken. If they put you in white, you'd want gray. I understand that. You need to get out of here. You need to go back to work. You need to sleep eight hours a day. You need to eat three meals a day." He said, "I can't do that. I don't remember." I said, "Whether you remember it or not they picked you up inside the store with a shotgun. Whether you remember it or not doesn't make any difference. They're not interested in your recall. They're interested in the people who saw you in there holding the store up." Well, he was on some kind of dope. The District Attorney really got hot with him when he went to trial; he was tried as a habitual felon and he got life.

When he got life he became a model prisoner. He was a trustee. At that time they had furloughs. The warden would write me a letter and tell me he would recommend Wimp for a furlough for ten days if I didn't object. I would never object to one.

He would always go on his furlough and come back like he was supposed to. Then I lost Wimp and I didn't find him until I learned he was in a nursing home in Jeffersonville. It was a sad ending to a friend. We were kids together. He had a chance to turn it around and he wouldn't.

CHAPTER 96

Ray Jr. was 17 years old and he had worked the summer before with the carpenter's union as a laborer. The second time he got out of school for summer I got him back with the carpenter's union. This time he wasn't working at the Pabst Plant. He was working at Plant Scherer. They were pouring forms, tearing them down, picking the big pieces of lumber up, moving them, and then pouring new forms. He was a laborer who carried the forms. He was strong and healthy and he worked in the sun.

He told me one day, "Dad, I'm working for a foreman up there and he's kind of crazy." I said, "Crazy? What do you mean?" He continued to tell me, "He's got all kinds of ideas about astrology and about stars and about the moon and about predicting things." A day or two later he came back and made another comment. I said, "What is his name, Ray?" He said, "Dad, his name is Bassett." I stopped what I was doing to look at Ray and say, "Is his name Jimmy K. Bassett?" Ray said, "Yes, sir." I said, "Great Scott. I put him in Reidsville for life and he's up there now? Don't even tell him what your name is and just go ahead and work with him this summer."

During that summer Jimmy came in to see me. He came in and shook hands with me and I told him to sit down. He said, "Ray, I'm going kill Jackie." Jackie was his brother and Jackie was nuts. He had what we called jail house tattoos. The inmates would take a needle and puncture the skin then rub the place with Indian ink. It stays with you like a tattoo. All around his neck he had a series of little dots tatooed. Jackie had also tattooed on him "cut along the dotted line." I knew Jackie as well as I knew Jimmy K. I said, "Don't let that get you in any trouble. Somewhere there's a way to work around the problems. You've been in enough trouble already."

I talked him into not getting into more trouble.

Not too long after he was on trial over at the Federal Building. He went before a jury and his argument was he had put on his withholding statement something like 30 or 40 dependents. They weren't taking a dime out on him. So he was on trial for income tax evasion. I don't know who represented Jimmy K. but darned if he didn't win the case.

He was arguing his constitutional rights; he didn't have to pay taxes and he beat the case. Later his brother, Jackie, was over at Family and Children Services trying to collect food stamps because all the minorities in this country—and he didn't call them minorities—were getting food stamps and he was entitled to them. They called and said they thought he might have a gun in his back pocket. I went over there myself because I could do more with Jackie than anyone else. About the time I was on my way over, a school class that I had scheduled to show through the courthouse came in, so I sent Phillip Mann and Lieutenant Billy Guy. I told them to take the sticks and don't take anything off of him.

Jackie grabbed Phillips Mann's gun, shooting him, and then shooting another fellow in the shoulder. Lieutenant Guy grabbed him and turned that gun. Billy was a big strong man. He turned the gun toward Jackie and when he did the bullet went straight up through his aorta. If he had shot him directly in the stomach Billy would have been killed also because the magnum bullet would have gone straight through Billy too. Jackie was on the floor and I rushed over there.

When I got there Phillip was laying in a pool of blood and Jackie was lying nearby. The paramedics were working on Jackie, who was dead. I don't know why they were working on him. Two or three of our patrolmen grabbed Phillip and put him on the stretcher. They rolled him down the elevator and took him to the hospital in the paramedic's ambulance. The paramedics were still in the building and our man was in the emergency room.

I got to the hospital and they said the name of some doctor who was going to do the operation. I said, "I've never heard of him. He's not going to touch him." I wanted the best surgeon available. Damon King, the CEO of the hospital, came down and he said, "Ray, he's all right. He's rated like a hotel with stars." The doctor told me Phillip would never walk again. However, when he had recovered, Philip returned to work at the sheriff's office.

That was two brothers. The one who told me he was going to kill his brother got straightened out and became a carpenter foreman; his brother died. I haven't seen Jimmy K. in years.

═══════ CHAPTER 97 ═══════

The old foundry lot was located where the Department of Family and Children Services is today. In the old days it didn't have the produce on the back of it or any of those buildings. It was flat. They ran a little barbeque in the front of the building. Carnivals would come to the area very often. The mill village boys would go to every carnival that came through town. Then the medicine man would do a show there, selling snake oil, with an Indian beating the drums. There were no lights. They had rambos soaked in diesel fuel on each side of the truck and had it covered over. I went to every show.

I was little so they always put me up front. The medicine man would say he needed a volunteer and they would throw me up on the stage. I would tell him my arm hurt and he would say they could fix it. He would take a little bottle of snake oil and rub it on my arm then I would tell him it felt much better. He usually gave me the remainder of the snake oil. I had two or three bottles of snake oil. I don't think it was anything but turpentine or something. They would always throw me up there, the older boys.

One particular year the boys and I went to the carnival, taking some of the staple shooters we had made. A favorite pastime of ours was to make staple shooters out of rubber bands and a coat hanger. We would bend the hanger like a sling shot except we would use rubber bands which weren't near as big as the old inner tube rubbers. We would borrow an axe and using the blade we would take baling wire, hitting it to make an indention in the wire, then move it over and hit it, move it over and hit it, and keep repeating. Then using a pair of pliers we made a staple. The staple could then be put in the rubber band and when you pulled back and released it, it became a pretty good weapon.

I was with the boys at the carnival, including a boy named Charlie Smith. There were about eight or nine of the Smiths. Charlie had real wiry hair. A man named Joe Simpson at the village would cut your hair on his back porch for a dime but his clippers pulled the entire time he was doing it. He would cut everyone's hair for a dime, except Charlie's. Charlie's hair was almost like cutting copper wire.

A boy named Buck Brown was leaning on Charlie's shoulders while we were at the carnival. Buck said, "Look, Charlie." It was a big woman with wide hips and he said, "Watch her jump. Hold steady, Charlie. I'm going to shoot her in the rump." He proceeded to pull that staple way back while resting his hands on Charlie's shoulder while aiming. Charlie also had big thick ears. When Buck released his staple it hit Charlie behind his ear. Charlie must have come three feet off the ground. Charlie didn't do anything but assault him. He was just beating the fire out of Buck, as if he had done it on purpose. Buck hadn't meant to catch Charlie's big ear but it just got in the way. I never did fool with a staple shooter after that. I was looking for the woman to jump up and down but she didn't know anyone had been shot.

CHAPTER 98

I got a call from W. F. Murphy at First National Bank. He said, "Ray, we've got a problem." I went to the bank to check it out. In those days if you wanted to know if you had any money in the bank, you'd call in and ask them. So this gentleman called in and said, "This is Sam Alton Smith with Equitable Life Insurance Company. I'm going to be making a call this afternoon on Dr. W. L. Smith and he's going to pay a premium. I would like to verify that there is $500 in his bank account." The person at the bank would then look it up and tell you whether it was good. When Dr. Smith did come into the bank he looked good. His shoes were shined and he was always very nice. Then he would disappear. One of the tellers got a tag number on him and it wasn't a Dr. Smith. They got me to run it down and I found out this guy was a bartender in Atlanta. I arranged to take Ray Stewart, W.F., and two tellers with me to Atlanta where this guy worked.

We arrived at the hotel's bar and took a table, then I went to the manager of the hotel. I was giving them the courtesy of getting a replacement before he was put in jail. The relief bartender came in and I told Smith he was under arrest and I put him in the Atlanta jail. Man, he was raising Cain. We were trying to run down Gilbert Don King—trying to get a handle on him but we were getting nowhere. Finally we broke the guy down a little bit, and he told us he knew Gilbert Don King and had borrowed his car. I said, "Well, you're going to have to produce him. Unless we get Gilbert Don King I'm taking you to Bibb County and charging you with forgery."

When he realized he was going back to Bibb County he said, "Let me get to a telephone." We had surveillance on an apartment that had been rented by a Gilbert Don King but no one had been there all day. We really didn't know if there was anyone he even knew there; we were both tired.

I took him to the jail and he started calling known places that Gilbert Don King frequented, such as bars. Once he located him, I heard him say to the person on the other end of the line, "You're not fixing to leave right now, are you?" We jumped in a patrol car and went over there with the Atlanta Police Department, driving as fast as we could. It was a real swanky place. I asked the manager where Gilbert Don King was. He hesitated. I showed him my credentials and my gun then I said, "I'm going to put every man in here against the wall and look in everybody's pocket until I find him." That man's face went white. He said, "Please don't do that."

There were big mirrors around the walls and a baby grand piano; everybody was wearing tuxedos. Gilbert Don King was sitting at the piano with some other people who were all drinking and singing. The girl he was with had on an evening dress with sequins sparkling all over it. I walked up and tapped him on the shoulder and called his name. He followed us outside but his girl came running behind us hollering, "Don't do it. I want to go with you. Don't do it." King said, "Let her go. She's a nervous person." I said, "Get out of here. Go."

The police officer flew back to the station. When we got back the bartender was still there so we let him go. We took King in and got him through the records. We were still booking him when all of a sudden the girl friend comes through the door in that big fine white evening dress covered in sequins. She was crying and carrying on. "Ohhhh. I've had a wreck." He said, "I knew it would happen." She said, "I hit the back of the police car."

By this time I can't believe all the fiasco and carrying on happening right there in the station. King said, "I told you she was nervous." She had run into the back of the police car on the way down to the station.

I gave him a minute with her and told him she was going to Macon. This man came up and introduced himself saying, "I'm

Gilbert Don King." We went back to his hotel room and found the records. He had a big box of records. We put him in jail in Bibb County. The next morning she was down there. W.F. Murphy and I were sitting in there with him. He knew she was going to be in there. He was spiffed up. He had on new clothes, was shaved and his hair was neatly combed. We let her come into the room with us. She came over there and put a smack-a-roo on him.

W.F. Murphy was standing there with his mouth open and he said, "I don't know anybody who thinks that much of me." I took all the tickets and receipts from the hotel. He had been doing this all over the southeast. Wherever he had been I sent them a copy of a check. He had been in Selma, Alabama, and Chattanooga, Tennessee. Basically, he had been all over the southeast, just flying from one town to another. Literally, he didn't use anything but a rental car. This time he got in a tight and we caught him.

His real name was Bob Perkerson and he was represented by an attorney. We got a trial and then we sent him somewhere else. I don't know how much time he got. He was convicted in Bibb County but I don't really know what happened to him. About six months after this thing occurred I got a call from Tom Greene at the First National Bank. I went to see him and found that the bank had been sued for $500,000. The bank was represented by the Jones, Sparks, Benton, and Cork firm, with partner Frank Jones, a fine, Phi Beta Kappa lawyer, handling the case. When it went to court the bartender from Atlanta came down.

We found out that he was from London, England, and had come over to take a job. He was here legally but was unfamiliar with our police system. They don't wear guns over there and they don't arrest anybody with a warrant. He had to testify in the case and Frank Jones came to me in the hall, saying he had to be able to make a motion of dismissal. The judge is going to grant it and if the jury rules on it, it can never come back. He was going to try to prove intent of anything wrong. I went down later to see Tom Greene and he said they had been sued again for $500,000. He said, "The next one who comes through here passing checks we're going to put in jail. They can sue all they want to." Tom and I were close friends from that day on.

We learned later Perkerson went to a turkey shoot on Thanksgiving and won two turkeys. He had been a big shot in his pre-criminal days. They were real nice, big, dressed turkeys. He went to the hotel chef and made arrangements to have those turkeys cooked, then carried to his girlfriend's mother's house with white linen cloths, chef hats, big white chef coats, and aprons. That girl's mother thought he was like Ted Turner. He got their attention.

Of all things, he kept records. He kept every record of his hotels, cars, and everything. I made a chart of all his hotel records, including the days he was there. With the evidence I had we knew where he was for months.

══════ CHAPTER 99 ══════

We had a new jailer on position at the old jail. I don't remember the circumstances, but somehow this jailer got locked out and one of the inmates escaped. We began to look for him, running down some leads. Our investigation led us to an old hotel, the Plaza on the corner of Third and Poplar Street. Harry Harris, Ray Stewart, and I entered the hotel and I told the hotel clerk what I wanted. You could see the planks through the carpet—it was old wool and was worn so badly. Walking through the center of the room you could see the boards through it.

The clerk gave me the room number of the man we were looking for so we proceeded down there and I knocked on the door. There was no response, so I said, "If you don't open the door we're going to kick it down." Still nothing. I said, "Okay. We're coming in there."

The doors to the rooms in the hotel were nine or ten feet tall. It was a big, old fashioned door made out of fine material. I stood back and kicked that door for all I was worth. When I did, my other foot went out from under me and I hit the floor like a ton of bricks. I could see dust coming up from every crack in that old carpet. Man, I was embarrassed. They said, "Are you hurt?" My pride was badly damaged but I said, "No." I was so mad I kicked that door again and, BAM, it opened. We didn't find our escapee. Instead, his brother was in there with some prostitute.

I asked Harry a while back if he remembered me kicking that door down. Harry said, to this day he doesn't know why it didn't kill me because of how hard I hit the floor. We have laughed about it all these years later.

CHAPTER 100

I had the opportunity to make the acquaintance of a woman who became quite a good friend. She was a fine, fine lady who had moved to Macon from Dublin, Georgia, for her husband, who was a doctor, to establish an office here. I had known her since the time I had been to Dublin as a delegate and we had ridden the train back to Macon together. Her husband and son-in-law had been on the train also. The son-in-law was well known in the legislature. While on the train she had insisted I eat sandwiches with them.

She called me one day and said, "I think I may have misplaced my ring. I have looked everywhere for it but I can't find it anywhere." I assured her I would send two investigators out there to talk to the yard men. In telling me all about the ring she had mentioned when she last had possession of the ring and about a couple of yard men she had working there. She said, "No. No. I'm not accusing anybody. I wouldn't hurt their feelings for anything."

The ring was platinum, with about a three carat stone and 20 or 25 stones around it. It was a very large ring. The investigators went to the house and talked to the men together and then they split them up to get each of their stories again. This time the truth came out.

My investigators called me with the outcome and I met them at Old London Gold. The owner of the store had bought the ring from the yard men for $300. When we arrived he had an eyepiece on and a diamond tip drill like dentists use. He had gotten the center stone out and was at work cutting the baguettes out. In just a few more minutes the whole thing would have been scrap. The little drill he had was cutting those tiny prongs so the stones would fall onto a felt cloth. We arrested him and took all the pieces he had.

I hated to tell this kind lady we had found the ring but it was in a hundred small pieces. I knew the ring held great sentimental value to her so I called John Baker, a friend of mine. John Baker is a goldsmith with a shop in the American Federal Building. I told John all that had transpired and asked him if he thought he could put it back together. John felt confident he could do it so I took the ring to him and left it. He worked on it into the night, making it look brand new. He charged her $250 for the repairs—dirt cheap for the extensive work he had done. All the little prongs had to be welded back in place with the platinum. He did them one by one.

I invited her to come down and eat lunch at the jail with me. She was as fine a lady as they come but extremely down to earth. Whenever I ran into her she would always speak to me. If she ever had any problem she would call me. Later she wrote a cook book entitled "From the Jail House to the Whitehouse." Her name is Louise Dodd. She had eaten from the jail house with me all the way to the White House with Jimmy Carter. I felt honored to be included in her memories.

CHAPTER 101

After I was elected Sheriff we began to get more and more prisoners who belonged to the state and we were all running out of beds. These prisoners had been sentenced in the court but the state would not pick them up because of a commissioner named David Evans. He had promised each governor he served under that if they would keep the politicians off him he would keep the state from being sued. He wouldn't pick up anyone unless he had a bed in the prison. He left them for us and we were being sued right and left.

A group of sheriffs got together through our organization and asked for an appointment with the Governor. For some reason they asked Cary Bittick, the Monroe County Sheriff, and me to speak, representing the group, to explain to the Governor our complaints. Cary Bittick was to speak first saying, "Mr. Governor, the cement in Atlanta is just as soft as the cement we have in Monroe County. We've got prisoners on the floor in Monroe County but you don't put them on the floor in the state." The Governor had heard that story before but he listened courteously.

When my turn came to speak I said, "Governor, each year we come here and each year we have the same story. We're overcrowded at our jails. We've got people on the floor and the Civil Liberties Union is suing us. We've got the same problems each year. You listen to us and you always say I'll look into it. Then you turn to Mr. Evans." Now, the room was filled with people from the Department of Corrections and reporters. Mr. Evans was sitting in there with all his subordinates from the big office. I continued, "You look over to Mr. Evans and you say the sheriffs have 3000 people backed up in the jail. What can you do to help them? Then he says, 'I'll look into it.' Then he comes back and says, 'Governor, if we take them we're going to be sued. We don't have any room ourselves.'" It had grown extremely quiet by this time but I was not to be intimidated. "Sir, Mr. Evans has not been totally honest with you, and his people have not been totally honest." About this time the Governor spoke up, "You stop right where you are and you tell me exactly what you mean by that." I said confidently, "I'll be glad to. In the '60s and early '70s the Milledgeville State Hospital had between 12,000 and 15,000 patients and a staff of 5,000. Now they have a staff of 5,000 and a patient load of 2,500. There's 10,000 beds over there somewhere. Everyone doesn't have to be in a Bastille. Mr. Evans comes back to you and says give me $12 million dollars and I can build a jail. Five jails will be $60 million dollars. He's quoting a Bastille. With very little money and minimum and median offenders you could put people at Milledgeville with just a few alterations to the windows and building making it conducive to prisoners. The building and mattresses are already there."

The Governor came out of his seat, "I'm not going to fill up Milledgeville with prisoners!" I calmly said, "Governor, before you make up your mind, those prisoners would fare better there than they would here where we've got them on the floor. Before you make up your mind, the Speaker of the House, Mr. Murphy, had two large dormitories built at West Georgia College that have never been occupied. No one has ever slept there." Once again he said, "I'm not going to do that!" I continued, "Before you make up your mind, the grass grows up there. Toilets get stopped up there. The prisoners could work at the college and the hospital, thereby taking the state's additional expense off of them."

He was mad. The conference was over and when I left I said to myself, the sheriff's organization won't ever ask me to speak for them again. I came back to Macon putting the matter aside and went about my business.

Later I got a call from Tom Perdue who was the Governor's Executive Secretary. I couldn't imagine what he would want with me. He said, "Sheriff, the Governor wants to know if you would serve on the Board of Corrections." I couldn't believe what I was hearing. I said, "Before I answer that, Tom, tell me why the Governor wants me?" He responded, "You're his secret weapon." Today in Milledgeville about 8,000 prisoners are in those beds which formerly had patients.

CHAPTER 102

I was in the hospital several years back and they wanted to put a pacemaker and a defibulator in me. My doctor recommended it, so I said okay. Whenever a doctor recommended something you generally just did what he told you to do. He said, "You're already here so let's just go ahead and admit you to the hospital and do it while you're here." I was admitted to the hospital and put into a room. Not too long after I was taken from the room to the operating room. They had taken my clothes and put a sheet over me. I think it was starched. It hardly touched me and it was cold as I don't know what.

I was under the sheet but I was unable to push or pull up with my shoulders. There were three orderlies with me, young white fellows. Some of them may have been medical students but they were present in the room acting as orderlies. I was trying to move but was unable so I asked them to assist me. I said, "I'm not going to be able to help you. Y'all are going to have to put me on the table." One of the guys said, "We'll do it. Don't worry about it." So they put their hands under me, palms up, and on the count of three they all picked up, moving me to the operating table.

They were most courteous to me and said, "Are you all right?" I assured them I was. One of them then asked, "Are you worried about anything?" Well, here I am lying on the operating table about to have my chest cut open and something inserted into my chest. I don't know exactly what they expected but I said, "Well, I am worried about one thing." One of them asked, "What is it?" I said, "I'd feel a whole lot better if I knew Dr. Sogade was going to be the person to put this pacemaker and defibulator in. I don't have any idea who you are. I've never seen you before." Those boys looked at me, then one of them realized I was joking and he said, "Well, we're not doctors and we're certainly not surgeons but we did stay at Holiday Inn Express last night." I liked his sense of humor.

CHAPTER 103

J.W. Smith had become the coroner, and was about to go on his first call. "Ray, go up there with me." We went to a room in the Macon Hotel where we found a dead man. He was kind of thin, and was lying in the bed with his mouth open. He had a bottle nearby and we surmised he probably just died while drinking. I was standing back a little, letting J.W. do his work. I knew J.W. hadn't been out on any cases yet. I asked, "Who is he?" J.W. said, "I don't know."

I could tell J.W. was having a little difficulty with the grossness of the surroundings but I said, "Don't you think you ought to turn him over and get his wallet out?" Well, the man had urinated all over himself. J.W. just looked at the man. There weren't any rubber gloves around. J.W. looked like he was trying to use two fingers with two joints to get that wallet out. He finally got it out and there was $2.00 in it. That's all he had but we were able to get his name.

J.W. was kind of real dainty about keeping his hands clean. He looked around the room and then looked at his hands. I saw him spot a wash basin in the corner of the room. It was about 12 inches across in diameter. He went over and turned the water knob but nothing happened. I looked down and saw that there weren't any pipes running to it. It was a cheap hotel, about $2 a night—no water provided.

======CHAPTER 104======

I have met some very interesting people in my life. One of those is Jimmy Jones. When World War II started, he was teaching English at Mercer University. I guess he volunteered for the Marine Corp. When they checked into his background they didn't put him in the field but instead held him back. There was a top secret operation going on and after some scrutinizing and background checks, they brought Jimmy into it. It was called the wind talkers, and was made up of Navajo Indians. The Marines were training them for the South Pacific. Jimmy said the Navajo Indians were the only Indian tribe in the world that didn't have a written language.

Jimmy worked with them, going in teams to the Pacific. As I understand it, they were sworn to kill themselves before capture because they couldn't let the Japanese know what the code was. It was an unusual language. Jimmy said the wind talkers would work in pairs with one in the front transmitting the company commander's message back to headquarters. Then they would call it back and he would record it on his pad and the message would go right to him. The Japanese would always cut the line. But they could never figure out what the wind talkers were really saying.

Jimmy and I would always drink coffee together. He was a friend of Young Stribling. Jimmy told of time when Stribling went to Columbus and fought the Champion of the World there. Someone said, "What does this Stribling look like?" The response was, "You just saw him. He passed through the lobby here." It was just a young kid with a Lanier sweater. The man said, "Him?" Young Stribling almost beat the man's eyes out. All the betters and gamblers figured he was taken real quick. They got on a train. He gave the fight to Stribling until he got on the train. The referee said he had been intimidated by the Ku Klux Klan and turned him around and said he wasn't the winner, it was the other man. They went back to Chicago.

Jimmy wrote a popular book about Young Stribling called "King of the Cane Breaks." That was a story I always enjoyed with Jimmy.

CHAPTER 105

As sheriff I was often called on to speak to different groups of people. Many groups also came to see the jail or City Hall. One time I received a call from a high school asking if I would speak to the Attitude Adjustment Class. I really didn't know what the Attitude Adjustment Class was but I agreed to do it. On the appointed day I went over to the school to speak to this class. As the students began to come in I looked at the crowd and observed that they weren't anything but a bunch of troublemakers.

One of them sat on the front row. He had on a large overcoat similar to the ones people wear while shoplifting. He sat down in the front row slumping way down in the chair. Then he threw one side of his coat to one side and threw the other side of his coat in the opposite direction and proceeded to go to sleep. I looked around and thought this adjustment class isn't anything but a group they're trying to straighten out.

As they were filing in a teacher was saying, "Come in, please. Please stop talking. Please, don't talk. Please, sit down. You're not going to get credit for last week because you wouldn't let Ms. Timsley talk." It seems they had a guest speaker the week before who couldn't even talk because of the disruptions. The teacher continued, "You're not going to get credit for it." I thought, huh, this is the crowd I'm going to be dealing with? She finally got them quiet enough to tell them who I was.

In those days I always wore a suit and a pair of Bostonian wing tip shoes with a sole on them that was pretty thick. I had seen and heard enough. I walked over about two steps to the place the fellow was asleep in the front row and I kicked him twice in the shin before he could even get his leg out of the way. Then I said, "Look. If you're going to sleep, it ain't going to be on my watch." The teacher looked like she was going to pass out when I kicked him. Everybody in the room sat up. The boy straightened up and looked at me like I had shot at him. He didn't know what to say.

I turned to the rest of them and I said, "You look like the crowd I just left in the Bibb County jail. The only difference in what you look like and what they look like is you're a little bit younger. But if you keep doing what you're doing I will have you one day." You could hear a pin drop in the room. From that point on they asked good questions. There wasn't any junk in there. I never did get invited back, though. I think the lady was afraid she was going to get sued or beaten up. I got their attention. I thought to myself, they run over her but they aren't going to run over me.

CHAPTER 106

A lady came in and told me she and her husband had been separated for four days and she thought he may have killed himself because she hadn't seen anything of him and he had been drinking heavy. She said she would like to go to their house to check on him but she was afraid of what she might find. I told her, no, you give me the key to the door. You can drive down the road and get close enough but don't come all the way. Tangling with one was going to be hard enough.

I got there and went to the side door, calling out to tell him who I was. Nothing. I took the key and put it in the lock and opened the door. I saw there was glass all over the floor. I looked up and saw the ceiling fan had been shot out. Then I saw bullet holes all in the wall. I put my hand on my gun and said, "I'm from the sheriff's office. I want to talk to you." I saw more broken glass and a shot-up television. I looked up and he was standing in the hall with a German Luger in his hand. He was drunk as all get out. He said, "The d--- thing is jammed." I said, "I'll take care of it for you." I took the gun away from him and then I put him in the car.

He thought I was going to take him downtown and put him in jail but instead I drove him to Milledgeville to the mental hospital and admitted him. I never did hear any more from him.

CHAPTER 107

Pearl, Ray Jr. and I had been out on a drive through Shurlington and down Highway 49 and had started home. As we were nearing our neighborhood, I saw a young woman I had known all her life crossing the street. Nothing would be unusual about that except she was wearing a nightgown and a coat. Pearl was always a very private person and she said, "Don't stop. Don't stop. That's Rennie May. She's got her nightgown on." I said, "Pearl, something's wrong."

I stopped the car and pulled up to her and said, "Rennie May, what's wrong?" She said, "Ray, get me to the hospital as quick as you can." She was holding a little boy in her arms. She jumped in the backseat and I turned the siren on. I heard her hit him in the chest and then I heard her breathing for him. I called ahead to the hospital to let them know we were on our way with a code pink.

When we arrived she went with the little boy while Pearl and I waited in the waiting room. Once the child was admitted into the hospital and the doctors were working on him, I took Pearl and Ray home. Later that night Rennie May told us she left the little boy there. He was in a coma and they didn't expect him to live. I felt like we had done all we could but I still worried about him. I checked on his condition from time to time but there was never a change. Things went on and weeks went by, then a couple of months went by and we had word he was back home. On Mother's Day the little boy awoke from the coma. He was crippled but there was no brain damage. He later went to Mercer and graduated.

Later when I was running for sheriff I was out waving. That was the cheapest politicking you could do. It was cold as the mischief, and I was standing in the drizzling rain at the fork at the Howard

Johnson Hotel. Some cars were going on I-16 and some were going into town. Someone touched me on the back. When I turned around I saw it was the mother of that child. She had seen me out there in the rain so she stopped her car and got a large cup of hot chocolate to help keep me warm. She and that young man were a steady help to me during my entire campaign.

CHAPTER 108

As sheriff I wore many hats. There were two occasions I had to wear the hat of King Solomon. I always tried to use wisdom in every case I dealt with. The hospital called me one day asking if I would come down. It seems there were two ladies, a Ms. Brown and a Ms. Green, who had just had babies. When it came time for them to be discharged Ms. Brown was given Ms. Green's baby and Ms. Green was given Ms. Brown's baby. The tags and footprints were all correct, the nurse had just handed each lady the wrong baby. It was just a case of the nurse carrying the baby to the wrong mother.

As soon as I arrived and checked everything and assured the mothers they had the correct child they were satisfied. They had panicked at first but when I came in and did a check it assured them everything was fine.

Then I had one more situation at the same hospital. There was a psychologist or psychiatrist from Milledgeville in the hospital delivering her fourth baby. I can't remember if she had three boys or three girls but at any rate she delivered a boy. She began raising Cain right there in the hospital. She said, "They told me in the delivery room I had a girl." They called me to come up to the hospital so I went. I checked the paperwork over two times before I ever went into her room. When I was sure everything was in order I took the paperwork to her and showed her the points of identification on the papers as I drew them off. When I finished doing that she was satisfied.

She was extremely reasonable after I finished. I think she was under anesthesia and only thought she had been told she had a girl. I just thought it so amazing how many people only needed the assurance of the authority to help them see what they really already knew.

CHAPTER 109

Many Christmases ago an event occurred that has left its mark on me until this day. Randy Candler was a sergeant at the police department. I hired his wife, Cathy, to be my personal secretary. She had extremely good typing and dictation skills. Because of those skills and several other qualities I wanted in a secretary, I hired her. She did a very good job for me.

Cathy wore her hair in a very short cut and she didn't wear any makeup. When people would ask me where they should put some project I had given them to do I would tell them to give it to my secretary. They would invariably ask, which one is she? I would say, "My secretary is the one who looks like a little boy in there." People would laugh, but Cathy really was a great person. She wasn't flamboyant or anything but she was one of the best secretaries I had ever seen.

She was highly enthusiastic. If something came along she wanted to be right in the middle of it. If some poor person was stranded somewhere I may have thought I wasn't going to be involved in it but sooner or later I would find myself right in the middle of things. She was always getting me involved doing something to help these people. She would say in no uncertain terms to me, "You're going to do something." We had that kind of relationship.

Maybe a couple or three years had gone by and they were going to hang Christmas decorations in the offices. Cathy was a real active person. She could hop up in her chair with her hammer and before you knew it the whole place was transformed. Cathy and several others were hanging Christmas decorations when some poor lady came into the office. Someone came in to tell me this lady wanted to see me. I told them to send her in. This poor lady came in and sat down and I could tell she had been crying. She started telling me a long sad story and in the middle of it she started crying again.

In the outer office they were still hanging Christmas decorations. There was only a wall separating my office from the office they were decorating. Cathy started putting up something requiring a nail in the wall so she hopped up in the chair and started hitting that wall with the hammer. She forgot the poor lady was in my office. I listened to her bang for a few seconds, thinking all the time the noise would stop momentarily. The noise continued and a minute later Cathy hit the area of the wall where I had a picture hanging. The picture fell off the wall hitting the poor woman in the head. It scared her to death. She jumped out to the middle of the floor. I hollered, "Cathy, stop."

Later after the lady left Cathy said, "I'm sorry, Sheriff." I good naturedly said, "I'm going to kill you. I'm going to kill you." I still tell her today I never had a person I worked with as closely as I had worked with her who I loved as much as I loved her but I wanted to kill as many different times. She was a great person. She had previously been employed at a printing company, setting type and working on books. She knew all the formats and punctuations. There really was nothing that I gave Cathy that she did not complete in excellent order. We still see each other and they come by every so often.

=======CHAPTER 110=======

I consider even in the serious moments humor can be found. It may not always be staring you in the face but many times if you slow down and take a step back you can see things you may not have seen to begin with. I have learned many things from many people. Some of those people were criminals. Even they taught me much. Others were important people such as presidents. In my career I have met six presidents of the United States. Each one of them left a different impression on my life.

The first President I met was Lyndon B. Johnson. Kennedy had been killed in Texas and Johnson had been sworn in to complete Kennedy's term. When he completed that term he had to run for President. During the 1964 campaign, he was in Alabama with his next stop either Augusta or Atlanta, Georgia. He was coming to Georgia and Secret Service was as nervous as a cat with a sore tail in a room full of rocking chairs. They didn't want any slip-ups. Secret Service had unlimited amounts of money. They could do anything they wanted to.

In those days we didn't have cell phones and the walkie talkies like we have now. At City Hall they brought a person from Secret Service in, housing him at the Dempsey Hotel and calling it White House Communications. White House Communications was a man sitting at a switchboard. When Secret Service got out of the car and entered the City Hall building on the police side he would find a telephone on the street, a telephone at the bottom of the stairs, a telephone at the top of the stairs, a telephone in the hall. About every twelve feet there was a telephone. When you picked up the phone you were instantly connected directly to Washington, D.C. to whoever was in charge of the problems.

We had to have a hospital room completely ready for a heart patient. They had to have a cardiologist and a heart surgeon there with all the equipment in that room. If anything happened to Johnson he would be rushed to the hospital into that particular room with the medical personnel on standby.

We also had to plan an escape route. The escape route was basically a plan of getting him out. Period. No matter what the situation we would get him out. In the event of gunfire we would have Johnson out of danger instantly. The plan was to put him into a car, taking him to the ball field at Mercer University where a helicopter would be able to land. The government had a helicopter flying over Central City Park. I had one of my officers in the helicopter with Secret Service. The Mercer ball field was Plan A. In the event they couldn't make a pick-up there, Plan B was to attempt a pick-up in the K-Mart parking lot on Riverside Drive (now the site of Hutchings Career Center). No matter what, we had to get him into the helicopter and back to Air Force One. It was all serious business to me.

One Sunday afternoon I came out of Hart's after attending a funeral when I received a call on my radio. Secret Service was looking for me. They wanted me to come to the Wilson Airport. When I arrived I saw a helicopter complete with Secret Service agents. They said they wanted to run the route again to inspect roof tops and that sort of thing. I had noticed there were a good many of them. Helicopters are not at all large and I really wasn't too anxious to fly in one. I had been in some before and they sound like they're going to come apart at any minute.

They all started piling in and I found myself being the last one left on the ground. This was a military helicopter. Finally, one of them said, "Come on. We saved a seat for you." Well, the seat they saved for me was at the door, right slap at the door. I climbed aboard and thought surely they would close the door. Little did I know the "door" was a nylon cord about the size of my forefinger. It had a hook on each end which fit into a loop on each side of the helicopter doorway. That was the only door on this thing. I thought, great Scott. I stuck my foot out turning it sideways to bridge my leg as if it were steel against the other side of the door.

We put on our helmets and speaking gear and then took off. When a helicopter takes off it does a nose to the ground. It then goes up and gains some altitude to begin actually flying. We went up and then made a turn. When it made the turn one of them pushed me on the shoulder. I said over the microphone, "I was just sitting here thinking, there aren't enough Secret Service agents on this thing to throw me off." We continued our fly-over, finding everything was ready to go.

On the day of President Johnson's arrival we were at Robins Air Force Base. Air Force One came in. A limousine had been brought in by a C-5 earlier in the day. Air Force One landed and the ceremonies began. The General stood there for all the hand-shaking, then President Johnson got in the car for us to proceed into town. We weren't supposed to stop at all but by the time we got to the main gate of the Air Force Base there was a big crowd of people. Johnson ordered the car stopped and he jumped out and started shaking hands with everyone. The agent with me was sort of in a panic. He said, "That's not supposed to happen or they would have had agents on the ground there."

We got back in the car driving into Macon. As we came inside the building I saw all the phones were lighting up. We got to the mayor's office where Mayor B.F. Merritt had invited a lot of distinguished and very strong members of the Democratic party. They were standing all around the four walls in the conference room. The mayor's personal chair had been brought in the room for Johnson to sit in. When Johnson came in the mayor introduced him to several people; then Johnson sat down. I was a little taken back when he sat. Most people would have gone completely around the room shaking hands. Instead he sat down, interlocked his fingers together, and put his hands behind his head. He then leaned back and went sound asleep. I just stood there staring in amazement.

The Secret Service agent gave me a very slight nod and look that said, don't do anything. He slept while everybody in the room was looking. You could hear a pin drop it was so quiet. Not a word was said. In about five or six minutes he sprung out of the chair and said, "Let's go." Of course, it stunned the daylights out of all of standing in the room. They gave me a shove on my back and before I knew it we were on the podium. Johnson gave his speech from City Hall. On each side of the podium was a teleprompter. He was speaking and all of a sudden he came off with a "Who shot John?" story. It was completely ad lib. The story was about his folks going through Georgia on their way to Texas. When he finished telling the story he picked back up on the next line on the teleprompter and kept right on going. I thought that was pretty amazing.

Youngblood, who was in charge of the detail out of Washington, was the agent who had covered Johnson's body when Oswald killed Kennedy. Johnson thought an awful lot of Youngblood. President Johnson had Youngblood in the car with him as we were on our way back to Air Force One. All of a sudden Youngblood said over the radio where everyone could hear, "Who was to remove the cover and unplug the flags?" The guy next to me said, "Somebody is going to be chewed." We were moving but we had to stop so we could get out and remove the covers from the American flag and flag of the President of the United States located on the windows. I thought, you know, with all the planning you can still make an error somewhere. I felt sorry for the poor agent who had forgotten his job.

We continued to the Air Force Base and it was all uneventful. When we started to leave I was introduced to him. He spoke to me, thanked me, and grunted and that was the end of it. The most memorable part was him asleep in the chair for those few minutes and then his abrupt awakening.

Secret Service had covered all the rooftops in downtown Macon with snipers. The Secret Service agents were all nervous. On anything that looked suspicious the snipers had them in a gun site. It was one of those situations where they didn't want anything to happen. One of the agents confided in me when they were in Dallas there was a little chrome platform made onto the bumper of the limousine for an agent to jump onto in the event the agent would need to cover the President. President Kennedy was sitting down waving from an open car. The agent was standing up holding on to a little bar so he could keep his eyes on everything. The president would wave to the right and he would wave to the left. The President said, "Get off, get off, get off, get off, get off," all while he was smiling and waving at the people.

The agent said twice he stayed on there and twice he was ordered off. He continually attempted to return to the platform of the car but because it was a Presidential order he would have to get off the car. That order may have cost President Kennedy his life. When Johnson came to Macon the assassination of President Kennedy had not been too long past. This time they wanted to take double care no problems arose. The car following Johnson was full of Secret Service agents. The car in front of Johnson was the news media with cameras. The car behind the Secret Service held a doctor, a nurse, and a cardiologist with everything he needed in the car to render aid in case of an emergency.

This was the routine in every place the president visited. It is still the same way today. There are people in this country today who would kill George Bush if they had half of a chance. There are people who would kill anyone who held that office because there are a lot of crack pots out there. Johnson was one of the most detailed and I can understand why. Because of the events in Texas with President Kennedy they wanted every base covered.

CHAPTER 111

President Nixon was coming to dedicate the library at Mercer University. This was to be one of his first times out of the White House since Watergate broke. The agents confided in me, "This Watergate thing has really put him in the pits. We're trying to make this a remarkable event to lift his spirits so he will have some feelings about the crowds."

When Air Force One landed and the President got off the plane he did the normal routine of shaking hands with the generals and the other high officials present. His limousine had come earlier by a C-5 as was the norm. We all got into the cars waiting to make the drive to Mercer. There were some women communication workers out of Athens, Georgia, part of an organization that was suspected of having a communist taint to it, that the Secret Service already knew would be demonstrating against Nixon. There might be trouble. When we got over there I was on the line with the Secret Service. We were making sure no one got through the line. I don't know how many people, deputies and others, were on the line.

Right below me was a woman who looked to be about five foot, four inches tall. She was husky, with legs that looked like she could play football at the University of Georgia. I was watching her scream and holler and then all of a sudden she broke through the line. When she did, the agent grabbed her by the nape of the neck and almost by the seat of her britches. Then he almost dug her into the ground. He put a pair of handcuffs on her and she was gone. I mean, the whole scenario didn't take three minutes. The dedication continued and everything was uneventful.

On the return trip to Air Force One, the president was being called by one of the agents in my car and he would say, "Look at all the crowds." A lot of people came out to see President Nixon. All the Watergate issues had not hit him here. I personally always thought the whole Watergate thing was blown way out of proportion. I still think if President Nixon had been a president who would chop your head he would have named all those involved, fired them and had charges brought against them. The only thing I have been able to find he said was, "I don't want any slip-ups." In other words, don't surprise me with anything in my background and that's when they decided to burglarize headquarters. That's my personal opinion.

When we got back to the airport the agent I had worked with in charge of the affairs came up to me and said, "Ray, I want you to meet the president. Stand right here. I'm going to bring him over to you." I thought it would be an honor so I said, "Okay. I would love to." I was standing off to the side while President Nixon was greeting generals and other important people. I noticed Colonel Coffer of the Georgia State Patrol look over in my direction. He came over where I was standing and said, "Hey, Ray. How are you doing?" And stuck out his hand for me to shake. Now I'm number two. I had been number one. Then Sheriff Talton, a good friend, Sheriff of Houston County, came over and said, "Hi. How are y'all doing over here?" Now I was number three. By the time all was said and done I was number five. I didn't move, I just got moved down by these others coming and now I was number five. When the president came over he started down the line with someone saying, "This is Colonel Coffer of the Georgia State Patrol. He provided a lot of troopers for us and covered all our roadways and blocked the roads for us, Mr. President." The president said, "Colonel, I really appreciate you coming out today and I really appreciate your help." Next he was introduced to Colonel Coffer, "I'm glad to meet you Mr. Copeland." They said some flowery words about all Colonel Coffer had done then he said, "This is Sheriff Talton." Once again the President said, "Glad to meet you, Sheriff." Sheriff Talton said, "Glad to meet you, Mr. President."

I was at the end of the line thinking, the whole world is caving in. The gold standard has stopped. The stock market is in a spin. And here the most powerful man in the world is going to be introduced to you in about ten seconds and what are you going to say? Here is Sheriff Ray Wilkes. He came out and helped us. Thank you so much. We really appreciate it. To which I would respond, thank you, Mr. President? I asked myself, is that the way it's going to go down? I quickly determined not.

The president finally appeared in front of me. We went through the routine of the agent doing the introductions then I said, "I'm glad to meet you, President Nixon. May I speak?" He looked a little shocked then responded, "Please do." I began, "Listen, the people who are out to destroy you are going to do it if this country is standing knee deep in ashes. You've got to fight and stop this some way. It isn't right, sir." I said a few other things then he asked, "What did you say your name was?" I told him my name once again. He stopped the whole show to stand there and converse with just me. I think if I had told him at that point you need one friend who you can count on so you will never have to watch your back and I will be that man, take me back to Washington, he would have put me on Air Force One and taken me with him. Everyone else he had met was interested in meeting them for themselves. I had told him, "They're out to destroy you. They don't care about this. It's political." And it was political. I think if I had asked him to take me with him he would have done it because he didn't trust anyone.

═══════CHAPTER 112═══════

A friend of mine, Neal Holton, was asked to pick Jimmy Carter up at the airport when he was running for Lieutenant Governor. Neal, in turn, got Gostin Freeney to go to the airport and then show Jimmy Carter around town. When Carter came through town a second time Neal leaned on Gostin again to pick him up. When the campaign got hotter Neal went back to him and said, "Gostin, he's going to have to be picked up again." Gostin immediately replied, "Get somebody else to pick him up. H---, that man can't even talk."

Jimmy had a way of talking that was quite unusual. He didn't have a natural flowing speaking rhythm and he stammered as he went along. Gostin Freeney, on the other hand, was an announcer for television and radio with a beautiful voice. He recognized quality in voice quickly. He declared Jimmy Carter couldn't talk.

At that time Jimmy was trying to get elected Lieutenant Governor but he lost the race. Later I was with Jimmy Carter again along with Don King. Phil Walden was also with us at Lakeside Park. Jimmy talked to me just like he always did.

Several years ago when Jimmy was in early politics he asked Fred Hasty if he would handle his campaign in Bibb County. Fred looked it over and said, "No. I can't do that. I'm not going to do it." When Jimmy got to be Governor of Georgia Fred could have shot himself. There was a vacancy for District Attorney and Fred wanted a chance at it but he had not helped Jimmy Carter with his campaign. Jimmy never forgot it. He's got an incredible memory of anything that goes wrong.

I talked to Jimmy on behalf of Fred Hasty and Jimmy Carter told me, "I wouldn't appoint Fred Hasty as dog catcher." I let the remark slide and said, "Well, I want you to look at someone else. He's just left office. It's Tyler Evans. He's a fine young man and he's a fierce solicitor. He is a serious and dedicated prosecutor. He would make an outstanding District Attorney." Jimmy told me to ask him to come for an interview.

I just knew Tyler would be thrilled about the opportunity. I went to Tyler and told him Jimmy Carter requested to see him about the position and Tyler said, "Ray, if you had asked me two weeks ago I would have jumped at it but I've made commitments to Baxter, my brother, and I can't break them." I had to go back to Jimmy Carter and tell him Tyler wouldn't be able to take the position.

I then told President Carter about another man who was a good friend of mine, Walker Johnson. Walker wasn't a show horse. I told Jimmy, "He's been a former assistant district attorney. He has worked for the United States Department of Justice and he's worked for the assistant district attorney and he's the newest assistant we've got." Jimmy Carter said, "Tell him I want to talk to him."

Walker called Governor Carter and was subsequently appointed District Attorney. Then Walker later got appointed judge of Superior Court, a position he held until his death.

Jimmy Carter was an easy fellow to get along with. We shared mutual friends. Many people don't know it but when Jimmy Carter was president he would stop in Macon unexpectedly and go into Phil Walden's office to talk to him. When Jimmy was running for president he ran out of money. Phil Walden convinced the Allman Brothers to do concerts with a part of every ticket being a contribution to Carter's campaign. There were $40 tickets and $50 tickets. For every dollar Jimmy raised he received two dollars of Federal money. Jimmy Carter never forgot about his friends helping him.

I met Jimmy Carter in the governor's office during his tenure as governor. The Sheriff Association was trying to get a bill passed allowing law enforcement officers' children an education in state institutions if the officer was killed in the line of duty, which was passed. We were having a reception for the legislature where Jimmy was in attendance.

The other occasions that I met Jimmy were just like the day he stopped for the emergency. When he got out of there he stopped at the grease rack and came over to me and we talked for a few minutes. I asked him how the family was doing, down home talk, that's all. He was very cordial. I never found him to be a person whose position went to his head, demanding some of the things that Johnson was accused of and of being a hard man to work for. My relationship with Jimmy Carter was good.

I never had occasion to meet Billy Carter. I saw him on television and that was enough. I met Rosalyn Carter one day at Central City Park. Amy was scheduled to be in attendance also. I don't remember what the occasion was but Secret Service was covering her. Amy was to meet her parents there and when she didn't show up Rosalyn began to get upset. Amy wasn't too easy to handle in those days. She finally arrived late. Her hair was parted directly in the center of her head; one part was black and the other part was red. I thought, great Scott. That was the family. Rosalyn was very cordial and very lady-like even when her daughter showed up looking strange.

Whenever President Carter came home to Georgia for a visit he flew directly into Plains. We never had to be of assistance unless he came to Macon for some special occasion.

CHAPTER 113

I also had the privilege of meeting President Reagan. He did not come to Georgia a lot but when he did, it was generally to Atlanta. I was at Air Force One when he landed in Macon on one occasion. I was also with him while he was speaking here. I was asked if I wanted to have my picture taken with the president. I told them I sure would like to. I said, "Mr. President, you're shaking hands with a Democratic sheriff who's doing all he can for a Republican president." He chuckled and said, "Keep it up. Keep it up." I never had opportunity to meet or be near President Reagan any other time.

I also met Nancy Reagan while she was in Macon with the president. She's a tiny little thing—very petite and pretty. I had my picture taken with her also. Secret Service told me they had a bullet proof vest to protect her but it was so heavy she couldn't wear it. They put the protective gear into a London Fog coat. An agent followed her with the coat on his arm and in the event that anything looked out of order he placed the coat around her shoulders then removed her from the crowd as quickly as he could. I'm sure the coat must have weighed 30 or 40 pounds.

CHAPTER 114

One of the most impressive men I have met is George Bush, the father of our current President, George W. Bush. I met him when he was vice president during a time he came to Macon. George Israel and I walked over to his limousine and we were introduced. He shook hands with me and he thanked me. I walked back to the Dempsey corner and he got out of the car, coming over to where I was standing. He said, "Sheriff, I want to thank you again for coming out here today. That really means a lot." He made a few other remarks as we stood there briefly chatting until it was time for him to leave. I thought, you know, that's really the quality of a man. He had met me once and paid me all of the respect I deserve and more. Then he gets out of the car to come do it again. I thought very highly of him. I have never met the young President Bush.

CHAPTER 115

I never had the opportunity to meet President Ford. Sara Jane Moore had tried to kill him at the Saint Francis Hotel. I stayed at that hotel and then I walked through the park in Sacramento where Lynette "Squeaky" Fromme had tried to assassinate him three weeks earlier. President Ford and I never crossed paths. From what I understand he was so dedicated to doing a good job he really didn't travel a lot. He stayed in his White House office and, before that, in Congress, a good bit of the time.

═══════CHAPTER 116═══════

When President Clinton came to Macon I was with my friend, Buster Williams, who was a Secret Service agent. Another agent was present and Buster said to him, "This will be the last detail Sheriff Wilkes is going to be on. He will be retiring in December." The agent said, "Really. How long have you been in office?" I told him I had been in the same office 40 years but I had only been Sheriff for 16 years and three months. He said, "40 years?" I replied, "That's right."

When we got to the airport this agent said, "I want you to meet President Clinton." After the president's formalities he began to walk in my direction and I walked towards him. We shook hands and the agent said, "This will be Sheriff Wilkes last detail, President Clinton. He's retiring. He has 40 years of public service." President Clinton, "I'm glad to meet you, Sheriff." We parted and got in the motorcade. When it was time for him to leave he was having group pictures made with Macon Police Department with different people who had participated and with some of the Democratic leadership. They were taking pictures with the president in groups of five or six.

The car I was in was parked perpendicular to the aircraft he would board. The plane could not be side-swiped and kill the president because my car would have to be hit first. There was a path he could walk in security. Buster Williams had the lead and he said, "Just stand right here and I'll see you later." I said okay and he left. I was standing alone when President Clinton finished the group pictures. He began walking towards me and I thought, I wonder where he's going now. The closer he got I could see he was coming directly to me. He stepped in front of me extending his hand. He grasped my handshake with his free hand and said, "Sheriff, there are a lot of people who will never appreciate 40 years of public service, which is a long time, but here's one who does. Let's have some pictures made." He was a charmer. He knew how to talk.

Within a few seconds a fellow came rolling up with a Roloflex camera, loading it with film. I knew enough about cameras to know that you opened it to load the film but that you couldn't take a picture with it open. I looked at President Clinton and said, "He hasn't got any film." He said, "Aw, he'll get some in a few minutes." The president was standing there with his arm over my shoulder. I realized then how tall he was. I'm sure he was at least six feet, four inches tall. We had pictures taken with his arm around my shoulder. Later I received four photographs from Washington. I didn't always agree with him but you had to give him an "A" for his charisma. He had nothing to gain coming over to me. His actions were very sincere.

CHAPTER 117

Early in my career I met Carl Vinson in Washington. I was later called back to Washington about two years before I decided to retire. I was slated to attend a protection school, learning how to protect dignitaries. At the school they covered every president, beginning with Andrew Jackson, when an attempt on his life was made. Jackson had walked over to the Congress to lobby for something. A fellow known as an office seeker wanted a job and Andrew Jackson had not obliged him. The fellow pulled out a cap and ball pistol; a cap and ball required you to pack it. He drew his pistol, pointing it at Andrew Jackson's head, and pulled the trigger but it didn't fire. The fellow pulled a second pistol out but it didn't fire either. There was no such thing as Secret Service in those days. The story goes that Andrew Jackson had a cane and one of the most disgraceful things to happen to a man was to be horse-whipped with a cane on the courthouse porch. It is told they had to pull Andrew Jackson off the man.

The school was extremely interesting. Part of the training is practice runs of different scenarios. One day we were told there would be a practice run for the security of the president. We were to be placed in a crowd but there would be some surprises. We were standing there waiting when along came the escort. The escort has the motorcade in the front. It has the motorcycles and Secret Service agents tht cover each corner of the car so all four corners are protected. Once the surroundings are secured they open the door.

When they opened the door, a young man who was about 25 years old stepped out of the car, wearing blue jeans. He started waving so of course we clapped for the president. He shook hands as he walked in the direction of the podium, working the crowds like the president does. When he stepped up to the podium people were still clapping. He held his hands up to begin a prepared speech.

He started speaking, "Law enforcement is the most underpaid organization." Of course, we gave him a big clap. He went on with his speech, then all of a sudden somebody shouted, "GUN!" There was a disturbance at one side. The agents had thrown a man who was posing as a gunman to the ground. While all the ruckus is going on they grab this young man posing as president and try to get him covered. When they do, a second gun comes out. They then grabbed him and threw him into the limousine. The car speeds away. I thought it was really interesting. They run those scenarios over and over and over. And they learn the slogan "Fight or Flee." A wise man knows which to choose.

Reagan was shot by John Hinckley as he was leaving a speaking engagement at the Washington, D.C. Hilton Hotel. Three others were wounded at the same time. When Hinckley began shooting the agent grabbed the President and shoved him into the back of the limousine. Without any fanfare it sped away, going to 1600 Pennsylvania Avenue, led by two Washington motorcycle officers. In communications they told them where to go. There were two agents behind them. All the other agents were on the ground with Hinckley. The agent in the back seat with the president asked, "Mr. President, did I hurt you when I threw you in the car?" The President responded, "I think you hurt my rib cage when I hit the middle of the car there but I'm all right." As the president was trying to sit up the agent looked at him and saw sputum at the edge of his mouth with blood in it. The agent said, "Washington Memorial Hospital, quick. We've got the president. He's been shot. Get somebody standing by to wait on him." Ironically, that very morning there was an important meeting at the hospital. All medical personnel with admission privileges were required to be at the meeting unless they had an extremely good excuse. This included all doctors and surgeons. When the president arrived at the hospital all the doctors were already there because of the meeting, so the president received immediate medical attention. He did not have to wait for anyone to be called in. The blood in the sputum indicated the lung had been punctured. I read later the president was told there was a surgeon present and he was going to take care of him. The president said, "I sure hope he's a Republican." Even at death's door he still had a wit.

CHAPTER 118

During one of my trips to Washington we were taken to the Oval Office. The president was not there, but we were allowed to go in and look. There were dogs in the parking lots. There were officers with mirrors checking under cars. They had a radioactive instrument used for checking. I asked someone, "What is he looking for?" I was told, "If someone had a piece of radioactive material the size of the end of my finger and they planted it in the back right there at the window where the president sits with his back to the window he would gradually become sick and no one would know what was wrong. The only symptom would be that he was being exposed to radioactive material and it would be coming from his own office. Putting it there is a very real possibility." Everything on the lot was checked and rechecked. Sweeping for radioactive material was done continually as a protection of the president.

After Pearl and I left the Oval Office we had an opportunity to have lunch with the staff of the White House in the dining room. So I've eaten at the White House and I've eaten in the jail house. Both ways have been good.

CHAPTER 119

I have also met Lester Maddox. Mr. Maddox was a devout Christian man but he had some crazy ideas too. The problem I ran into was when the Grand Jury was in session. The first X rated movie coming to Macon was "The Vixen," to be shown at a local drive in theater. I'm told "The Vixen" was made in Canada for $60,000. It had nude scenes in it. The Grand Jury was demanding something be done about it.

Fred Hasty came to me saying we had to do something. He thought we needed to have it shut it down due to some research in the law he had done. We went out to the drive-in and waited until the particular scene came on the screen. We went into the little office and told them they were under arrest. We made them take it off the list and we seized the film. Within a short time they made bond.

I thought that would be the end of it until one day we were served papers. They slapped a lawsuit on me. Well, the county didn't say anything. The suit wasn't against them. It was against me. I was served a lawsuit for $40,000 or $50,000. The amount was so far out of my concept. If I sold everything in the world I owned I would have only been making a down payment on it.

Fred Hasty called down to the County Attorney's office asking them to furnish us a lawyer. They wouldn't do it because the suit wasn't against them. So we didn't have a lawyer. That was the final word: it's not against us and we only furnish lawyers when it's against the county. I had no idea what I was going to do.

We decided to go to Atlanta to see Governor Maddox. Tully Bond, who had been a lawyer in Macon, was now working in the governor's office. Tommy Irvin was the governor's executive secretary. Tully Bond, Fred Hasty and Oliver Bateman went with us to see Governor Maddox.

When we entered the governor's office Lester was in there with a face as red as a fox's tail. Someone explained the problem to him; Irvin said, "Governor, it's one of those things where they're trying to enforce a law. It's like segregation. You can't enforce that." Oliver Bateman spoke up, "No. It's not like that." Then Fred spoke up. Finally Lester said, "We're going to furnish them a lawyer." So the Attorney General represented us.

As it turned out we gave them back the film but they promised not to show the film any more. They dropped the lawsuit. I didn't live happily ever after but I did get through the lawsuit.

That was Lester Maddox but I always liked him. He was easy to get along with. He was a common man and an extrovert. He loved to do things to get the crowd. When he was running for governor I was told he had an older model station wagon loaded with signs and a ladder. He would climb a tree and put "Maddox Country" signs everywhere. They were putting those signs all over South Georgia.

He often visited civic clubs at their lunch meetings where he would make some remarks and eat lunch. Then on the way back to Atlanta they would stop all along the road posting the signs. He had a one-horse operation in Atlanta. After a long day of nailing up his own signs he opened his own mail then went to bed. He didn't have staff working for him like so many others did.

CHAPTER 120

Everyone in our country has heard of the event called Woodstock. What most have never heard of, even those within our own town, is the Byron Pop Festival. I had just returned from the FBI Academy traveling through Atlanta when I saw a music festival was coming to our area. I talked to the colonel of the state patrol and the commander of the GBI. Both gave me the same advice, "Ray, if there is any way you can stop it then by all means do so. Anyway you can, stop it."

As soon as I was back in Macon I began trying to get the word about the festival coming here. The newspapers did not care at all. They had freedom of assembly and freedom of speech and all those kinds of things. I could not believe the response of people. It was beyond my comprehension why anyone would want that type of event coming here to our own backyard. No one realized just how this would impact our town.

When I saw no help was to be found on the local level I attempted to ask the governor to intervene. There were no laws on the book to stop the event from happening. The Rotary Club wanted to hold a debate between me and the man sponsoring the festival at a Rotary Club meeting. Alex Cooley and a fellow named Brian, who was an Associate Professor at Georgia State, are the ones who pulled it together. I did all I could to fight the festival happening. When I got no support from the newspaper, Jimmy Bloodworth said to lay off of the whole situation because of all the controversy.

I was on the drug council at that time. I heard through my connections with the council that Dr. Bobby Donner, a friend and pathologist, would be setting up a health clinic at the festival site to help those people who might overdose on drugs. When I finally realized there was no way to stop the event I went out on my own, hiring a fellow who had a week's vacation. I asked him to go to Byron and film the events with a 16 millimeter camera. I paid for the purchase of the 16 millimeter film and getting the film developed. I also gave him $100 for his time and labor but he had a good time too. He told me people would approach him while he was filming to ask where he was from. He would tell them BBC. I was surprised to learn BBC was actually there too.

All the top names in rock and roll had come. As the festival actually began the only thing legally we could really do was set up a perimeter at the Bibb County line. The actual land the festival-goers were using was in Peach County but the Bibb County line was in very close proximity. When they came into Bibb County and violated the law we put them in jail. One day I was at the area and I spoke with a girl standing there just like she came into this world—completely naked. The sun was shining. People were walking all around and here she stood in her birthday suit. I said, "Can I ask you a question?" She said, "Sure." She spoke very politely and with good diction. I asked, "Where are you supposed to be right now?" She answered completely honestly, "I'm supposed to be in some part of Texas taking my final exams for the semester." I stared incredulously at her and said, "You walked out on your final exams after spending a whole semester working on your courses to come here?" She said, "That's right."

I could not even fathom the mentality of someone who could do something so irresponsible. I'm sure this young lady had parents somewhere who were utterly heartbroken. Sometimes I would ask one of the kids where they were from. Ocassionally they would tell me but many times they would not.

Right before the festival started I went to see Virgil Shepherd. He owned a big old colonial home in Byron adjacent to the site the festival-goers were to use. The house was fenced in but I knew a fence would not keep anyone out who wanted to go in. I said,

"Virgil, we're going to have to do something. We need to stop this thing." Virgil said, "Ray, Brown is promoting this thing and he's one of the best friends I've got. My furnace went out in the dead of winter and he came out and fixed it. I can't do that."

I really couldn't believe he would actually want all this going on right in his own backyard. I asked, "What are you going to do when they come on your property?" He answered, "You see that bull right yonder?" I said, "Yeah." Virgil said, "He will take care of everything." I still didn't believe he thought it would be as easy as that. I said, "You take a good look at that bull because it's probably the last time you'll see him alive. They'll eat him, horns, hooves, and all. They'll eat everything about that bull. There are so many people they're like locusts." He said, "No. No. No." I could not convince him any differently.

We did many hours of filming to have a documentary of all the events happening in Byron. Oliver Bateman took the newspaper editor, Bill Ott, and someone else out there one day. As they were getting out of the car they saw a guy with a cord around his arm and someone was giving him a shot of heroin. Bill Ott's eyes could not have gotten any larger.

As they walked through, that scene was to be repeated over and over again everywhere they went.

One morning while I was out there I saw a beautiful girl near the long row of portajohns they had lined up. She opened the door, closed the door, opened the door, closed the door, opened the door, and closed the door. I thought, what in the world is she looking for? I walked over there and opened the door she had opened. The odor would gag a maggot. Human feces was piled up 12 to 15 inches, not in the hole but still on the bench. There wasn't anything you could do but use a fire hose on them. They had 100 portables out there and those didn't even scratch the surface.

People would just use Virgil's place whenever they needed to go to the restroom. When they wanted sex they just laid around out there in his grass. Virgil's wife had a nervous breakdown around that time. The festival goers drained all the water out of his well. Virgil was ready to leave until the whole thing was over but he had to stay there to protect his house and belongings.

When they finally left Virgil told me he had never seen anything in his whole life to equal what he had just experienced. He had a trailer he pulled behind his tractor. The day I spoke with him he was pulling trailer loads of trash, debris, and crap, and all that kind of stuff off his property. He said, "I've hauled 47 loads and I haven't cleaned it all up yet."

They didn't eat his bull. I never saw it again but I wouldn't have put it past them. I know they would have done anything. All they were serving out there was brown rice and maybe some bread. I'm not sure Virgil ever completely recovered from having people do so much damage to his property.

The crowd migrated toward Vinson Valley in south Bibb County. The man who owned the place had five men with shotguns positioned on his property. The crowds just went over the top of the fence pushing it all the way down to the ground. There were so many people the men were not able to fire a shot. Festival attendees swarmed the entire place, going into the swimming pool. When they left the swimming pool was completely void of water.

After all was said and done and the festival was over Jimmy Bloodworth received a call from Mississippi. The same festival was planning to hold another shindig but this time it was to be held in Hattiesburg, Mississippi. The officials there were requesting I call them. They wanted me to go to Mississippi and speak to the Sovereign Commission. I was told they would pay all my travel expenses plus food and hotel while there, in addition to an honorarium of $100 a day. I didn't make $100 a day so I thought that was pretty classy.

I did go to Mississippi to speak to the Sovereign Commission. The meetings were to be held a big amphitheater. I really had no idea who the Sovereign Commission was so upon my arrival

I was expecting to be attending a rather small meeting in some conference room.

When I saw the size of the amphitheater I began to wonder what this was really all about and just how many people I would actually be speaking to. I asked the plain clothes officer who they had assigned to me who this Sovereign Commission consisted of. The officer said, "Sir, the Sovereign Commission is made up of everybody who is anybody in the state of Mississippi. Here comes the lieutenant governor and his staff. That man sitting in the back is the FBI agent in charge of the state of Mississippi. The general sitting next to him is the General of the Reserves. The general over there is the General of the National Guard." I thought, great Scott, what have I gotten into? All these people and here I am, little chief deputy sheriff of Bibb County, speaking to all these high ranking officials. The officer continued, "The governor and his staff are coming in now." I began to mentally rehearse the topics I had prepared, making sure I kept everything factual. I had brought the film with me also to show the reality of my words and give them a visual image of just how severe the situation really was.

I was introduced and then the film began to be shown. I narrated the film, trying to give details of what was going on. When we finished a fellow stood up and said, "Governor, I think we should call the National Guard out." The governor said, "I'll let General so and so respond to that statement." The governor turned to the general, giving him the floor to speak and the general said, "The National Guard is budgeted so much money for training. By the time this festival is slated to arrive here the training money will have been spent. You would have to supplement three million dollars a day to keep the National Guard in the field." Then he sat down. Another man stood up with a different idea of how to stop the festival. This time the governor let the adjunctant general respond. Then a little thin fellow with a red face and thin red hair said, "Governor, I believe I know the people of Hattiesburg, Mississippi about as well as anyone in here and there's enough d--- dynamite in Hattiesburg, Mississippi, to blow this d--- thing off the map." I said to the officer next to me, "Great Scott, who is he? The sheriff?" The officer said, "That's the district attorney."

They paid me to come to Mississippi to speak to this group and they paid me to go to court for them. Mississippi was able to thwart the efforts of the festival so it would not be held in their state. It was later held in New Orleans. I was glad my work on the film and documentation of all the happenings in Byron were able to help the state of Mississippi keep the festival from coming to any of their towns. It was a great reward for me after seeing all the destruction so close to home with none of my own state officials taking me seriously before the festival began.

The film I made belonged to me. I took it to the state capitol and showed it to a senate sub-committee. I showed it to the governor and the floor leaders. Because of that film, we now have a law which says you can't hold a gathering unless you provide so many portable toilets per 100 people at any given function. There must be so much medical personnel per 100 people. We never had another festival after this but it really left its mark on the city of Byron and Bibb County as well. I was extremely satisfied with the film. I was glad for the documentation and I still own the film to this day. We had provided evidence with this film that resulted in a law being passed, prohibiting this kind of event in the future.

There is a bright side story to this whole thing. I was driving out Gray Highway one day when I got a call on my radio. The dispatcher asked if I could go to a pay phone then call back with the number of the phone. He continued, saying I had a call coming in from England and he would get the call transferred to the pay phone for me. I said, England? Great day. I whipped into Shoney's and called my office to give them the number. Within a few seconds the phone rang. Well, the man I was speaking to had been to Macon.

There was a big event celebrating the music of Jimi Hendrix and a man who was working with the Jimi Hendrix Foundation had come to town. While in Macon he had visited WMAZ and Dodie Cantrell showed him the film I had made of the Byron Pop Festival. I had given WMAZ a copy of the film to keep in their archives for future reports. After introducing himself he told me he would like to see the film. I called Dodie and she acknowledged the man had inquired of her about the film and he indeed did want to use it. Dodie would not let him have it without my consent, telling him the film didn't belong to WMAZ, but to me. She told me, "They'll pay you to use the film." I asked Dodie, "How much?" She said, "I don't know but they'll pay good for it." When he called and asked if I would let him use the film I told him I would send it to him.

I sent the film to England where he cleaned it, eliminating the scratches and making the places we had put it together smooth. Then he sent me a cassette of what Jimmy Hendrix used as part of the anniversary and how it was celebrated. He said, "You can count. We only used five minutes and you can count the five minutes as you see them. We're telling you the truth. We'll pay you the going price, $1000 a minute." I said, "I'll tell you what. I'll give you a price. You give me $10,000 and I'll give you the whole shooting match." He would not accept my offer, "No. I'll give you $5000." So he did. He told me I was really a gentleman, sending it to him like I said I would. I had about 30 still pictures, the whole film, and several other pieces of memorabilia I had collected from the festival.

Jimmy Hendrix and the Allman Brothers had been in attendance at the Byron Pop Festival. There were many other rock groups but I can't remember who they were. The $5000 I received from sending the film to England was about a half year's wages for me. I was very glad I had taken the time and spent the $100 to have the film made in the first place. I bought Dodie Cantrell a $5 gold piece with a chain and gave it to her. I gave the girls in the office $100 each for all their help to me.

CHAPTER 121

The Allman Brothers were managed by Phil Walden. Phil and
I got along very well. He seemed to respect my position. I
helped him when one of his people had gotten into a fracas. His
father came in to see me. Otis Redding had shot Katie McGhee's
son. Mr. Walden, Sr. told me of the situation with Otis and how Otis
was out on bond. They were binding him over to Superior Court
but he had to be fingerprinted and photographed. Mr. Walden told
me that he had a plane sitting at Wilson Airport ready to go to New
York, where Otis was opening in New York that night at a club's first
opening. Mr. Walden felt if Otis did well at this club his career would
skyrocket. Mr. Walden said, "He's got to be there tonight." I told
him I would take him first and we were able to rush him through,
getting him to the airport right on time.

Later we had a riot in the jail. Twiggs Lyndon, who was road
manager for the Allman Brothers, approached Phil and said, "The
prisoners don't have anything to do all day. It's easy to see how riots
can happen. We ought to buy them some televisions."

So Twiggs Lyndon and the Allman Brothers came to me saying
they wanted to give $5000 towards building racks in the jail and put
televisions in. I thought it was a great idea. It was a bad jail, at that
time located in the courthouse. There was no ventilation so it was
hot in the summer and cold in the winter. I found someone to build
the racks and install the televisions. The Allman Brothers and I met
to do a press release about their donation of the televisions. They
were all together then, and were always appreciative of what I did to
support them. So many people said 'no' to them.

When they gave us $5000 I asked a Lutheran priest to accompany
me to the bank to open an account in the name of the "Bibb County

Jail Prisoner Relief Fund." It required his signature and mine. The priest came to the jail everyday so he knew first hand of the conditions there and the morale of the men. He thought the television idea was good also.

Judge Stevens was a member of the Elks Club. After they had played cards with a deck about three times they would throw the deck away so no one could recognize bends and alterations to the cards. Judge Stevens would bring the cards to the jail, and this gave the prisoners a little something to do, but they could not occupy themselves all day with card playing. The televisions still didn't change the structure of the building. The members of the Allman Brothers Band and Phil were very fond of me.

CHAPTER 122

Roy Dale Billingslea was probably one of the most dangerous criminals ever to be in this area. Roy Dale, along with two accomplices, robbed the Sears Roebuck store. They were in the office when a Wells Fargo truck came in. It has not been determined how the hold-up started but a Wells Fargo employee was present. It is assumed he reached for his gun and was then killed.

There was another murder at the Ramada Inn, where a Cuban exile was employed. The Cuban spoke only enough English to get by. Roy Dale and his men came in carrying a sawed off shotgun. It scared the poor man so badly he resorted to speaking in Spanish. I think it frustrated Roy Dale so they just killed the Cuban man. Roy Dale went to prison for 20 years. While in prison he was given no good time and no early out.

I was notified by the State Prison Parole Board that Roy Dale was going to be released. I called the Parole Board and everyone else I knew telling them how dangerous this man was. They called me back saying, "Ray, there's nothing we can do. He served his 20 years. He's finished. We've got to release him." They held him an extra two weeks while I was trying to stop his release. I'm sure he didn't have any love for me for making him stay in prison two weeks longer.

During my tenure as sheriff I had always maintained an open door policy. Anyone wanting to see me could come to my office. I never denied anyone. I didn't ask for names unless they volunteered the information. Mrs. Jones walked in my office one day and said, "There's a man out here to see you. His name is Roy Dale Billingslea." I said, "Really? Tell him to come on in." I checked my top drawer making sure I had my .38 lying in there. When he came in he asked, "Do you mind if I shut the door?" I said, "No. Go right ahead." He closed the door behind him. His next statement stunned me. He said, "Sheriff, I'm a changed man." He stuck his hand over the desk and shook my hand. He said, "I've served my time. I'm an expert welder. I've taken every welding course they had. I sure would appreciate it if you would help me get a job." I listened to him and we talked a few minutes. When we finished I walked to the door with him.

The sight I saw as I opened the door astounded me. Jerry Modena and whole SWAT team were standing just outside my door. They were waiting for the word to blow him out. Roy Dale left Macon and went to New Jersey. He killed someone there and he is in prison for that crime.

CHAPTER 123

Jimmy Waters asked me one day if I would drive to Atlanta
to pick up Colonel Jim Irving at the airport and bring him to
Macon. Jim was a Christian astronaut, the third man to walk on
the moon. Colonel Irving was scheduled to speak at Mabel White
Baptist Church and it would be broadcast on television. I told him I
would be honored to do the favor for him. I took the pastor's son-in-
law Richard Green, the pastor's son Jimmy Jr., and my son Ray, Jr.
with me to Atlanta. I wasn't too familiar with the Atlanta airport.

I was sweating. One wrong turn on the Atlanta interstate system
and you end up in Eastpoint or on I-85 north. I called the police
in Atlanta telling them who I was and who I was meeting. When
I asked them to escort me to Interstate 75 they gladly obliged. A
police car met me and I followed him to the correct terminal to
await the flight coming in. We were waiting directly in front of a
door in a no parking zone. Of course, his plane was late so we had
a little wait.

He finally arrived with his bag. We made introductions and he
sat in the front seat next to me. I introduced him to the others in the
car but he really didn't say very much. He was polite but extremely
quiet. Within a few seconds the siren on the police car in front of us
began to wail and we took off. He had a look on his face that said,
'why the police escort' so I said, "I wanted to make sure we got to
Interstate 75 South without any problems." That seemed to answer
his unspoken question.

As we traveled on I-75 South I was going in excess of 80 to
85 miles an hour because we were running late. I knew what time
Brother Waters was expecting him at the church so I was kicking it
in the pants. We got to Macon and he said, "Take me to the hotel.

I'm going to stop there for a minute. I've got to take a bath." I said, "A bath? You don't have time for a bath. Your plane was late and they're expecting you at the church." He didn't blink an eye but cool as a cucumber he said, "Oh, it will be all right." He checked into his hotel and took his bath.

When he came back down I drove him on to Mabel White. As soon as we walked in the door Jimmy Waters was waving him in. When Jim Irving walked in everyone gave him a standing ovation. When the clapping died down Colonel Irving said, "As you know, I was the third man to walk on the moon. Going to the moon is the fastest travel you can ever do other than the trip I just took coming from the Atlanta airport today." I did a double take and chuckled. He continued, "Sheriff Wilkes brought me from Atlanta to Macon almost at the same speed you can go to the moon."

I was spent about an hour and a half or two hours with him, and it was obvious that he was a devout Christian. Later he contracted with National Geographic to take part in photographs of the search for Noah's Ark or the evidence of it. He spent a lot of time in Turkey and along the borders of a few other countries looking for Noah's Ark. He was one of the nicest guys I ever met.

CHAPTER 124

When I became sheriff I never realized the many different people I would meet. I knew Senator Talmadge when he was elected. We had been on a security detail together at an earlier time. He had always been very nice and cordial to me. From all evidence Senator Talmadge was a gentleman. James Whitmore, the movie star, was in the area making a film and his producers wanted Mr. Whitmore to meet Herman Talmadge. Senator Talmadge had been in the U.S. Navy. I made the arrangements for them to meet. They talked together for quite some time, all the while the Senator was very cordial to Mr. Whitmore.

At one point Mr. Whitmore told Senator Talmadge, "When Adlai Stevenson ran, you were a Democratic Governor. He came to the mansion for a conference with you. The next morning you both walked out for a press conference and some of the slick New York boys said, 'Well, Governor Talmadge, you've been with Governor Stevenson all this time and we're sure you've been talking to each other. Right now what I'd like to know is, do you agree with him?'" Herman Talmadge said, "I met Governor Stevenson and we did talk for hours. We have found out we agree on some things and we disagree on other things. One thing is for certain though, we agree on more things than we disagree on." I thought that was one of the best answers anyone could have given to a question like that.

Jack Flynt, from Griffin, Georgia, was a good friend of mine. He represented the 6th Congressional District. Dwayne Gilbert, who became a U.S. Marshall, initially introduced us. The first time I met Jack was when he picked Dwayne and me up at the airport, and took us to his house for dinner that evening. We became very good friends. He was person I could always count on when something needed to be done.

The first time I ever saw Ernest Vandiver occurred when I went to Atlanta with Ollie Perry and Robert Perry, who were lobbying for brick trucks. Their argument was that they weighed their bricks on fair bank scales, which are the most accurate scales for tonnage. But when the State Highway Department weighed them they jacked a little thing under two wheels and the weight came up differently. That was improper because if your weight was correct when you left the yard and you were certified as having the correct amount of loads, you shouldn't have to be weighed again with a Mickey Mouse set of scales that say you're overweight. If they found you to be overweight you had to pay a fine.

I went to Atlanta with my two friends and we spoke to Ernest Vandiver about it. He had a suite in one of the big hotels in Atlanta. Mr. Vandiver told a story of how someone had come in the room next door and said, "Who in the h--- has been in my room? What's all these d--- clothes in here?" Ernie Vandiver said, "I'm terribly sorry. I thought we had been given the double room. I'm Ernest Vandiver and I'm running for governor. I'll be glad to get you to wherever you want." The man said, "Oh, no, Governor. You don't have any problems with me. Just make yourself at home. You don't have any problems with me." When the man realized who he was talking to he changed his tone of voice very quickly.

Mr. Vandiver was an extremely nice man. He said to me, "Ray, I want you to meet the strongest supporter I've got." I looked over and there was Paul Anderson in Governor Vandiver's room. Governor Vandiver was from the Toccoa area so he knew Paul. I had a chance to talk to Paul while the Perrys did their business with Mr. Vandiver. Paul told me when he started out he used auto parts like chassis, wheels, and axles to make his weights. He told me how he finally made the Olympics and went to Russia and was in a stadium packed full of people. The Russian competitor bent down and lifted, over his head, the most weight that had ever been lifted by a man, then dropped them down. His coaches came to him and said, "We do not want to embarrass you. You don't have to go on. He's already won. He's already lifted more than anyone." Paul said, "I think I ought to have a chance." So he walked out there and took the bar the man had just lifted and added more weight to it. He reached down, grabbing the bar, and then lifted it to his chest. After a few seconds he lifted it over his head. He held it for the required time then dropped the bar. Then he just stood there. Nobody said anything. He said, "I did more than he did and no one even applauded." He continued, "Then it was like a bust of thunder. The people shouted I had picked up the bar like it was a match stick." He won the World Championship, the strongest man in the world. That's where I met Paul and we became friends after that.

Governor Carl Sanders was a fine fellow. Carl was from Augusta, a handsome guy and very articulate. He always knew what he was doing. I did not have any real strong contact with Carl Sanders, but we knew each other. He made me a member of his staff. We were not close friends but I did know Mr. Sanders.

Peyton Anderson was the owner of the Macon Telegraph and News. He was a very wealthy fellow. If he couldn't see something visible to put his money in then he didn't do it. I had several encounters with Peyton and I was probably one of the few people in Macon, Georgia, who could pick up the telephone and say, "Peyton, we're having lunch over here at the jail today and we're having such and so and I thought you might want to come."

One such time when I called him he said, "Ray, I'm going down to Dunlap's. I'm getting my car fitted with a gas tank large enough to hold enough gas so I can drive all the way to West Palm Beach. As soon as I leave there I'll come over there and we'll have lunch." And so he did. Every time I met him Peyton would say, "What do you need?" and I would say, "Nothing." Then one year he sent me a check for $500. I wrote him a letter thanking him for the money and sent it back, telling him I didn't need it. I said, "We're making out fine without it." A few days later he telephoned me and said, "Take that money. It won't be long before somebody will be on your doorsteps needing some help and you won't have the means to be able to help them." I said, "Peyton, I would take it if we needed it but we don't need it." As he hung up the phone he said, "That's the first d--- check I've ever gotten back." When he died he left over $25 million dollars to establish a foundation. The last I heard there was $100 million dollars in there. Peyton didn't like to fund anything unless there were some matching funds. He wanted someone else to have an interest also.

Peyton was a very smart man but he wasn't someone you could push around. He was actually a common man. I walked into his office one day and I said, "Peyton, that's a nice looking coat there." He stood up and said, "This is a regular and I wear a long but I got it at such a good price I don't care whether it's a long or a regular." He watched his dollars. I think we became good friends when I put a stop to the stalking of one his family members. He never forgot my help.

Another person I highly admire is Zell Miller. Zell called me and said, "Sheriff, I want you to do something for me." I said, "All right. You know I will." He said, "I want you to serve on the Board of Corrections." I had not considered he might ask something like this of me. I said, "Governor, before you go too far you need to know Governor Busbee appointed me to the Board of Corrections and Governor Joe Frank Harris threw me off." Mr. Miller said, "I don't care anything about that. I want you to serve a five year term."

I served my five years on the Board of Corrections but it took six years for him to replace me. I was glad to get off of the board, though. It was almost like still being sheriff.

Sam Nunn and I were tight. Back in 1972 Sam asked me to meet him at Hadden's Restaurant on Houston Avenue. I met him there, with a member of his staff. We sat down and talked about his chances, should he run for United States Senate against a fellow named David Gambrell from Sea Island, Georgia, who was serving under the appointment of President Carter. He had served the unexpired term, and now he was running for the full term. I supported Sam and did everything I could to help him.

Ever since that time, we've been friends. Every time I was in Washington I would go by his office to see him. If he was in office he would want to see me. If there was something I needed and he was in the Senate, he told me to come to the door and tell them who I was and they would see me.

The Drug Enforcement Administration is the czar of dope in the United States. They run airplanes and they run boats and everything else. The man who was in charge in Atlanta and I were good friends. He sent an emissary and said, "Do you think it would be possible for you to arrange a meeting between me and Senator Nunn?" I told him I didn't know but I would see what I could do. He told the time he would be here. I called Senator Nunn's office in Atlanta asking an aide if Sam Nunn could squeeze in a few minutes to meet with this fellow.

The aide confirmed Sam would meet him at 7. He had another meeting at 7:30 so he would meet in his room. I said all right and I called the fellow back, giving him the information. Senator Nunn would be staying in a certain room at the Ritz Carlton and he would see him at 7. Everything was set up and I thought everything was okay, when all of a sudden everything fell apart. The fellow called me back and said, "Stop the meeting. Stop the meeting." I said, "What in the world is the matter?" He just kept ranting, "Stop the meeting. Stop the meeting. Don't go any further. See if you can cancel it."

I called the aide back and told him there had been a change and a meeting wouldn't be necessary. I was extremely put out until the fellow told me he was a district manager for DEA. He was a law enforcement officer. There were about 40 different places similar to this in the United States. He found out that William Bennett was the person meeting with Senator Nunn at 7:30. Bennett was the drug czar, appointed by President Bush to serve in that capacity.

The officer realized if he met with Senator Nunn first and Bennett met with him second, there was a good chance Bennett would find out about it. Should that happen the agent would not be around long. He wanted to get out of the whole situation.

John Knight was part owner of Knight-Ridder newspapers. At one time they owned about 28 newspapers from one coast to the other. John was a very well thought of fellow and a multi, multi-millionaire. His daughter was Beverly Olson. She was married to Ed Olson who had been publisher of the Macon Telegraph at one time. During Cherry Blossom Festival one year there was a dance at the City Auditorium. Beverly caught my arm and said she wanted me to meet her father. There was an empty chair so I sat down with her father and Peyton Anderson to talk with him. We chatted a few minutes. Peyton had previously told me what a fine fellow her father was.

When Peyton decided to sell the Macon newspaper he called one person and one person only, John Knight. John Knight made him an offer of something like $30 million dollars. Peyton took it. Part of it was in stock. They shook hands on it that night and then John Knight paid him more than the agreed amount because the stock had risen and had more value to it. But the deal was made over a handshake. I always thought that was the way gentlemen really did business.

I had admired General Scott since I was a teenage boy. I mentioned earlier I was ranked number four in the city selling U.S. Savings Bonds. Because of that I got to sit on the stage with him when the premier of "God is My Co-Pilot" came to Macon. General Scott was a Boy Scout too. He earned every merit badge except two, sign language badge and the music merit badge.

Our friendship really began when General Scott was introduced to me by Mason Zuber. General Scott and I became good friends.

His father was in his 90s when General Scott moved to Sun City, Arizona. I would check on his father for him to make sure he was being taken care of appropriately. General Scott was always so grateful to me for showing kindness to his father.

At one point I had been trying to get in touch with General Scott but I couldn't reach him. I called his brother Roland in California who in turn gave me General Scott's number in Arizona. When I finally talked with him he told me he had been locked in a room writing for about three weeks. He was writing a story about walking the Great Wall of China. "Reader's Digest" had already indicated it to be a best seller for them. They wanted it as Book of the Month. He was writing the history of the wall and telling about his experience in walking it. When I went to the board meeting at the Scout Headquarters later that evening I told them, "I talked to General Scott today and he's writing a book on the Great Wall of China." The executive of the Scouts said, "Yes, we know. "Reader's Digest" called here to verify he had received all the badges except two and that he was an Eagle Scout." I thought more of "Reader's Digest" after that, because I knew they checked the credentials of those writing stories for their publication.

The Museum of Aviation was later named for General Scott. Several of us convinced him to come back to Macon, and he made his home here. He was a great American and a great Patriot. I had many long conversations with him. The idea of writing this book about my experiences started because of General Bob Scott.

One day he said to me, "Ray, why don't you write a book?" I said, "General, I don't know how to do something like that." He said, "Well, you write down your thoughts, edit it, then rewrite it, edit it again, and then rewrite it until it reads smooth. Then you've got a book." He gave me one thing, his personal belief I could do this, so I owe General Scott an awful lot. He ate lunch with me in the jail on several different occasions. He was one of the main people who encouraged me to run for sheriff. I consider General

Scott a true hero.

I met Strom Thurmond when he came to Macon as the senior senator of the United States. It was a Democratic visit to Boeing Company. There was definitely a lot of hand shaking. When he approached me shaking my hand I said, "I understand you and Herman Talmadge are related." He informed me that his mother and Herman's mother were sisters. We talked for a few minutes then he said, "Call Herman up and tell him to vote for such and so bill." There was some bill the Independents and the Republicans were pushing. I told him I would do it. He was a very nice fellow—very feeble when I met him so he had people with him to keep him from falling, but his mind was good.

I went to Virgil Powers School. It was only a block from the mill village. A brick school, it was probably one of the poorest in the county. We did not have a playground or a lunchroom. When we needed space for any type of school play or production, a partition was removed from between two of the classrooms. The two rooms combined created our little auditorium.

My first grade teacher was Ms. Ruth Elder. I can't remember the name of my second grade teacher. My third grade teacher was Ms. Gwendolyn Allie, and my fourth grade teacher was Ms. Lottie Smith. I possessed very little appreciation for my teachers. Maybe they did their best.

I didn't have a binding relationship with a teacher until I went to Ann Maria Domingos' fifth grade class. Ms. Domingos had graduated from Wesleyan and was doing her first teaching assignment. She was so very nice. Everyone respected her. She worked extremely hard to help her students with any weakness she saw. She became a very special teacher to me. At the end of our fifth grade year she went to Washington, D.C. and sent every student in her class a post card from Washington. Mine had a picture of the Tomb of the Unknown Soldier. I kept that post card for 25 years then it got misplaced. I have always hoped I would find it somewhere among my things. I would run into her from time to time during my life and we would chat.

She once told me how proud she was of me for being elected sheriff. On one occasion I had called to invite her to join me in the jail dining room for lunch. She accepted my invitation, and we had a lovely lunch. She was always so pleasant. Another time she called to ask if she could bring some foreign guests to the jail dining room and I told her certainly. Our bond of friendship was one that continued throughout the years.

I had another friend, Whoop Bennett, who lived across the street from Ann Maria. One Christmas I was invited to attend a Christmas reception at his home. Much to my surprise Ann Maria was there also. I was sitting there with my arm around Ann with the Christmas music playing and I said, "Ann Maria, I used to call you Ms. Domingos. Now I call you Ann Maria. I don't know what happened, if you got younger or I got older but I think you got younger." She laughed. I then asked her, "Did you ever think when I was in the fifth grade we would be standing here with my wife and all these guests with my arm around you?" She said, "No." She was such a sweet person.

We kept that friendship through the years. I picked her up from her house one year and brought her to our house to have Christmas dinner with us. When she finally gave up her home, Ann Maria, along with her brother and his wife went to Carlyle Place on Zebulon Road to live. I kept thinking I would go to see her.

Then one day I talked to her brother Billy whom I knew because we had served on the Boy Scout Council together. I told Billy I wanted to go see Ann Maria. He said she had been moved to the area housing people with dementia. That made me want to go see all the more. When I got to her room I found her asleep. She was still pretty to me at 82. The associate working there said it was time to get her up but I said, no, I would come back another day. They kept insisting it was time to get her up so I said, "All right. I'll sit right here. I've got the time. But don't come get me until she is dressed and has her hair the way she wants it to be. I want her to feel completely comfortable before I come in."

When I entered, she remembered me immediately. The dementia had not progressed to the point she didn't know me. She was tickled I had come to visit her. At one point I said to her, "Ann Maria, your brother Billy told me when you finished your first year at Virgil Powers he made arrangements with the school board to have you moved to Joseph Clisby." Joseph Clisby was an elite school in a much better section of town. I continued, "He already had it worked out to remove you from the mill village crowd and the poverty kids." He didn't mean it derogatorily but that was what our school was. She had told him she could not do that, saying, "All those kids love me and those kids need me. I've got to stay." She stayed at our school because that was where she wanted to be. I cared for her even more when I learned of her love for our school.

The last time I saw Ann Maria I held her hands and said, "I'll never forget the kindness you showed me. Ann Maria, I love you because of what you did for me and my family." She said, "I love you too." It wasn't a honeymoon love. It was a love and respect for each other. Two weeks after seeing her I received a call she had died. I would not have taken $1000 for having gone to see her the day I went. I was real happy I did see her. She was such a good person.

James I. Wood was sheriff and I was still a deputy when he came to me and said, "Senator Walter George is going to be here tonight and I've got a ticket for it." I don't remember if the tickets cost $50 or $100 but he was getting ready to run again for the Senate. Herman Talmadge had been running a number of years for the office. Senator George was old and he had been out of Georgia politics a long time, making his chances of being elected slim.

I went to the Walter Little Room of the Dempsey hotel one evening and saw an old fellow sitting down on a couch. I recognized Mr. George so I sat down to talk with him. We talked at random about how things were going. We were both there early so we talked about 20 or 30 minutes. He shared some of his views with me and I shared mine with him. I thought, here is this man who sits on the Senate Foreign Relations Committee, a very powerful committee chairman, and any day he opened his door his office would be filled with people wanting to see him for just five minutes. I sat with him and just talked, without wanting anything at all from him. It was sad to see such a prominent man sit here all alone. He soon withdrew his hat from the race and retired, never to run for office again. I will always remember him. He was a very distinguished gentleman who was so nice to me. I was very glad for the opportunity to meet him.

A person I greatly admired was Bill Fickling, Sr. I had great admiration for him because he was a self-made man and an honest one. He also had something no one else in the real estate business here in Macon had, which was vision.

We had become friends a long time before I ever ran for sheriff but when I did run I went to see him to ask for his support. He immediately agreed to support me and became a tremendous help to me. He was always at my side for anything I needed. I could count on him day or night. His office was located one floor below a law office where I quite frequently had to attend to business so I would stop by his office to speak to him. Peyton Anderson's office was two doors down from Mr. Fickling. In one trip to that particular office building I could see three people I respected and loved.

Whenever I stopped by, Mr. Fickling was always glad to see me. I stopped to talk with him when he was 86 years old. He said, "Ray, this will probably be my last Cherry Blossom Festival." I said, "Mr. Fickling, don't say that. You're probably going to be around for a lot more. We can't let you go like that." He said, "Well, I'm 86 years old and in the health I'm in, this will be the last one." I said, "I certainly hope not." Mr. Fickling was a prophet because he died before the next festival was held.

One of the first things he would ask me whenever I went to see him was, "What can I do for you?" I would say, "Nothing. I just came by to speak to you." Then he told me something. He said, "Ray, people think I'm smart. I'm not smart. All I've ever done is look which way Macon was growing then jump ahead of the growth and buy land. When I bought land I waited for it to come to me. That was it." When Mr. Fickling died his son asked me to be a pallbearer and I told him I would. His son dropped me a card to thank me and in the card he wrote, "My father always considered you one of his best friends." I thought of him in the same regard. I never asked him to sponsor anything. I only wanted to be his friend. So many people would ask things of him and he and his wife were both gracious people. I just wanted to him to be comfortable with me knowing I wanted nothing from him in return.

I was once asked by a magazine reporter from a national publication what one thing I could think of that made the Ficklings different from all the other people who are in their status in Macon, Georgia. I thought for a few minutes then I said, "Mr. Fickling's family is the only family I know who is as wealthy as they are and the least affected by their money. They talk to everybody." Mr. Fickling had three black Americans who paid him rent. When these men would come to his large executive office he treated them like they were in the State Capitol. When they paid their rent he would take a pad out of his desk drawer to write them a receipt. This was repeated each month.

A person who probably affected me as much or more than anyone else outside of my family was a man by the name of Dallas Mobley. Dallas Mobley came from Rockdale County. He was a lawyer and a small claims judge. When the FBI was formed he was one of the first people hired so he went to Washington D.C. Dallas was probably one of the smartest agents in the legal field. He taught banking laws and banking procedures at the FBI Academy.

He became an investigator.

Laws changed and times changed and eventually Dallas was transferred to the training division. Politics had grown in Bibb County and I was on the bottom of the totem pole in the political arena. The people who had supported Sheriff "Rock" Robertson were making all the changes. The changes included not retaining me as a deputy sheriff. They intended to get rid of me. I think they had a fear of me because I could do so many things. I could read fingerprints. I could develop pictures. I could work wreck scenes. I could do investigative work. I had been exposed to a lot of different aspects in the law enforcement field.

When I was appointed as identification officer I went to the Ident Division not knowing one finger from the other. No one in the department made a move toward me to teach me how to read fingerprints. I called the FBI and went into the training division where I met Dallas Mobley. I first talked to him on the phone. He told me if I got a class of ten people the FBI would send someone here to teach it. I thought that was great because a lot of other officers were in the same shape as I was.

I asked Dr. Maffeo at Mercer if we could borrow a room at the university where the first class could meet. Then I starting telephoning about 25 guys who I thought would want to learn to read fingerprints. Dallas Mobley and Carl Clayborn came to Macon to teach us how to read fingerprints. At the end of the first week all in that class were classified finger printers.

Carl Clayborn had been an expert witness all over the United States. He and Dallas Mobley later came to me asking if I knew a certain person in the Ku Klux Klan. I did know the person and he knew me. He was openly a Ku Klux Klansman because there were mask laws at that time. Everyone just saw who you were. I arranged a meeting between the FBI and the person and later this person became an informant for the FBI. There were no arrests and no one was put in jail. They were basically wanting to keep tabs on it: was it getting any bigger, was it getting any smaller, all this sort of thing.

Dallas and I continued to see one another on occasion. One day he said, "Ray, I'd like to see you go to the FBI Academy." I said, "I can't get in." He was very encouraging to me and said, "Yes, you can." Through his efforts and the contacts he had, along with my background, the FBI accepted me so I received an invitation. The only way to attend the Academy is by invitation from Mr. Hoover.

I went to the FBI Academy and when I came back home politics had become a little bit worse. Some of the men in the FBI Academy were from of New York. Their commanders would send telegraphs stating upon graduation that person was being promoted in their division. I sure wasn't looking for a telegraph saying those words. In fact, it was just the opposite. When I returned I found out my salary had been cut. It took about six months to get my salary back to what it had been before going to the Academy. I'm sure they thought if they cut my salary they would surely get rid of me.

The person responsible for cutting my salary has never apologized but 30 years after the fact he spent at least half an hour telling me he had changed his life and he wanted to spend the rest of his life working for the church. We parted as friends. Even back then I can honestly say I have never had any bitterness or hate for him. Dallas Mobley was the person responsible for pushing me forward in my career so later I would become the sheriff of Bibb County. I will always be grateful to him for what he did for me.

Many friends have encouraged me to write a book about my 40 years experience in the sheriff's office from the start to the end. One of the people who has spent much time pushing me to write this book is my good friend, Jack Caldwell. I would see Jack from time to time and he would always encourage me to get started with my memoirs. Jack had bought an old antebellum-type home on College Street, built right after the Civil War by a Civil War hero. I don't know anyone who could have done more with the beautiful home than he did. Jack didn't change the house but rather restored it to its grandeur, just about like it was originally. The house was graced with furniture when Jack purchased it. Every Southern Memorial Day Jack hosts a lovely dinner in his home. There are usually people from reenactments present, along with someone playing the bag pipes.

It was always an entertaining evening remembered long after the night was done. The festivities would begin with the "Star Spangled Banner" and then "God Bless America." At some point during the night everyone sang "Dixie." Every time I saw Jack he would ask, "Have you done any more on your book?" I would say, "No, Jack. I'm still thinking about it." Then he would say, "We've got to do it, Ray. We've got to do it."

I knew this conversation would be repeated at Christmas, Southern Memorial Day, and 4th of July. I knew he would be on my case about the book. Finally he said, "I'm coming to your house Thursday night. I'm bringing a tape recorder and tapes and we're going to put down these stories so your children's children can know about their grandfather and grandmother." Jack has been dedicated and faithful. It is through his commitment that this book is being written. I will never forget Jack for the things he has done for me.

Another person I am indebted to for the rest of my life is Dr. Clyde Kelly. In 2005 I got sick. I began losing weight but the doctors couldn't determine what was wrong with me. Finally, they brought in a team of specialists and I was diagnosed with lymphoma in the left pelvis. I had lost a considerable amount of weight causing me to be very weak.

I told Dr. Schnell at the time he diagnosed me, "Dr. Schnell, listen to me. This is the way I believe. This is not in my hands. It's in the hands of the Good Lord. I'll tell you something else I believe. I'm not going to leave this earth one day early and I'm not going to stay here one day late. I don't question your medical integrity or your ability or your education. I have no question at all. I think you're the best and I appreciate everything you've done for me but I want to go to M.D. Anderson in Texas." He said, "All right. I'll help you make the arrangements."

I entered M.D. Anderson for a week of testing and procedures. The diagnosis they gave was the same diagnosis Dr. Schnell had given me with the same prognosis, it's treatable but not curable. Dr. Kelly, a dermatologist who had retired, came to see me while I was in the hospital. We had occasionally had coffee casually together over the years. I did not know him well but I did know him.

When I was released from the hospital he would call every so often to check on me. He said, "Ray, I can carry you anywhere you need to go. I can take care of you." Since he was retired, he did not have his busy schedule.

One day I got in a tight with my radiation appointment. It seemed everybody was tied up and they had forbidden me to drive down there because you never knew how it might affect you. If the radiation made you sick you would need someone to drive you home. I called Clyde Kelly and asked him if he could give me a lift to radiation. He said, "I'll be there in a few minutes." He came right on over. He drove me to my appointment and walked me to the building. I told him, "You can go ahead now. I'm going to walk down here. I'll be all right." He said, "No. No."

I had multiple chemotherapy treatments and radiation treatments. I had learned with the chemotherapy treatments you never knew how long you would be there. It could take three or four hours depending on how your body reacted to the medication. I said, "Dr. Kelly, I'm here. My daughter, Cathy, will pick me up. I appreciate you getting me down here." He was adamant, "No. I'm not going to leave you." I said, "She'll come along after she gets off work and pick me up. You don't have to stay." Once again he said, "No. I'm not going to leave you." He had brought a book to read but the nurse recognized him. She said, "Dr. Kelly, you can come on back here with him."

Dr. Kelly stayed with me for my entire treatment, which took three to four hours. They had to give it to you very slowly. Dr. Kelly ended up going with me to every doctor's appointment I had. When all was said and done, I finished the chemotherapy and I asked the doctor if I was going to lose my hair. He told me I would lose some of it. I said, "Well, it doesn't bother me. Whatever you have to do, don't worry about the hair. It can be gone." He said, "All right." I always call it a blessing because I never got sick in radiation. I never got nauseated in chemotherapy and I never lost my hair. I thought, that was really something.

Dr. Kelly made notes at every doctor's appointment. He has a copy of every report each doctor has. He told me one time, "Ray, I'm not treating you but I'm going to stay close enough to you to make sure nothing falls through the cracks." He has stayed right with me through all this time and I'll never forget him for it. I've tried to put gas in his car. I've tried to reimburse him. He would never take any compensation from me for all the things he has done for me. The only thing I've been able to do for him is obtain a football autograph from University of Georgia football coach, Mark Richt, and a big nice barbecued Christmas ham. I can never repay him for all he's done for me.

CHAPTER 125

There have been three major crimes in Bibb County that have caught not only the locals' attention but also national attention. The first is the Woolfolk murder case. The Woolfolk murders took place in 1887, when Tom Woolfolk killed nine members of his family with an axe. He then sought out a black tenant farmer, telling him someone had come and killed his family and he had just barely escaped. His plan was to get the tenant farmer to his house, kill him, then tell everyone the black man had killed everyone in his family but him.

The black man was so scared after the man finished telling his story he took off running. No one saw him for a couple of days. Tom Woolfolk had to go to a different plan. He decided to dump the bodies in a well.

Eventually people became suspicious. An investigation was launched and he was arrested. He had a trial and the jury was hung. He had another trial, this time ending in his conviction. In 1890 he was hung at Mulberry and Fifth streets where the Green Jacket Restaurant was later located.

The next one bringing world-wide attention was Anjette Lyles. People came from all over the world. The London Daily Mirror was here. They came every day to the trial. I was assigned to the trial to take care of the jury. Taking care of a jury at a trial of those proportions is very tedious; you can't let the jury become tainted in any way in order that they may reach an impartial verdict. Before I let them see the newspaper I cut out the story with a razor blade; when they opened the paper it had a big hole in it. There were many responsibilities I had to undertake to help keep the jury on task.

I heard every witness who testified in the case. I also heard

Anjette and everything she said. I remember that Hank O'Neal and Charlie Adams had both been appointed prosecutors for the State of Georgia but recused themselves. Neither Hank O'Neal or Charlie Adams was anyone's fool. Both of them were smart as crickets.

The prosecution brought in nationally recognized Dr. Richard Ford, who had written three or four books on arsenic poisoning. Dr. Ford was chief pathologist for the Massachusetts State Police and had degrees you could hang the length of a clothesline. He looked like a lot of other people who are brilliant. His suit was about two sizes too small. It was hot weather but he was wearing wool herringbone. When they called this Dr. Ford to the stand I looked up because I thought someone had gotten into the courtroom who didn't belong there. Just as I started to stand, one of the lawyers stood up and said, "Go ahead and take the stand, Dr. Ford." I would have never thought this man to be an expert witness or a professional. He started giving his credentials as an expert.

When a lawyer on the other side knows the expertise of a witness they will generally try to get him off the stand as fast as they can. This lawyer gave Dr. Ford's qualifications and listed the books he had written. He then stated Dr. Ford was chief pathologist for the state of Massachusetts. They got all that out of the way.

The prosecution asked some questions, then turned the witness over to the defense lawyer, Bill Buffington. Bill had spent a lot of time in the hospital library researching arsenic poisoning. He thought he would add a little humor to the questioning. He walked to the stand and lazily leaned on it and said, "Dr. Ford, is it true that y'all have people up there in Boston, Massachusetts, who take this stuff too? Is that true?" Dr. Ford said, "We have our fools and villains too." The defense lawyer got his bristles up a little and he came back asking Dr. Ford about a medical term adding, "Isn't that true?" Dr. Ford said, "I wish you had not used those terms. It confuses a jury and it confuses a lay person. It only means pot ash."

Bill realized he had problems. He had a stack of all kinds of reports he had brought with him. Bill asked, "Dr. Ford, have you read all of these?" Dr. Ford responded, "I certainly have. I finished at 2 a.m. this morning." Bill lost out. He couldn't handle Dr. Ford. He was an expert witness who helped the prosecution with the technical and medical tests he ran.

Anjette sat there during the whole trial. A really nice looking woman, she pulled her hair back in a ponytail. Some of the press wrote that her hair turned white over night. I read that and I thought, her hair has been white for a long time as far as I know. The jury was sent out and the other bailiff and I waited until we were notified the jury had reached a verdict.

Our lawyers had a terrible week. They went to the VFW, which was across the street. I think they began to bend their arms over there. After 55 minutes Carl Wheeler, who was foreman of the jury, said, "We've reached a verdict." I went to the VFW and told the attorneys a verdict had been reached so they were needed back in the courtroom. None of them were in any condition to go back but they did. They all took their place going through court procedure. The clerk of the court read, "We the jury find Anjette Lyles guilty of murder in the first degree with no mercy and recommend the electric chair."

The governor didn't want to be the first man to send a white woman to the electric chair. There had only been one other woman executed. He brought in some psychiatrists to evaluate her. Their evaluation concluded that she was not able to aid in her defense at this time. She died in the Milledgeville State Hospital.

CHAPTER 126

There is one story in my life which has been very memorable for me. I was at City Hall on some kind of a case one day and as I stepped out in the hall I noticed a lady. She was poorly dressed and it was very cold outside. With her was a boy of about 12 or 13 years of age whom I assumed to be her son. He was poorly dressed as well with no shoes.

I saw her talk to the clerk in the City Hall where fines are paid, then they left. I approached the clerk and asked her what they lady was there for. She said, "Her husband is in jail. She's trying to find out how much the fine is to see if she can get him out."

I decided to look at the record to find out who this man was and what he had been incarcerated for. He was a cab driver who had been arrested drunk. He had a 16-year-old girl in the car with him riding at night. Records showed he had been in and out of jail on numerous occasions. His family was living off Old Jeffersonville Road.

The following day I drove to their home so I could speak with the lady. She was weather-beaten and was very thin, so her clothes just hung on her. She had five or six children. As I talked to her she began to tell me how she needed to try to get him out. I listened to her then I told her I didn't think his release from jail was the answer to the problems.

I drove back to the office and began to think about this family. I dug into my own pocket. Then I called others and I got some money from this one and that one. Before long it began to pick up speed. I went to Mr. Markwalter who was in charge of Macon Housing Authority and I told him about this family. He said, "Ray, we've had them here before. That man has done nothing but cause problems." I said, "Give them a three-bedroom apartment and I'll guarantee you he won't be here." Markwalter asked, "He won't be here?" I said, "No, sir. And paint it for them." He said, "Great Scott, what are you going to do to me? Here I am taking in a family and now you want me to paint the apartment too?"

I then went to see Judge Baldwin. I was able to put a hold on the husband. They bound him over to state court and they put a hold on him. I said, "Judge Baldwin, if you give him a fine then he'll be back some way and then he'll be back in that family. I can't get her any help as long as he's there." The Judge said, "I'll handle him." They called his case on Friday morning and Judge Baldwin gave him 12 months in the penitentiary. That got rid of him.

Next I went to Family and Children Services to get them qualified for assistance. It was Christmas so I was able to get some emergency money from DFCS. I had to get them out of the dump they were living in. I went to see Mr. Smith, who owned Dixie Auto Parts on Broadway, and who owned the rental house they occupied. I told him I would pay their rent of $50. He said, "No. They owe $150. They ain't going nowhere until they pay the $150." I had to pay him $150 for the dump they were living in on Walnut Creek.

After that was squared away I went to see Walter Cannon. I said, "Walter, you've got to help me. We've got to move those people to Pendleton Homes." He said, "We'll do it, Ray." Walter took a truck and a crew out there. I can still see them picking up cotton mattresses and putting them in boxes. You would have been better sleeping on the boxes and throwing away the mattresses. The men put the mattresses in boxes and treated them like they were Beauty Rests. They got everything in the truck and drove the furnishings to the new house. All the furniture was put in the house in the proper place.

I made arrangements to take all the children to Dannenberg's. We didn't have a K-Mart. The cheapest place to get anything was Dannenberg's. Pearl and Cathy went with me. Ray, Jr. had not been born yet. Pearl bought underclothes for the children—panties, slips, and socks, and all the other things she thought they needed. We also bought them some clothes. After we chose clothes for each of them we dressed them, then bought them each some shoes and took them home.

I really wasn't satisfied so I went back out and bought nine toothbrushes, nine tubes of toothpaste, nine hair brushes, and all types of other sundry items I thought they might need. We wrapped the items in gift wrap and put together a food basket. On Christmas Eve we took it to them. They had new clothes and all these personal items and that was their Christmas. I got them all settled in their new home and hoped I had helped them.

About ten years later my secretary came in and said, "There's a fellow out here who wants to see you." I told her to send him in. The Korean War had just ended. When I looked up an Army sergeant had walked in. I figured he wanted to see someone in jail who was related to him. I invited him to have a seat and he said, "I wanted to come by here to meet you and tell you what you meant to me." He was the little boy who was standing in the hall with his mother at City Hall the day I had first seen them. He had come to my office to thank me. He was now a sergeant in the Army.

Then one day I was at Pine Forest Baptist Church where Ms. Frances Mann was in charge of the senior citizen programs. The Cherry Blossom had just finished and Ms. Mann asked me if I could get any Cherry Blossom ice cream for the senior citizen's dessert. I said, "I don't know but I'll see what I can do." I called the manager of Borden's, who was a good friend of mine, and told him my request. He said, "We don't even sell it any more. Another company sells the ice cream now." I asked, "Do you know anybody who works there?" He told me he knew the manager so I asked if he would call him for me and ask if he would give us any for the senior citizens.

When he called me back he said, "The manager knew you. He used to work for us at Borden's before he became manager there. He said anything you ever want you can get from him." I said,

"Who is the manager?" Then it came back to me who the manager was. He had the ice cream delivered and then later he brought his wife and his son to see me. He was one of the children in that same family I had helped. He was the oldest boy. When I had first met his mom she was trying to find out how to get her sorry husband out of jail. We're still friends.

My friend is a devout Christian and one day I asked him about his father. The young man said he wasn't allowed to go back there again. He told me about a time at the house when his mother said something that apparently angered his father; she was bending over and the husband kicked her flat on the floor. The young man said he hit his father so hard he knocked him out cold and he was forbidden to come back to his house. Later, his father was living at McAffee Towers and dying of cancer. He went to his father to tell him that he held no grudges against him and he had forgiven him for everything he had ever done. He was able to lead his father to the Lord, and now his father was a Christian. You never know when you touch someone's life what type of domino effect it will have, negative or positive.

I could always pick up the phone and raise $200 or $300 within a few minutes to help someone out. I never expected anything. The only thing I knew was Pearl and I had almost been there. The big difference was that my parents weren't like those parents. This lady was a good woman; she was weather-beaten and abused, but we were able to help her during her bad times.

CHAPTER 127

There are some places of notoriety remembered by those of us who lived here. I never will forget the Chicken House. Steve was a crippled man who ran the Chicken House. There was a slot machine near the front door and there was a sign over the slot machine. It read, "In case of air raid stand near this slot machine. It hasn't been hit yet." That was the Chicken House.

The Marines were stationed at the Naval Ordinance Plant. I later hired a sergeant who had been in the Marine Corps and he told me the story of a Marine who went to the Chicken House one night. He started drinking and before long he had quite a few beers. Someone started a fight and pulled a knife; it cut the Marine's blouse open and cut his arm. The sergeant was on the gate that night; when he looked up Guy Paine Road, here came a Marine hollering, "Bring reinforcements, bring reinforcements." He said he ran to the gate and grabbed the Marine, asking him what was wrong. This Marine was telling him they needed reinforcements at the Chicken House because a gang of thugs had beat him up. They had to take him in and get him patched up.

The DAV was a rough club and rough people went there. As a general rule we could go to the DAV and get a drunk out of there or separate a fight or arrest someone in a cutting or occasionally a shooting. The DAV was not as bad as the Chicken House. It took an unusual man to run the Chicken House and Steve was that man. He would sit at the cash register and watch for the money; nobody ran the register but Steve.

Steve was sitting at the register one night when a guy walked up to him, pulled out a pistol, and said, "This is a stick-up. Give me the money." Steve said, "No. You don't want to do that. Put that gun back in your pocket and go over there and sit down. Hazel, Betty, come here a minute. This man needs something to eat. Give him anything he wants. Get him some eggs and ham." The man looked at Steve then walked over there and sat down. They started bringing food to him and Steve kept ringing the cash register. The man started to leave and Steve said, "Look a here. This will help you get on your feet." And he handed him $20. The man walked off. That was the way the Chicken House operated.

Willow Springs was run by the Smiths. The guy had glasses that looked like bottoms of Coca-cola bottles. Glen kept a big handle and a pistol behind the counter. Willow Springs didn't really get cranked up until about 11:30 at night. The fish eaters had come in to eat and had already gone.

After they were gone this other crowd came in from all over. Anyone with a difference to settle would come. It would be open until 2 or 3 o'clock in the morning. Whenever any trouble started Glen would come out from behind the counter with the pistol in one hand and the stick in the other. He would hit everything in front of him.

A friend of mine, Willie Andrews, did everything you could think of in the country of jobs. He hauled cars. He ran a restaurant in the Farmers' Market. He drove a taxi cab. He and Johnny Lamb were big buddies. Willie was a little fellow who kept a cigar stuck in his mouth all the time. He stayed parked at the Terminal Station.

Back in the day there were 40 or 50 trains stopping at the Terminal Station. Many of the travelers were military. Sometimes they had to catch another train going a different direction but sometimes they had a layover. One night two paratroopers approached Willie about taking them somewhere.

Willie parked at the Terminal Station and they would come out and say, "Hey, cabbie. Do you know any places where any action is at?" Willie would say, "Yeah. I know some places where there's action." They would get in Willie's cab and say, "Take us out there where there's some action." They had their boots polished; they were paratroopers. They got in the back of the cab and Willie took them out to the Bloody Bucket. When they got of the car they said, "Pick us up at 2 o'clock. Be sure and be here." He would always say, you really ought to be there a little early because someone else would get your fare. So about 1:30 he began to ease back to the Bloody Bucket to pick them up.

He was driving up Millerfield Road about 1:15 or 1:30 in the morning when he saw two soldiers flying down the road. They were running toward Macon. He stopped the car and watched them run past him and keep on running. He turned the car around and pulled up to them and said, "Are y'all going to ride back in the cab?" They said, "H---. Get us out of here." They jumped in the backseat and said, "Go. Go. What kind of d--- place did y'all take us to?" Willie said, "Y'all said you wanted some action. What happened?" They said, "The booths were lined up. We were in the middle. The juke box was going and folks were dancing and liquor was flowing and we had a drink. About that time the man in the back booth cursed the man in the front booth and said, 'You are too.' And the other one said, 'You don't have a gun on you.' And the one in the back said, 'POW.' We hit the floor. The one in the front started shooting the one in the back and we were between them. We got out by crawling out of there. When we got to the road we started running. We were planning on running back to Macon."

Willie Andrews was never involved with the slot machine business but he wanted to be with the crowd. Sam Turner, Billy Watson, and Big Willie worked machines. They went over to the Veteran's Club in Athens, Georgia. They had a drill on their finger made to look like a ring. All they had to do was push that little drill in there and move the hand back and forward. The little drill would drill a hole in the machine. They would drill it at just the right place and then they ran a wire hidden in their shirt up through the hole. Their other hand would be on the machine pulling the lever. They were fishing until they caught the little lever and they hit the jackpot.

The bartender behind them heard the jackpot hit. A few minutes later he heard another jackpot hit. He picked up a pistol with a six inch barrel on it and he picked up a big stick he kept behind the counter. He left his place at the bar and started hitting them until they were down on the floor. They were bloody as pigs when he got through beating them. Then he took a card out of his pocket and handed each one of them a card. He told them if they had any friends or business to send them over. They came back to Macon and their lawyer, Virgil Shepherd, said, "Ray, it was the worst mess I've ever seen. I've never seen such abuse in my life. They all had to go to the hospital. All of them were being sewed up. I called the police and told them they were going to take out warrants. They said we were wasting our time. They had no evidence of anything like that going on. You can't get no justice nowhere." Virgil was upset justice could not be served.

═══ CHAPTER 128 ═══

In the old days we had the boys of the slot machines. Sam Turner and Joe Coco were arrested in a telephone booth. They were robbing telephone booths of the money. In those days there weren't any cell phones or any walkie talkies. The only thing we had were telephones and public pay phones. Public phones did a tremendous amount of business.

When they first came out it cost a nickel to use the phones, then the price went up to a dime. Sam and Joe had leather jackets with inside zippers and a pocket so they could put the money from the phone into it. They locked the box and would be gone.

Sam and Joe got caught so they hired the former lieutenant governor of the state of Mississippi to defend them. Southern Bell had already sent some big shot Mississippi lawyers to the governor, giving him money so he wouldn't drop the charges but he said no dice. He had already been compromised with a campaign contribution, I think. Sam and Joe had a bond on them. The bond Sam was under was somewhere in the $10,000 and $20,000 mark. Joe appeared in court but Sam jumped bond. He came back to Macon just like they always do.

The man came over from the bonding company and asked, "Do you know him?" I said, "Yeah. I know him." The bondsman continued, "He's in Macon but I don't know where he is. I'll give you $500 if you can put him in jail for me." I said, "Give me your name and number and I'll be in touch." I had pictures from our files that I circulated throughout the community. I went to Lee and Eddie's. I went to Club 159. I went to all the places the thugs hung out and showed his picture.

About 2 o'clock one morning it was pouring down rain when I

got a call. It was from Lee and Eddie's and he was whispering, "He's in here now. Come to the back door." The front of his establishment was a barbecue place but it was closed at night. It was located at the corner of Riggins Mill Road and U.S. 129 South, Cochran Short Route. It's still there today.

I quickly drove to Lee and Eddie's and went around to the back door. I knocked lightly on the big steel door. Lee opened the door and oh, man, they were going. Liquor was flowing. Lee said, "He's over there." Sam was playing at the monkey machine, which didn't pay off in cash but rather in games then the money would be paid.

He had a roll of quarters feeding the machine with one hand and holding another roll of quarters in his other hand. I walked up to him and said, "Sam, you're under arrest. You jumped bond in Mississippi and I'm going to take you in." He turned around to look at me. I had seen the roll of quarters in his right hand and I knew very well how hard his fist would be with it in his hand. I was wearing a coat so I threw it back and put my hand on my pistol. I said, "Sam, you're about to make the biggest mistake of your life. I won't take no foolishness off of you. You're under arrest. Get over there." And I pushed him over against the wall.

Just as I pushed him he took the roll of quarters and threw them against a cement block wall. Quarters went flying all over the place. No one even moved to pick up one. I put a pair of handcuffs on him and put him in the car and took him to jail. I called the man in Mississippi and said, "Do you have that money?" He asked, "Do you have Sam?" I said, "Yes. He's here waiting." To which he responded, "I'll be there in the morning." He was there the next morning to take Leon back to Mississippi. He paid me my reward. The bond fee he had charged Sam was twice what he offered in reward money.

CHAPTER 129

Domestic violence was forever rearing its ugly head in my world of law enforcement. It knew no race or status. We received calls for all kinds of disputes. Bill Shelton, who was no more a law enforcement officer than a Coca-Cola man, was always interested in what someone else was doing.

One night a rough looking old cab driver came in to the sheriff's office all upset. He was at the counter whining, "They won't let me get my wife. My wife's in that trailer park and they won't let me get my wife." Bill asked, "Who?" The cabbie continued, "They're holding her. They won't let her out." Bill inquired as to what trailer park the man was speaking of, to which the cab driver answered, "Houston Avenue. They've got her out there." Bill instructed the man to get into the car and they rode out to the trailer park.

When they got to the trailer Bill noticed it was pretty run down. The trailer didn't have a deck on it, only three or four steps going right up to the front door. Bill was holding his flashlight as he walked up the steps, leaving the man standing on the ground. Bill banged on the door and said, "Open the door." While he was waiting for someone to come to the door he noticed holes all in the front door. He said, "These look like bullet holes." The fellow said, "Yeah. They shot at me when I was standing at the door a little while ago." Bill jumped off those steps in one quick motion. He said, "You didn't mention any shooting and bullet holes in the door." Bill left as quick as he had come. He lost interest in the case. The woman was inside drinking and not being held by force.

CHAPTER 130

I can honestly say I feel I have been truly blessed. God has been so good to me throughout the years. One of the greatest blessings He has bestowed on me is my family. We have stuck together through thick and thin, the good and the bad. I am so proud of my children and all they have accomplished in their lives. My son, Ray, Jr., earned his Eagle Scout and now my grandson has as well.

There was a time I thought Ray would not complete his work toward earning Eagle Scout. He had worked so hard in Scouts and then all of a sudden he wasn't interested in putting the effort into completing the course. I had tried to talk to him but to no avail. I was in the FBI Academy and I had a friend there who was a police supervisor in the New York Police Department. His name was Looney. He was Italian with a very large extended family. One day he and I were talking and I told him about Ray and the Scout predicament. I said, "He has almost completely quit and I've tried to get him to go on. I feel like I am butting my head against the wall trying to get through to him." Looney said in his New York Italian accent, "No. No. You can't do that. Let me tell you how to do it." He began hitting his fist into the palm of his other hand. He said, "You've got to hit them, knock them, beat them. No. No. Go. Go."

I came back home filled with vim and vigor. I asked Ray, "Have you gotten your merit badge in emergency preparedness yet?" He said, "No, dad. But I'm working on it. I'm working on it." The next day when I got home from work I said to Ray, "Oh, by the way, Ray. I got you an appointment on Friday with Mr. Beasley at the fire department for emergency preparedness." Ray went into the normal teenage conniption fit. "Why did you do that? I'm not ready for that.

Why did you do that?" I just listened to him then I calmly said, "I don't care. You're going. I don't care if you're ready or not, you're going. If you want to go down there and sit like a cluck, that's all right with me. But you're going to go."

Friday came along and Ray had been sulking all week. I took him to the fire department and turned him over to Mr. Beasley. Mr. Beasley told me to come back in about an hour to pick Ray up. When Ray got out of the car he about tripped over his lip it was drooping so low. When I returned to the fire station Ray came out grinning from ear to ear. After that day I never had to take matters into my hands again concerning Scouts. Ray continued to work earning his other badges and then becoming an Eagle Scout.

It's really a funny thing. After he was married and had become vice president of an automobile agency with his own office he was prowling around one day in his old room. Pearl asked, "What are you looking for, Ray?" He said, "Mom, where is my Eagle Scout badge?" She was able to locate the badge for him. He had the Eagle Scout badge put into a shadow box with a picture of his troop. He hung that on the wall of his office. He was extremely proud of earning the badge.

Pearl and I didn't drink or go to clubs. We didn't party when others were. We tried to be extremely careful with our money and didn't spend on extravagances. When we first started out we spent everything giving Cathy an education she could be proud of. When Ray came along we were in a little better shape financially and did not have to struggle quite as much for his education. We sent both of them to college. Cathy went to Georgia College in Milledgeville. She graduated from Georgia College then earned her Master's Degree from the University of Georgia. She continued her education receiving her doctorate at Georgia State in Atlanta. She has a Ph.D. in education. She worked 18 years at Central Georgia Technical College in several positions before becoming the director of admissions. After leaving there she went to work for the Georgia

Department of Corrections. While working for them she continued to work with vocational education programs and for a while she worked in Atlanta, evaluating vocational programs in the state prison system. She was first hired to assess inmates for academic and vocational training and later ran the law library and general library for one of the prisons.

Cathy married Danny when she was 19 years old. They've been married 37 years. I couldn't ask for a better son-in-law than Danny. Whenever I have had a need or have been sick they were there for me. Cathy left her home and moved in with us when I came home from the hospital for the fourth time. She moved into her old bedroom in the front room to be here at night in case anything happened to me. She has always been a very dedicated daughter. You cannot buy the love of a woman and you cannot buy the dedication of your children. The things I have accomplished in my life have been due to the support of my family. I have always said "we" were in law enforcement.

Cathy and Danny have a child, Danny, Jr. When Cathy was pregnant with little Danny we were all sitting on pins and needles because she was overdue. Dr. Brown was with me and I was running for sheriff. He said to me, "Ray, Cathy is overdue and I'm suspecting the umbilical cord is wrapped around the baby's neck. I'm going to induce labor and if she doesn't deliver within two hours I'm going to do a C-section. I don't want to take a chance on having a bad baby or a bad mother." So I was prepared for that.

Pearl is a natural born worrier. She can pick out something to worry about in any situation. She said, "Oh, Lord. That cord is around his neck. His oxygen is cut off. He's going to be retarded." She was just all upset and wringing her hands worrying herself sick the whole time we were in the waiting room during the delivery. Dr. Brown delivered the baby and we all got to hold little Danny. He seemed healthy and well.

Danny was around three or four years old and he and Pearl were doing something with money and he said, "Grandmamma, give me this and I'll give you that, and then hand me this one and I'll give you this one." That continued for a few minutes before Pearl looked around and realized she wasn't holding any of the money. He had all of it. I asked, "Do you think he has a bad mind now?" Pearl answered, "Yeah. A criminal mind."

Dan Jr. was a Boy Scout and then earned his Eagle Scout. I wanted to pay for him to go to college also but college was not for him. He graduated from First Presbyterian Day School and was at least above the middle of his class. He had a good education from Presbyterian and went to college for several years, but he really didn't want to go to college. He wanted a restaurant. Although he is very talented in cooking dealing with people, he learned quickly restaurants didn't make any money. And he found out there are many other ingredients that go into a restaurant to make it successful. The restaurant ended up being a lesson learned for him. Because he was in the restaurant business he applied for a job with Sysco, a wholesale food company. There must have been 30 people who applied, most with degrees. Danny was chosen because of his three years of experience in the restaurant business. He became a sales representative for Sysco. He went to Atlanta for training then he began working for them. They started him off at a good salary and full benefits. He lived in Macon and serviced this territory. He was employed with Sysco for about two years. Recently Dan had an opportunity to improve his income and return to the restaurant business as a manager with Applebee's.

Once I helped Dan when he had some debt needing to be paid off. Danny came to me one day when he was about 21 years old and said, "Granddaddy, how can I get out of debt?" I said, "How much do you owe?" He said, "I really don't know." I said, "You can't get out of debt. If you don't know what you owe you can't get out. You go and figure every nickel you owe and come back to me." He came back and said it was about $2,000. I said, "I'll tell you what

I'll do. I'll pay your debt." He was working at Jim Shaw's Seafood Restaurant at the time. I continued, "I'll pay all your bills for you. In return I expect you to repay me all the money I give you for your debt. The deal is, every penny you earn comes to me. Then I'll write you a check for $35 each week. That $35 will fill your gas tank up and give you $1.50 a day to get a Coca-Cola or something but that's it. Don't tell me what you'll do. You think about it because I'm expecting you to do whatever you say." He went home to think about it then came back to me and said, "I'll do it." He did ask if he could pay for his telephone. I told him I would let him do that one thing. I put the clamp on him so tight. When we had a family get-together at Thanksgiving at Danny and Cathy's house on Plantation Drive I said to the crowd, "I have an announcement to make. Danny, Jr. is completely out of debt and has $1000 in the bank. If you put $500 in the bank I'll put $500 more." Everybody clapped for him. He learned a lesson at the school of hard knocks. He had something to do and he stuck with it and accomplished his goal in about seven weeks. Danny Jr. is now married and has a little girl named Hannah.

Ray Jr. was in school and had a job at Pabst Blue Ribbon building tanks in the ground with cement to pump the mash out of the big stills where it fermented. The year he completed high school at Monroe Academy I got him a summer job as a laborer with a construction company. The temperature was going up to 105 that summer. Mayor Ronnie Thompson opened the Coliseum so that people without air condition could go there to stay out of the heat. I came home one afternoon to find Ray Jr. lying on the sofa. He had showered and was plopped onto the sofa. His tail was worn slap out. He had been carrying lumber that day. They were building columns, then tearing down the ones they had built two days before. They were two by tens and two by twelves and all of them had some cement stuck to them. The cement would rub your shoulder when you carried them. His grandmother, Pearl's mother, was sitting in here with him. When I came home from work I walked through where he was collapsed on the couch and he said, "Dad, six more carpenters quit today." I said, "Really? I know one that isn't going to quit." As I walked on through I heard Ray Jr. say, "I know one who would sure like to quit." His grandmother busted out laughing. He worked there in the summer for two years then he worked for Frank Amerson carrying sheetrock up in the Grand building.

The fourth year he was a senior in college. I said, "Ray, this year I'm going to get you a job in a bank." He said, "Dad, I don't want to work inside." I said, "Yes, I'm going to put you in a bank." He still wasn't satisfied, "Dad, why do I have to work inside?" I said, "Ray, I interview a lot of people for jobs. When I find someone who has a background of working hard as a laborer and then has worked in a bank, and I see he's never been in jail, has a college education I can make anything I want out of him. If he knows what work is and he's honest he can go anywhere in life he wants to go."

Ray Jr. met Pam while they were in college together. He came to me and said, "Dad, Pam and I are going to get married." So Ray married Pam and they lived in Macon. Ray worked for the bank as an assistant branch manager. Then Pam's grandfather died. Ray's father-in-law and his father owned the Chevrolet dealership in Winder. It has been in that family since 1939. He wanted Ray to go up there and join him in business so Ray went. It was a good move for him. I had my doubts about it at first but it has proven to be a good move for him. Ray learned the business and now he's been with that company for over 20 years. He and Pam have done well. They've never had any domestic problems. They've always been able to have good jobs. She worked for the Board of Education in the human resources department for approximately 12 years. She now works for a consulting firm in Atlanta.

Pearl and I have four grandchildren. Melanie is the oldest. We paid for her to go to college. We paid for Katie, her younger sister who will graduate in December, to go to college, and we've taken care of Chad. He'll be a senior in high school next year and we'll probably pay for him to go to college. Melanie now wants to go to graduate school to become a physical therapist. Last Christmas I said, "Pearl and I have talked and we have agreed we want to pay for you to go to graduate school and anyone else in the family who wants to go to graduate school we'll pay for them to go too. I have always felt money was no good if you couldn't pay for things for your family. I never wanted money so it could sit in the bank. I never want it to become an idol to sit in the bank. My family is very important to me and I want to give them everything I can, not to spoil them but rather to help them be all they can be. The best way to spend your money is on your children's education. I never bought new cars but helped them buy a home.

Ray and Pam have remodeled a house they are getting ready to move into. It's right on the county line with 28 acres. Atlanta is growing in the direction of Winder. He has a good investment in the house and property. There is land all around him selling for a lot more than he paid for his. In all probability the land will be worth two or three times what they paid for it in just a few years. If they want to keep it they can or if they want to sell it they can. I suggested they enjoy it now then one day use it for a retirement fund.

I have watched my children and now my grandchildren grow through the years. I love them and want to do what I can to help them. I did not have the luxury of an education past high school but I know how important it is today. I was ridiculed many times for trying to improve myself over the years. I tried to always look ahead and prepare for a future even though I did not know what that future would be. I wanted a good life for my wife and children with a stable home where love abounded. I hope I have succeeded in giving that life to them. I have been blessed abundantly and I know it. I could not have accomplished anything I've done in my life without Pearl. She was good for me.